PR
2983
.S44   Shakespeare, the
1984   tragedies

DATE		

89018791

TWENTIETH CENTURY VIEWS

The aim of this series is to present the best in contemporary critical opinion on major authors, providing a twentieth century perspective on their changing status in an era of profound revaluation.

Maynard Mack, *Series Editor*
Yale University

SHAKESPEARE:
THE TRAGEDIES

NEW PERSPECTIVES

Edited by
Robert B. Heilman

Prentice-Hall, Inc. A SPECTRUM BOOK Englewood Cliffs, N.J.

Library of Congress Cataloging in Publication Data

MAIN ENTRY UNDER TITLE:

Shakespeare, the tragedies.

(Twentieth century views)
"A Spectrum Book."
Bibliography: p.
1. Shakespeare, William, 1564-1616—Tragedies—
Addresses, essays, lectures.   I. Heilman, Robert
Bechtold (date).   II. Series
PR2983.S44   1984   822.3'3   83-21262
ISBN 0-13-807918-8
ISBN 0-13-807900-5 (pbk.)

To the Robert W. Kings

This book is available at a special discount when ordered in bulk quantities. Contact Prentice-Hall, Inc., General Publishing Division, Special Sales, Englewood Cliffs, New Jersey 07632.

A SPECTRUM BOOK

10   9   8   7   6   5   4   3   2   1

Printed in the United States of America

Editorial/production supervision by Jane Zalenski
Manufacturing buyer: Edward J. Ellis
Wood engraving © 1984 by Vivian J. Berger

ISBN 0-13-807900-5

ISBN 0-13-807918-8

PRENTICE-HALL INTERNATIONAL, INC., *London*
PRENTICE-HALL OF AUSTRALIA PTY. LIMITED, *Sydney*
PRENTICE-HALL CANADA INC., *Toronto*
PRENTICE-HALL OF INDIA PRIVATE LIMITED, *New Delhi*
PRENTICE-HALL OF JAPAN, INC., *Tokyo*
PRENTICE-HALL OF SOUTHEAST ASIA PTE. LTD., *Singapore*
WHITEHALL BOOKS LIMITED, *Wellington, New Zealand*
EDITORA PRENTICE-HALL DO BRASIL LTDA., *Rio de Janeiro*

Contents

Introduction

by Robert B. Heilman

Shakespeare: The Tragedies (New Perspectives) is inevitably a supplement to *Shakespeare: The Tragedies: A Collection of Critical Essays*,
edited by the late Alfred Harbage and published in 1964. The role
of *New Perspectives* is to sample the criticism of the last two decades.
To represent this criticism adequately in limited space, I have
arbitrarily excluded critics who appeared in the earlier volume,
though several of them have continued to write. The critics appearing in *New Perspectives* include both older hands in the vineyard and
some younger laborers. The proportion of American and British
contributors is identical with that in Harbage's volume—a fact that
I discovered only after I had decided on the essays to be included.
However, one difference shows that *tempora mutantur*: whereas in
Harbage's collection the proportion of men to women was seventeen to one, here it is eleven to five—again a fact discovered only
after my choices were made (the proportion happens to be almost
identical with that in the membership of the Shakespeare Association of America). Finally, the list of publishers represented in the
bibliography reveals one interesting fact: although the numbers of
British university, British commercial, and American commercial
publishers remain constant, American university presses have
increased from fourteen to twenty-two. At least from the university
perspective, publishing Shakespeare is evidently a growth industry.

The essays in this volume come mostly from single-author collections, a field that one can have some illusion of sampling respecta-
bly, rather than from periodicals, where the production is so
spectacularly vast as to demand anthologies far larger than this one
can be. (Only two of my selections—Adelman on *Antony and
Cleopatra* and Skura on *Hamlet*—come from book-length studies,
which, as Harbage remarks, "resist excerption.") Perhaps because

book publishers do not limit the length of chapters as periodicals ordinarily limit the length of articles, the essays in many volumes tend to be too long to use *in toto*, and I have had to take the risk of cutting some of those that I selected. I hope to have managed excisions in such a way that the parts reproduced constitute reasonably independent and coherent essays; these should stimulate readers of this volume to seek out the full originals. I have cut some essays by omitting passages dealing with nontragic or non-Shakespearean plays, cross-references to other chapters or parts of the discussion, and so on, when this could be done without excessive local awkwardness. (All omissions are indicated, of course, by appropriate typographic methods.) I have retained only footnotes identifying materials in the text or intimately related to the progress of the author's thought, and have omitted those that contain parenthetical observations, extensions of the text, notations of parallel or opposing thoughts in other critics, and general surveys of critical opinion on the issues canvassed by the essayist. Still, I have not managed or found the shorter selections that enabled Harbage to include a slightly larger number of critics than appears here (the compact general essay is less frequent in our period, more given to elaborating special points of view).

In making selections, an editor inevitably operates with both a sense of quality and a sense of representativeness. Not that there is an unpassable chasm between the two; I have included no essays that speak for points of view needing representation but that seem qualitatively inferior. On the other hand there simply is not room for all the first-rate essays that one would like to include; it would not do to have, say, five essays on *Lear* and to shortchange the rest of the major tragedies accordingly. In judging quality I have tried to keep in mind the criterion of style: I have intended to include only essays written in a lucid, unaffected prose, free of in-house mumbo-jumbo that intimidates all but the innermost circles.

Critics refer to various editions of Shakespeare. Since, for the most part, differences in lineation by different editors are not great enough to cause much difficulty for readers who want to check cited passages, it has seemed advisable to let stand the references to different editions. To shift all references to a single edition would have no compelling advantage, since the single edition used might be unavailable to a given reader, or not preferred by him or her.

Despite the great variety in recent Shakespeare criticism, certain attitudes recur. The concept of role-playing has been popular enough to appear in critiques otherwise dissimilar. New ways of doing things are often accompanied by repudiation of older ways. As Harriett Hawkins nicely observes, "what was yesterday's fashion is today's taboo" (*Poetic Freedom and Poetic Truth*, 1976, p. 119). The yesterday fashions that are the most frequent objects of today's fashionable pummeling are Bradley character analysis, often called old-fashioned; New Critical discussions of texts, widely supposed to ignore history, the stage, and dramatic structure; and thematic criticism, usually called reductive. But anathema does not guarantee amnesia. One is struck by the survival power of modes officially ruled outmoded. Somehow Bradley remains the predecessor with whom critics—English perhaps more regularly than Americans— need especially to come to terms; one reads "as Bradley says" about as often as one reads "Bradley is not entirely wrong" or "unfortunately, Bradley, etc." John Bayley and René Wellek have recently paid tribute to his durability; one may say that he has undergone metamorphosis from progenitor to target to quasi-monument. (Other forebears who have moved into the target phase of the evolutionary sequence are T. S. Eliot and F. R. Leavis, notably as observers of *Othello*, and Wilson Knight and L. C. Knights have acquired some status as refutands.) And of course character analysis has never been in a real slump. We may come to it with different tools—stage conventions, psychoanalysis, doctrines of the day, socio-politico-economic bearings, symbolistic habits of mind, linguistic predeterminations—but rarely do we wholly bypass the issue, to use recent idiom, of "who Hamlet is." We do, of course, complicate the problem; we have come to think of a character as several things, even contradictory things, at once.

At bottom the New Critical approach was simply to assess the role of poetic language, especially when marked by reiterative usage, as a constituent of the dramatic reality. Normal Rabkin and Thomas McFarland have conceded some merit to this practice, and, as G. R. Hibbard has observed, it has quietly moved into the mainstream of critical activity and is employed by many critics who may be primarily concerned with other things. Likewise, the effort to identify themes has hardly disappeared—naturally, for themes are there, and the problem is to spot them, not as ultimate essence but, in the manner of the late Rosalie Colie, as constitutive elements.

Ringing out the old may be either a way of justifying the new or a phase of the skepticism that has a good deal of strength now. Such skepticism has been codified in Richard Levin's systematic attribution of error to whole schools of criticism—the discovery of irony, the identification of themes, and even a historicism intent on anchoring Shakespeare firmly in the ideas of his day. A section of Levin's work serves, in this volume, to represent repudiation at its most inclusive.

Repudiation, however, is only one of the prevailing attitudes to forebears, immediate predecessors, and colleagues. A few critics seem to have read everyone else and to concentrate on what is best in them—Rosalie Colie, for instance. Others feel enthusiasm only for figures who have evoked enthusiasm elsewhere. Then there is the normal enthusiasm for the like-minded, reflected in the familiar gesture of reassuring companionship, "as Professor So-and-So says." A few hard-bitten assessors such as A. L. French can find little to praise and much to question in the critics read. On the other hand, Kenneth Muir is that rather rare figure, the very detached critic who maintains an overall view and assesses merit and error with great balance of judgment. His essay on *Hamlet*, reprinted here, shows a firm mastery of the text and of various commentators on it.

Muir's judicious general evaluation is not much attempted now, when a sense of how much as been done leads naturally to the pursuit of novel and special points of view. The critic with a new angle may attack or not attend to prior criticisms. At times the critic opposes some specific idea but ignores the general context of thought in which the idea is stated. Or the critic says approximately what *A* has said but seems not to know that *A* said it. American and British critics tend not to notice transatlantic voices, though Americans ignore English less than English ignore Americans. More than one critic, reading some work that postdates his or her own, must share the feeling of the graffito writer commenting on an earlier inscription he sees: "But that's arrant plagiarism. I wrote that on a wall three years ago." Professor Brents Stirling has wittily observed, "Any idea about Shakespeare that survives is stated anew and independently every five years."

But quinquennial renewals are subject to changing modes of perception. It is perhaps only in a post-Artaud world that one critic can term *Titus Andronicus* a "greater play than we had thought." Perhaps something in the contemporary air gives unusual vigor to the antiredemptivists on *Lear*, such evangelical zeal to their insistence that the play ends in desolation, total loss, *nada*. Perhaps A. L. French is reacting against bardolatry when he argues that Shakespeare was often a bad artist, making up his mind as he went along and not bringing what he had written earlier into line with new turns decided on later. Perhaps no current critic could speak with the assurance of the late Harold Goddard and the late Sigurd Burckhardt, who in different decades explained what Shakespeare "had" to mean or be saying or showing. More in the temper of our times is the idea, articulated by Normal Rabkin, that we must live with indeterminacy in the plays, with "complementarity," that is, the copresence of meanings and implications that are consistent or even contradictory. Thus, in criticisms of *Antony and Cleopatra*, the long debate between romantics and realists (or moralists) has apparently yielded to a new view held in different ways by Norman Rabkin, A. L. French, H. A. Mason, and Janet Adelman (who appears in this volume) and leading to different conclusions—the view that the play is marked by a problematic division between drama and language, between characters as represented in action and as presented in poetry.

The "Shakespeare industry" might well be called an industrial complex or a consortium or a conglomerate, since the enterprise has many phases and they are all notably productive (stressing the diversity rather than the productivity, Rosalie Colie and F. T. Flahiff use a different image, "prismatic criticism"). A number of the allied industries are represented in this volume. The representatives of general skepticism and complementarity have already been mentioned. Sigurd Burckhardt seems to have been one of the earliest exponents of the idea that a play is in some sense about itself, that the language and drama make implicit comments on the arts of poetry and drama. This "metadramatic" approach is reflected in the essay by James Calderwood, who does not limit himself, however, to a tight ideological discourse. E. A. J. Honigmann is concerned with the way in which the actions and speech of characters encourage kinds of responses in the audience—a phase of the "process" criticism that is also practiced by Nicholas Brooke, a contributor, and Ruth Nevo, among others, and indeed is implicitly present in many analyses of character and dramatic movement. Psychoanalytic criticism has become big business. Meredith Skura gives a sober outline of its possibilities, with recurrent comments on *Hamlet* that I have brought together as a continuous discussion, and Normal Rabkin invokes it, with a restraint that gratifies G. K. Hunter, in his study of *Macbeth.* Various critics look at major plays in terms of earlier ones seen as anticipatory sketches; a special form of this is the reading of tragedies as transmutations of a comic substance. There is something of this in Emrys Jones, H. A. Mason, and Susan Snyder, whose essay on *Lear* appears here. That essay may also be said to reflect the more hopeful side of existentialist thought. While literary people may turn philosophical, philosphers may turn to literature; in this volume they are represented by Stanely Cavell's inquiries into *Othello.* The Shakespeare consortium includes a considerable theological operation, split among those who, bringing some sort of faith to the reading, believe that Shakespeare brought some sort of faith to the writing, or believe that indeed he didn't (much sectarian warmth here), or use theological keys in explication—for example, Robert G. Hunter, who illuminatingly uses Pelagian, Augustinian, and Calvinistic perspectives and shows how they lead to different readings of a text (and for whom I wish there were space here). Shakespeare-as-theater is a very productive business, practiced by John Russell Brown, Marvin Rosenberg, Richard Levin, Muriel Bradbrook, and others; against the critic who wants to treat a play as only a script for production, Rosalie Colie wisely reminds us that it is also a text for reading and hence subject to inspection as a work of literature. Historical study continues, represented here, if somewhat distantly, by Reuben Brower, who views *Titus,* along with other plays, in terms of the classical heroic tradition. Michael J. Warren's essay on *Lear* quarto and folio not only provides a taste of textual study but hits on an issue of considerable significance and interest. Finally, I have included an essay of my own. Since it deals with virtually the same materials discussed, from a different point of view, by G. K. Hunter, our essays are neighbors in this volume. In this juxtaposition I take a risk that is a kind of penance for my "exercise," as Harbage calls it, "of the inalienable right of anthologists."

Whatever the variety in this volume, it can only partly reflect the welter of ideas about the plays and of ideas said to be present in the plays. Ideas about tragedy fluctuate between two extremes: that tragedy means total loss, and that moral survival triumphs over the losses incurred. Tragic heroes may evoke enthusiastic admiration (from some writers Hamlet, Othello, Antony, and even Coriolanus elicit extraordinary tributes), a sense of their mixed human reality, or even more disparaging views. (Though Reuben Brower has said that the "recognition of greatness" is more difficult for us than for the Elizabethans, antiheroic readings are often followed by vigorous efforts at rehabilitation.) It is Shakespeare's fate to keep evoking in print every kind of response to every aspect of his plays. The record includes not only critics responding to plays but critics responding to one another in multiple ways and thus helping to produce an enormous crazy quilt of revisions, overlaps, oppositions, and even novelties. They may use the voice of cool technical expertise or of impassioned partisanship. Some interpretations appear to flow out of what may be called, a little heavily, attitudinal predisposition, the perhaps undefined loyalties with which, for the critic, the play seems to cohere. One senses the presence of both religious temperaments and antireligious temperaments in some critiques of *Lear,* and the presence of romantic and antiromantic sensibilities in critiques of *Antony and Cleopatra.* Arguments from the text become extensions of personality into the critical process (e.g., glorification of the lovers in Egypt may express a basic "romantic" cast of mind—anti-Rome-ism, or in modern terms, hostility to "the system," administrators, and so on). But that this may be so, and sometimes is so, does not relegate criticism to the rivalry of diverse subjectivities. The only justifications for a volume such as this are that the plays are objective realities, not mere stimuli to idiosyncratic modes of response; that in each there is an essence or truth to be sought; that the best criticism is the self-corrective pursuit of that essence or truth (i.e., the ideal or total reading); that the closer a reading comes to this, the longer it survives through the mutabilities of fashion.

Shakespeare's plays have been seen variously as metaphors for, or expressions of, reality in general (mimesis), the conventions of the mode (theatrical styles, plot patterns), contemporary history (political, social, intellectual), aesthetic tradition and innovation, creative problems and process (metadrama), the biography of the playwright, and characters—unique or archetypal—in action. The fate of some of these approaches in our century has been recounted by Dr. Peter Wenzel of the University of Bochum in his analysis of fifty modern studies of *King Lear, Die "Lear"-Kritik im 20. Jahrhundert* (Amsterdam: B. R. Grüner B. V., 1979). Since Wenzel's major conclusions are generally applicable to studies of the tragedies, I quote, with his permission, a number of passages from the "Summary" of his book (in Supplement to *Anglia*, 1980, pp. 59-61:

> The various critical approaches . . . have constantly influenced each other in what may be called a dialectic process. Thus, critical dissatisfaction with Bradley's character analysis has given rise to the development of both the historical and the textual approaches to Shakespeare, which, in the course of time, have not only criticized but also influenced each other, laying the foundations for a definite tendency towards methodological pluralism in modern criticism. Since the sixties, increasing dissatisfaction with the historical and textual approach has led to a far-reaching rehabilitation of Bradley's methods. This rehabilitation, however, is not an atavistic relapse into an earlier stage of criticism but rather an attempt to find a synthesis between the character approach and other types of criticism. Finally, it can be shown that even the most recent approaches to Shakespeare (such as the numerous "structural analysis" of his plays) grow out of the older methods in an organic way.

Wenzel finds that Shakespeare criticism is making "progress . . . in a few general methodological tendencies":

> To begin with, modern critics tend to deal with special aspects of *King Lear* rather than with the play as a whole. Second, there is an ever increasing interest in methodological questions. Third, modern critics tend to regard a Shakespearian drama as a pluralist work of art, stressing its variety and ambiguity. Sometimes this affinity for relativism verges on the point where the critic is no longer able to offer any conclusive interpretations at all. Fourth, Shakespeare's dramas are nowadays more willingly regarded as plays written to be performed on a stage rather than to be read in a study. Fifth, modern critics for the most part have a sound understanding of the fictional quality of a play. They hardly ever fail, for instance, to attribute a symbolic meaning to Lear's division of his kingdom in the first scene of the play, while their predecessors were usually obsessed with the question of this scene's probability. Sixth, the technique of interpreting seemingly central statements in the play has also changed: While former critics have generally understood such statements as the embodiments of Shakespeare's message in the play, recent critics tend to interpret them only in relation to their speaker and to the precise moment of the dramatic action. In addition, one

can trace several less significant tendencies in Shakespeare criticism, such as a pronounced dislike of value judgements and the complete abolition of the biographical method and metaphorical style.

Wenzel sees an improvement in the "practical tools" of criticism:

> Both the methods of textual analysis [and] the critical terms . . . have been considerably refined. Such terms as, for instance, "pattern," "image," "ritual," or "paradox" each have their own history in twentieth century Shakespeare criticism. Furthermore, there have been shifts in the evaluation of the importance of background knowledge supposed to be valuable for interpreting the plays. Thus, in the exploration of . . . meaning . . . the intellectual and literary background of the time has proved to be much more helpful than knowledge about the structure of an Elizabethan stage, the composition of an Elizabethan audience, or the teachings of Elizabethan psychology.

These changes in method may or may not influence the "concrete results of . . . interpretations. . . . (Two critics may, for instance, rest their interpretations on exactly the same methods and yet achieve different results, simply because they select different data from the text under discussion.)" There have been changes "the interpretation of the play's general meaning":

> In the wake of modern intellectual currents, the Christian or "optimistic" view of the play's ending, which was almost universally accepted during the forties and fifties, has in recent times been replaced by much more skeptical or even plainly pessimistic interpretations. Moreover, recent critics are much more willing to admit that a Shakespearian drama can be viewed from very different angles and that its meaning, therefore, cannot be reduced to any incontestable dictum.

However, in this connection a serious problem arises: the "present inability [of Shakespeare criticism] to cope with the difficulties arising from the modern notion that any reading of the play is relative to its perspective. What is required here is a definition of the pluralist nature of art which does not imply that the various aspects of a work of art are detachable and arbitrary." Still another problem is that since critics do not keep up with the "bulk" of prior criticism, they run "the risk of overlooking important arguments in the previous discussion" and even "take issue at length with positions which have, strictly speaking, long since become antiquated."

Of the post-1965 critics represented in this volume, mentioned in this introduction, or listed in the bibliography, most proceed from a principle, generally a limited one, but few from an embracing system. There is more "practical criticism" than "literary theory." Perhaps many of the critics could say with Leonard Dean, in his delightful essay "Theory and the Muddle" (*Critical Inquiry*, 1980, pp. 752-54):

> I was not surprised to find that I had been muddling along for years with very little theory . . . A muddler naturally feels flattered by any kind of praise from the world of theory, as, for example, by Robert Scholes' generous remark that "muddling along, in literary theory as in life, is often more humane and even more efficient than the alternatives offered by political, ethical, or aesthetic systems." . . . In dealing with drama, the oldest and newest critics agree that it is best to start not with theory but with actual plays and learn about literature and life by attending to such practical things as stage types. . . . The muddle, in short, is full of examples of critical inquiry, and it is also lots of fun.

Shakespeare or the Ideas
of His Time

by Richard L. Levin

The term "historical" has been applied to the criticism of
English Renaissance drama in so many different senses—many
more than either "thematic" or "ironic"—that we cannot hope to
survey them all here. Historical knowledge of one kind or another
is involved in every attempt to interpret these plays. On the most
basic level, it gives us the very meaning of the words in our texts. It
even gives us the texts themselves, since analytical bibliography is a
form of historical reconstruction. And it supplies the facts about
the authorship of the plays and their chronology, the sources they
drew on, the theater where they appeared, the dramatic or literary
traditions and conventions that influenced them, the society they
portrayed, and various other aspects of the very extensive context
which we bring to bear upon them, often quite unconsciously, and
without which we could scarcely be said to understand them at all.
To the extent that we do understand them, therefore, we owe an
immeasurable debt to the labors of the historical scholars in these
fields. But this type of knowledge, essential though it is, does not
constitute an approach to interpretation. It is really prein-
terpretative, since it underlies any informed reading of a play, but
does not in itself define the nature of that reading.

If we limit ourselves, then, to the kinds of scholarship which do
produce distinctive "historical readings," and so can be considered

"Shakespeare or the Ideas of His Time" by Richard L. Levin. From *Mosaic: A
Journal for the Interdisciplinary Study of Literature and Ideas*, University of Manitoba, vol.
10, no. 3 (Spring 1977), pp. 129–37. Reprinted by permission of the editor of *Mosaic*.
Several short passages not dealing with the tragedies are omitted. The essay was
reprinted in Richard L. Levin's *New Readings vs. Old Plays* (Chicago: University of
Chicago Press, 1979), with a few verbal alterations and expansions used here.

approaches to interpretation, I think we will find that they are all based upon the contention that the real meaning of the plays is wholly or largely determined by some component of the extra-dramatic background and can only be apprehended in relation to it. There are several approaches of this sort, which can be differentiated in terms of the increasing particularity of the historical component they employ. On the highest level of abstraction we have the "zeitgeist approach," wherein the play is treated as an embodiment of a very generalized intellectual or emotional atmosphere said to permeate every facet of life in the period. Next come those studies that interpret the play in the light of certain specified attitudes or "ideas of the time." Below them is the "topical" approach to the play, which sees in it a commentary upon contemporary individuals or events. And the extreme of particularity is reached in what I call "occasionalism," where the play is viewed as a kind of private communication directed at a special audience, outside of the commercial theaters, at a special time and place.

This classification should be adequate for our purposes, so long as we recognize that the categories are oversimplified approximations and necessarily overlap. In fact, the lower ones often seem to depend on those above them—almost all occasionalist readings make use of topical references, topical readings frequently invoke the ideas of the time, and many readings based on these ideas derive them from a more general spirit of the age. It would therefore be more accurate to think of these approaches as roughly demarcated areas along a single continuum, with some individual readings falling between two of them or encompassing both. This need not trouble us, however, since we will only be dealing here with two approaches which are not contiguous—the second and the fourth. I have chosen to concentrate upon them because they have become the dominant modes of "historical criticism" in our field. The zeitgeist and topical approaches seem to be less fashionable now, but occasionalism and, especially, the ideas-of-the-time approach are flourishing and bringing forth a bumper crop of new readings that we should investigate.

Before beginning our examination of the approach it will be necessary to make another distinction, for the study of the connection between these plays or their authors and the ideas of the time can take two very different forms. In one of them the critic tries to ascertain how the ideas or attitudes which he finds in the plays are related to the mental climate of the period. This kind of study has an obvious value in its own right, and has taught us a great deal about what is usually called "the history of ideas," and about the dramatist's place in that history—about the ways in which he followed or modified or departed from the intellectual traditions he inherited and the intellectual movements of his own day. However, it is not an approach in our sense, because it is postinterpretative; it relies upon a prior interpretation of the plays and does not (in theory at least) influence that interpretation. But the study of a dramatist and the ideas of his time is also commonly understood to refer to another pursuit which proceeds in the opposite direction, since it does not treat the plays as independent data to be related to the ideas, but starts with the ideas and uses them to interpret the plays. And this clearly is an approach, for we shall see that it determines the principles and methodology and even the conclusions of a certain kind of reading.

It is of course possible to combine these two forms of study in various ways within the same book or article, but that does not affect the distinction because they are logically separable procedures. And since we are concerned with the ideas of the time here only when they are employed in interpretations of these plays, our investigation will be limited to the second pursuit. I should acknowledge at the outset, however, that much of what I have to say about it will not be new. For this approach, unlike the thematic and ironic approaches, has provoked considerable discussion, and a number of incisive criticisms of it have appeared, with which I am happy to associate myself, if their authors will have me.[1] But since

---

[1] See especially Edward Hubler, "The Damnation of Othello: Some Limitations on the Christian View of the Play," *Shakespeare Quarterly* 9 (1958): 295–300; Robert Ornstein, "Historical Criticism and the Interpretation of Shakespeare," *Shakespeare Quarterly* 10 (1959): 3–9; William Empson, "Mine Eyes Dazzle," *Essays in Criticism* 14 (1964): 80–86; Herbert Howarth, "Put Away the World-Picture," *The Tiger's Heart: Eight Essays on Shakespeare* (New York: Oxford University Press, 1970); Harriett Hawkins, "What Kind of Pre-Contract Had Angelo? A Note on Some Nonproblems in Elizabethan Drama," *College English* 36 (1974): 173–79; and Arthur H. Scouten, "An Historical Approach to *Measure for Measure*," *Philological Quarterly* 54 (1975): 68–84. See also the historical survey of this approach by J. W. Lever, "Shakespeare and the Ideas of His Time," *Shakespeare Survey* 29 (1976): 79–91 and the theoretical analysis (which does not deal directly with Elizabethan drama) by Ronald Crane, "On Hypotheses in 'Historical Criticism': Apropos of Certain Contemporary Medievalists," *The Idea of the Humanities and Other Essays Critical and Historical* (Chicago: University of Chicago Press, 1967).

the flow of new readings issuing from it has not perceptibly abated, there would seem to be a need to restate their position. And I have been able to add some further considerations which may help to clarify the case against this approach and to place it within the larger framework of the critique developed [earlier].

We will begin then with a convenient summary provided for us in a survey of the major trends in recent Shakespeare criticism by Patrick Murray, entitled *The Shakespearian Scene*, which can serve as our introduction to the ideas-of-the-time scene.[2] Murray calls one of these trends "the historical approach," and he finds that it has made a "singularly impressive" contribution "to our understanding of Shakespeare's plays," because

> it has rescued and brought into the full light of day matters of fact as well as patterns of thought; by restoring to view things lost or obscured by the passage of time it has provided new and productive ways of looking at the plays and . . . has corrected numerous errors of interpretation and helped to put some of the wilder theories of impressionistic criticism firmly in their place.

He goes on to supply several examples of this impressive contribution, from which I have selected three to illustrate the approach. In the first he explains that "the Elizabethan philosophy of hierarchy described in such books as Tillyard's *Elizabethan World Picture* and Lovejoy's *The Great Chain of Being* adds a whole new dimension to one's reading of *King Lear*" and enables us to appreciate, "in the light of common Elizabethan assumptions," the cosmic significance of Lear's abdication. In the second we learn that the "examination of Desdemona's role in the light of Elizabethan courtesy-books and canonical literature suggests that a contemporary audience would have had stronger reservations than those generally expressed nowadays about . . . some aspects of her behaviour [such as] her defiance and deception of her father [and] her breach of matrimonial conventions." And in the third he informs us that "a proper understanding of Elizabethan pneumatology" is required to explain the Ghost in *Hamlet*: "Without the insights of the historical approach, without constant reference to Elizabethan theological and philosophical speculations concerning spirits and their dis-

[2] *The Shakespearian Scene: Some Twentieth Century Perspectives* (London: Longmans, Green, 1969), pp. 145–49.

cernment, it is difficult to see how a modern reader can make much sense of . . . the ghost-scenes."

These examples—and most of his others are similar—have several elements in common that are characteristic of the approach in general. In each of them the claim is made that certain ideas of the time are essential to the correct interpretation of a major point in the play, and so must determine that interpretation. Moreover, this point is not simply a matter of fact but will vitally affect our judgment of the character involved (Lear, Desdemona, Hamlet). And it is clearly implied that the result will be a quite different judgment of this character from the one we adopt when we do not know these ideas—for if there were no significant difference, the approach would not be making an impressive contribution to our understanding of the play. An examination of all the problems raised in any one of these interpretations is beyond the scope of this [essay], but that will not be necessary in order to see what light they can shed upon the approach itself.

The first example should be very familiar by now, since a number of critics have recently been telling us how Lear's abdication violated the Renaissance world picture and concept of hierarchy. One of them asserts, for instance, that "as a king, it was not Lear's prerogative to abandon his rule . . . he could not abandon his royal obligations without disturbing the natural order." Another puts this more strongly:

> An act of betrayal is also committed by Lear when, in the play's opening scene, he divests himself of kingship and gives up the divinely-appointed duties of monarchy. We must here remember precisely what kingship meant to the Elizabethans, if we are to comprehend the magnitude of Lear's ill-doing. . . . Here is the Lord's deputy divesting himself, most sinfully and criminally, of his divine duty.

And a third is even more vehement:

> To understand the enormity of Lear's sin, we must recognize the peculiar position of the king in the highly ordered world which Renaissance Christian humanism carried over from the Middle Ages. Lear's resignation of his throne . . . would have been regarded by a Jacobean audience with a horror difficult for a modern audience to appreciate, for . . . [it was] a violation of the king's responsibility to God, and . . . could result only in . . . chaos on every level of creation. . . . By his resignation of rule Lear disrupts the

> harmonious order of nature . . . [and the] infinite good of God's
> order which decrees that the king rule for the good of his people
> until God relieves him of his responsibility by death.

Now one is immediately led to wonder why, if this idea is so crucial to the play, it is never once mentioned there. Lear's abdication is witnessed and commented upon by a great many characters, but not one of them expresses the least bit of horror at it. Indeed, Kent and Gloucester have apparently been consulted about his decision in advance and have accepted it. Moreover, Lear himself later in the play comes to acknowledge many failings, yet he never acknowledges this one, which is very strange if it is supposed to be his worst sin of all.

There is some reason to doubt, however, that the Jacobeans really would have regarded it as a sin. King James himself presumably would not, for in his *Defence of the Right of Kings* he raises no objection to the idea that kings may "renounce the right of royalty, and of their own accord give over the kingdom."[3] And Herbert Howarth points out that when the Emperor Charles V abdicated in 1555/56 his action was greeted, not with horror, but with admiration.[4] He also points out that King David abdicated in favor of his son Solomon. According to 1 Kings, David did this with the approval and assistance of Nathan the Prophet and Zadok the Priest, and thanked "the Lord God of Israel, which hath given one to sit on my throne this day, mine eyes even seeing it."[5] Nor does the ensuing narrative record any calamities resulting from this disruption of the harmonious order of nature, which ushered in the golden age of Israel's history. And Shakespeare and his

[3] *A Remonstrance of the Most Gracious King James I . . . for the Right of Kings and the Independence of Their Crowns, Against an Oration of the Most Illustrious Cardinal of Perron* (Cambridge, 1616), p. 270. In this passage James denies the Cardinal the right to cite William Barclay in support of the Pope's power to depose kings: "Barclaius, alleged by the Cardinal, meddles not with deposing of kings, but deals with disavowing them for kings, when they shall renounce the right of royalty, and of their own accord give over the kingdom. Now he that leaves it in the King's choice, either to hold or to give over his crown, leaves it not in the Pope's power to take away the kingdom." (Spelling and punctuation have been modernized.)

[4] *The Tiger's Heart: Eight Essays on Shakespeare* (New York: Oxford University Press, 1970), p. 170. Marvin Rosenberg, in *The Masks of King Lear* (Berkeley: University of California Press, 1972), p. 41, also cites Charles's abdication in this connection and notes that it was praised by Montaigne in the *Essays*, 2:8.

[5] 1 Kings 1:48 (King James Version).

audience, as Howarth suggests, were more likely to have read that biblical account than to have read Tillyard. Even if it could be proved, however, that the doctrine of the unresignability of kingship actually was an idea of the time, I would still have to argue that it is not relevant to *King Lear*, for the simple reason that it does not figure in the play.

The second example, Desdemona's marrying without her father's consent, is on a different footing, because we know that the duty of daughters to obey their parents, especially in the choice of a husband, was explicitly affirmed at this time in many of the courtesy books and moral and religious treatises. One critic has assembled some of this material in order "to examine Desdemona's conduct against a background of Elizabethan attitudes" and to demonstrate that "the predictable audience reaction" to her would be unfavorable:

> The conduct of a young lady in the courtesy books is also a far cry from that of Desdemona in her matrimonial arrangements. She marries against the precepts of both courtesy books and canon law, without consulting her father. . . . In terms of Venetian practice and Elizabethan precept the behavior of the lady is unfilial and unnatural indeed. . . . [She] is not the ideal young lady of the precept books, and the audience, especially the male members of it, could here be expected to judge Desdemona harshly.

Another asserts on the same basis that her action was "an incredible breach of normal decent behavior," and warns us against the modern tendency to side with her rather than with her father:

> To us at least, his anger that she should have chosen to wed Othello without first asking his leave is unseemly, unsympathetic, and crude. This was not the view in Shakespeare's day. . . . Brabantio was . . . a much-wronged man, and Desdemona was punished, albeit too brutally, for committing a sin against what at that time was regarded as a fundamental decency.

And this kind of evidence has been used to condemn not only Desdemona's marriage to Othello but also Juliet's to Romeo—in fact one critic equates these two "sins" in his discussion of Desdemona: "As with Juliet so here we must allow for the weight given by Shakespeare to the sin of disobedience to parents." Another critic explains that Juliet's behavior would have "shocked" Shakespeare's audience, because of "the fact that in thus boldly asserting her own will she violates a sacred canon of Elizabethan life; namely, that children, and especially daughters, owe obedience to the wishes of their parents." And another has been quoted as saying that "a prolonged study of a cache of Elizabethan social documents" left him "with one overriding impression: that the average audience of *Romeo and Juliet* would have regarded the behavior of the young lovers as deserving everything they got."

This alleged "sin" presents us with the same problem as Lear's, however, because it is not condemned in the play itself. The marriages of both Desdemona and Juliet are judged by the authority figure in their respective worlds, who do not find their behavior at all sinful. In *Othello*, I. iii., the Duke of Venice presides over a kind of trial and exonerates Othello and Desdemona, without any reference to her incredible breach of normal decent behavior; and in the final scene of *Romeo and Juliet* the Prince of Verona, after hearing a full account of the events, places the blame not upon the young lovers but upon their parents, and certainly never suggests that Juliet deserved everything she got. Apparently neither the Duke nor the Prince had a chance to study that cache of Elizabethan social documents. . . .

The third example, the Ghost in *Hamlet*, presents a more complex problem, but I believe the same principles apply to it. A number of critics have sought to determine the nature of this ghost by consulting Elizabethan pneumatology. They certainly have not settled the question, for they reach quite different conclusions, the most remarkable being that it is not really a ghost at all but a demon pretending to be a ghost. This view has now been advanced in several studies, but it will be enough here if we look at the argument of the most thoroughgoing and best known of them, which runs as follows: Protestant theology held that all ghosts were either hallucinations or else angels or demons in disguise. Catholic theology admitted a fourth possibility, that they could be souls temporarily released from purgatory. Now the Ghost in *Hamlet* certainly cannot be a hallucination or an angel. And it fails its purgatorial qualifying test, derived by this critic from two French books on spirits (neither of which, incidentally, had been translated into English at the time of *Hamlet*). According to them, purgatorial ghosts asked for alms, fasts, pilgrimages, prayers, or masses, which this ghost never does; moreover, it asks for revenge on Claudius instead of forgiving him, as Church doctrine required. Ergo, it cannot come from purgatory and so must be a demon.

There seem to be two basic errors in this line of argument. One is the assumption that the ideas of the time about ghosts were limited to what the authorities stated in their treatises—an assumption that leads another critic, for example, to assert that "no Protestant could admit that the spirit of the dead might return, since Purgatory was ruled out and Heaven and Hell were closed to departure." But we have conclusive evidence in the play itself that many must have admitted this, since they believed—in direct contradiction to the authorities—that the spirits of the dead, or at least some of them, did not go to heaven or hell or even purgatory but remained in their graves, to emerge at night or on special occasions. This belief is expressed in Hamlet's first reaction to the Ghost:

> Let me not burst in ignorance, but tell
> Why thy canoniz'd bones, hearsed in death,
> Have burst their cerements; why the sepulchre
> Wherein we saw thee quietly interr'd,
> Hath op'd his ponderous and marble jaws
> to cast thee up again.
>
> (I. iv. 46–51)

And it is repeated later in Horatio's comment. "There needs no ghost, my lord, come from the grave / To tell us this" (I. v. 125–26). We also learn in *Hamlet* (I. i. 113–16) and in *Julius Caesar* (I. iii. 63–75, II. ii. 18–24) that on the night before Caesar's assassination ghosts emerged from their graves to walk the streets of Rome. In *Henry VI, Part II* we are told that at night "spirits walk and ghosts break up their graves" (I. iv. 18), and in *A Midsummer Night's Dream* that at dawn "ghosts, wand'ring here and there, / Troop home to churchyards" (III. ii. 381–82). And one could cite much more evidence of this widespread belief, which still survives in our uneasiness around cemeteries at night. It is not relevant to the Ghost in *Hamlet*, who does not come from the grave, but it does prove that there were more ideas of the time about ghosts than were dreamt of in the official pneumatology.

We have the same kind of conclusive evidence in Shakespeare of another idea of the time about ghosts which is also not found in the treatises, but which is very relevant to *Hamlet*—namely, that the ghosts of murdered men could seek vengeance either by plaguing their killers or by encouraging their revengers. The ghosts at the end of *Richard III* do both (V. iii.), and earlier in the play Richard's mother tells him that "the little souls of Edward's children / Whisper the spirits of thine enemies / And promise them success and victory" (IV. iv. 192–94). In *Henry VI, Part II* Duke Humphrey's ghost is envisaged as an agent of retribution against two of his murderers, the Duke of Suffolk and Cardinal Beaufort (III. ii. 230–31, 373–74). And Richard II speaks of kings "haunted by the ghosts they have depos'd (III. ii. 158). Caesar's ghost appears twice to Brutus to foretell his doom (V. v. 17–20), and Juliet imagines that in her family tomb she will see Tybalt's "ghost / Seeking out Romeo, that did spit his body / Upon a rapier's point" (IV. iii. 56–58). It was even thought that these ghosts could torment their kinsmen for *failing* to avenge them: The Duke in *Measure for Measure* asserts that if Isabella should ask him to pardon Angelo, "Her brother's ghost his paved bed would break / And take her hence in horror" (V. i. 430–31); and Macduff fears that if Macbeth is "slain and with no stroke of mine, / My wife and children's ghosts will haunt me still" (V. vii. 15–16) . . .

Nor can I find any suggestion that any of these ghosts—either those referred to in the dialogue or those presented on stage—are supposed to be demons; they are all regarded as the genuine spirits of the victim, the official pneumatology of the time to the contrary notwithstanding.

The second basic error in this line of argument is the assumption that we can deduce the playwright's meaning in such a crucial matter from the ideas of the time, or from any external source, instead of inducing it from the play itself. For Shakespeare has very carefully established the Ghost's authenticity by twice voicing the demonic hypothesis within the action, and twice refuting it. In I. iv. Horatio warns Hamlet that the Ghost may tempt him to the summit of the cliff and there assume some horrible form to drive him mad; but it does not, and Hamlet returns from his encounter to assure Horatio that "it is an honest ghost" (I.v.138). Later, in II. ii., Hamlet himself wonders if it could have been a "devil" operating more subtly, by lying to him about Claudius's guilt rather than driving him off the cliff; but his mousetrap play proves that he can "take the ghost's word for a thousand pound" (III. ii. 274–75). And thereafter no doubts about a "damned ghost" are raised by anyone in the play; nor have they been raised, so far as we can tell, by the overwhelming majority of viewers and readers down to the present. Surely, if Shakespeare had wished his audience to regard the Ghost as a demon, he would have tried to make such an important point clear to them, instead of leaving it to be revealed by one of our new readings. I think we must conclude, therefore, that the Ghost is what the play says it is, and not what the ideas of the time, as expounded by these critics, say it should be.

What light, then, is shed by the three examples upon this sort of historical approach to the drama through the ideas of the time? They certainly do not support the claim, quoted at the outset, that it provides a corrective to the vagaries of impressionistic criticism, for we have seen that it is itself highly subjective and selective in its use of historical evidence. It is in fact doubly selective. It chooses which ideas of the time it will apply; from the various beliefs existing then on some subject, it singles out one to be designated as "the Elizabethan attitude" toward that subject. And it also chooses the plays to which it will apply this attitude: the idea that daughters must obey their parents is used against Juliet and Desdemona, but not Anne Page or Moll Yellowhammer; the idea that victims must forgive those who wronged them is used against Hamlet and his father's ghost, but not against Malcolm or Macduff or Lear or Cordelia, and so on.

It is no coincidence, furthermore, that in each of these examples the application of "the Elizabethan attitude" is supposed to make the character involved much less sympathetic than he would otherwise seem to be: Lear becomes a horrifying sinner before the play begins, and presumably remains one to the end (since he dies without repenting or even recognizing this horrifying sin); both Juliet and Desdemona become unnatural, indecent, sinful, etc.; and Hamlet, in accepting the demon-ghost, will himself become damned. We [have seen] that this was the general thrust of any attempt to impose upon the play an external standard of judgment derived from the ideas of the time. For in selecting the ideas that will constitute "Elizabethan attitudes," these critics are almost inevitably drawn to the orthodox pieties which they can confirm in the theological or homiletic literature, and which therefore usually turn out to be some exalted ideal that the character falls short of, or some exacting prescription of conduct that he violates. Thus we found one condemning . . . Montague and Capulet because their reconciliation is "far short of a heavenly peace" described by Augustine. . . . Another critic censures Romeo for not attaining "true love . . . by Paul's definition"; and another uses Plato's definition for the same purpose: "As Socrates proves in Plato's *Symposium*, love which is not directed toward some demonstrable ideal cannot be said to exist. . . . This is Othello's case (and indeed the case of Claudio and Orsino too)." And, he might have added, of just about every other lover in the drama of this period.

Many more examples of this sort could be cited, in which the ideas of the time, conceived of either as specific rules or general ideals, are invoked to denigrate a character. . . . [Other critics] have similarly attacked Hamlet (and his father's ghost, as we just saw) for not "joyfully forgiving" Claudius. Desdemona also runs afoul of the Christian ideal (Calvinist section), according to another critic, when she protests that she never trespassed against Othello's love, "Either in discourse of thought or actual deed, / Or that mine eyes, mine ears, or any sense / Delighted them in any other form" (IV. ii. 153–55):

> Her reference to her "discourse of thought" and to her "senses" as having been perfectly pure is another example of pride, since the mind and the senses were notoriously fickle from the Skeptical and Calvinistic points of view. . . . A virtuous person was expected to acknowledge and thus control his sinful impulses (thought and sense) rather than try to deny them as Desdemona does.

Another finds that Othello's account of his courtship—"She lov'd me for the dangers I had pass'd, /And I lov'd her that she did pity them" (I. iii. 167–68)—is concerned with "bad fame" (reputation among men) rather than "good fame" (glorifying God), a traditional distinction "which Shakespeare's contemporaries would recognize": "Judging from these lines, Othello's love for his wife would seem to be based on her acclaim of his military reputation, and there is no attempt by Othello to offset this by referring his love, on the model of good fame, to God." Other characters have been censured by other critics for failing to maintain the proper subordination of the passions to reason, as orthodox doctrine prescribed (we learn from one of them that "any humanist of the 17th century would have appreciated" this), or for trusting in the sufficiency of reason instead of properly subordinating it to God (the audience, we are assured, "would have understood such a preoccupation with the sin of 'self-sufficiency' . . . [which] every school boy would have known" from his catechism). And one critic has even anathematized Polonius's advice to Laertes on clothes because it violates the biblical admonition to "take no thought . . . for your body, what ye shall put on" (Matt. 6:25).

Still others have argued that contemporary attitudes toward (invariably against) certain specific actions were much harsher than our own, and so require an unfavorable judgment of characters whom we would otherwise regard favorably. The Elizabethan attitude toward suicide has been employed in this way to condemn Romeo and Juliet and Othello; . . . the attitude toward adultery to condemn Antony and Cleopatra ("Elizabethan audiences were more hostile to adultery than the 20th Century".) . . . It would seem, then, that the marked change in our judgment of the character which this approach is supposed to produce (and on which, we saw, rests the claim that it is making an impressive contribution to our understanding of the play) is always a change for the worse. The ideas of the time have become a club with which to clobber the character.

This reductive effect would suggest a relationship to the ironic approach, which also left every character it dealt with much worse than it found him. . . . [T]he two approaches can be employed together. But they are theoretically distinct. While some ironic readings enlist an idea of the time in their attack upon a character (since it is so easy to find one severe enough to condemn him), others do not; and there are ideas-of-the-time readings which never allude to irony or explicitly challenge the "face value" of the play, because their rationale is quite different. They are not claiming that the playwright deliberately concealed his real meaning; on the contrary, they will insist, if they consistently follow the principles of the approach, that this meaning seemed perfectly obvious to him and to his original audience ("Shakespeare's contemporaries would recognize," "every school boy would have known"), and is not obvious to us only because the ideas of our time are not the ideas of his. Thus instead of the ironic critic's distinction between the hidden real meaning and the deceptive apparent meaning, they distinguish the true historical meaning from the anachronistic modern meaning. But while this is an important difference in theory, the result is much the same, since both approaches ask us to reject our felt experience of the play and to substitute for it an interpretation we have not experienced— specifically, as we saw, to regard with antipathy a character whom we found sympathetic. In practice, moreover, if the historical critic tries to confront the facts of the play, he almost always has to resort to methods of the ironic critics in order to negate them, since in each of the examples these facts are clearly ranged against his interpretation (if they were not, there would be no need to invoke the ideas of the time and he would not have a "new reading"). The distinction between the two approaches, therefore, may seem to be more a matter of their rhetoric than of their actual procedure.

Although these historical readings often employ some strategies of the ironic approach, they do have one that is uniquely their own—the parading of the "authorities" endorsing the particular idea (or ideas) of the time which they intend to apply to the play. These are the contemporary theologians and philosophers and moralists, or earlier ones who influenced contemporary thought, and they serve as the principal weapons of this approach. The critic scores points against the character by citing the authorities who would disapprove of his conduct, and the more of them he can cite, the better for him and the worse for the character. In order to convict Othello of addiction to "bad fame," for example, the reading just quoted draws upon Augustine's *De Civitate Dei*, Boethius's *De Consolatione Philosophiae*, Petrarch's *Africa*, Erasmus's *Enchiridion Militis Christiani*, and Vives's *Introductio ad Sapientiam* and *Christi Jesu Triumphans*. And the reading . . . which undertakes to prove that Hamlet is "a soul lost in damnable error is able to muster an even more formidable battery against him, including Agrippa, Aquinas, Augustine, Boethius, Calvin, Dante, Peter Lombard, Francis de Sales, Nicholas Trivet, and Ludovicus Vives, along with seven books of the Old and New Testaments. With all those impressive voices proclaiming Hamlet's damnation, who will hear Horatio say, ᴦood night, sweet prince, /And flights of angels sing thee to thy t"?

ᴴis type of historical critic will not hear those words, because he listening to the play but to the ideas of the time, which will settle the matter for him a priori. The deductive inevitability of his conclusion is in fact built into the typical organization of these readings, which is explained to us in the introduction to the study of the Ghost in *Hamlet* discussed earlier:

> The reader will retrace the path taken by my own investigation, and take the same steps in the same order: first, defining conventional attitudes toward revenge in Shakespeare's day; next, ascertaining audience attitudes toward revenge in the plays of Shakespeare and his contemporaries; then testing the Ghost according to criteria familiar to both Protestants and Catholics; and, finally, analyzing the play itself in the light of some surprising discoveries.

We begin, in other words, with the ideas of the time (as defined by those "authorities"), which become the unquestioned premises of the argument, and so when we finally get to "the play itself," the analysis of it "in the light of" these ideas will necessarily be determined by them, as the conclusion of a syllogism is determined by the premises. It is therefore not at all surprising that this critic's discoveries about contemporary views of revenge and pneumatology should be mirrored in the play and should require the condemnation of both the Ghost and Hamlet. And numerous other historical readings proceed down this same path—first establishing "the Elizabethan attitude" toward some aspect of life, and then censuring the character for failing to measure up to it.

Sometimes these Elizabethan attitudes are employed to determine not only the judgment of a particular character but even the form and overall effect of the play. The reader will have noticed that the interpretations produced by this approach regularly transform the tragedies of the period, with their sympathetic and pitiful protagonists, into a kind of villain-hero drama where we are supposed to watch with grim satisfaction the punishment of sinners "deserving everything they got." But such a conception of tragedy has itself been deduced from the ideas of the time, by certain historical critics, and then used to deduce the need to apply other ideas of the time in order to prove that the characters are sinful. The earliest example of this double argument that I could find appears in an influential book on Shakespearean tragedy published in 1930, which is presented in three parts following an irresistible logical progression. The first section deals with "the purpose and method of tragedy" as "Shakespeare's contemporaries thought" of it, and demonstrates, through extensive quotation of the authorities, that they saw tragedies as *"exempla* by which men are taught the lessons of moral philosophy" on "how to avoid ruin and misery." The second section surveys "moral philosophy in Shakespeare's day" in order to show, again by extensive quotations, that this philosophy found "in men's passions . . . the cause of the evil which they bring upon themselves." And the third examines Shakespeare's major tragedies and discovers that they "made concrete" the "philosophical teaching of the period," since in each of them the protagonist's downfall is caused by the excess of a particular passion, which instructs us to avoid it. Trapped within this two-pronged historical necessity, Hamlet, Othello, Lear, and Macbeth are thus reduced to "slaves of passion," and their tragedies to edifying lessons in how not to behave. *Quod erat demonstrandum.*

The principal objection to the use of the ideas of the time in all these readings is the same one that we [have] raised . . . to the illegitimate use of sources (which is not strange, since these ideas are treated as a kind of source)—namely, that it leaves out the artist. For he becomes nothing more than a conduit through which the idea (or sources) are transmitted from the historical "context" or "background" to the play. And it is assumed that this transmission must occur regardless of what he may do or not do in the play itself, because he presumably is unable to ignore or modify that context (if he could, then it would not be possible to deduce his meaning from the ideas of his time). . . . [Thus one critic] finds that the same "orthodox" doctrine informs *Measure for Measure, Othello, Lear, Macbeth, Antony and Cleopatra,* and *Coriolanus.* Nor can we stop there, for the historical context which governed Shakespeare had to govern his contemporaries as well, and the result must be that all of the works of all of the writers of the English Renaissance will embody the same set of ideas and attitudes and therefore will have the same meaning. That is the logical conclusion of this approach, and its reductio ad absurdum.

I hope it is not necessary to argue that this is absurd. It should be obvious, for instance, that very different judgments of revenge are called for in *Hamlet, Antonio's Revenge, Hoffman,* and *The Atheist's Tragedy* (which were all written in a space of twelve years), and that \o monolithic "Elizabethan attitude" toward revenge, however it is formulated, could be applied to these plays without distorting some of them beyond recognition. . . . In fact very different attitudes can function within a single play, for we often find that one standard of judgment is being applied to the main action and another to the subplot, especially when it centers around a clown character (as may be seen, for example, in the treatment of Faustus's and Robin's dealings with the devil). And there would be no possible way to account for all of these differences if the artist were controlled by the ideas of his time. He therefore must have been able to choose, within fairly wide limits, the specific ideas in terms of which he wanted the action to be judged, and he also must have been able to establish them within the play itself.

The establishment of such an internal standard can be a very complicated and subtle process, one which I have never seen satisfactorily explained (and which I could recommend as an area of investigation likely to yield far more valuable results than the production of another new reading). But fortunately we do not need to understand its mode of operation in order to respond to it. And the fact is that in most of these plays we do know how to respond—we know whether a character is meant to be sympathetic or antipathetic, whether we are to laugh at him or with him, and so on. We know this without the benefit of of those historical readings based upon some idea of the time (indeed such readings can only confuse us, since we saw that they set out to refute our actual experience of the play). And this must mean that the playwrights, or at least the best of them, have been careful to incorporate into the play the relevant ideas and attitudes that are to guide our reaction. And if they have, then the critic's task is clear—that is, if he seeks to interpret the author's intention. He must induce each play's standard of judgment from that play, and not try to deduce it from the ideas of the time or any other external source.

Titus Andronicus:
Villainy and Tragedy

by Reuben A. Brower

The later quartos and folio of *Titus* have an ending also typical
of the Roman plays and tragedies:

> See iustice done on Aron that damn'd Moore,
> By whom our heauie haps had their beginning:
> Then afterwards to order well the state,
> That like euents may nere it ruinate.

Less nobly Roman, but thoroughly typical of popular Elizabethan
drama, is the "iustice done on Aron." "Breast-deep in earth,"
Lucius decrees, "let him stand and rave and cry for food" . . .
(179–80). However we regard Aaron's end, whether with revulsion
or amused satisfaction at seeing the villain "get his," we can agree
that he is the most entertaining and most individual character in
the play. His special voice is heard when he recounts his crimes
with the robust cynicism of Marlowe's Barabas:

> Even now I curse the day (and yet I think
> Few come within the compass of my curse)
> Wherein I did not some notorious ill . . .
>
> (V. i. 125–27)

this scene and elsewhere that "incarnate devil," as Lucius calls
is very like Iago. Both villains are scornful of "honest" men,
·oth juggle pious language with finesse. To a command from
that reminds us of Othello, Aaron gives Iago's sort of

'ronicus: Villainy and Tragedy." From *Hero and Saint: Shakespeare and the
Heroic Tradition* by Reuben A. Brower (New York and Oxford: Oxford
·, 1971), pp. 194–203. Copyright © 1971 by the Oxford University Press.
·rmission of the Oxford University Press.

> *Lucius.* Bring down the devil, for he must not die
> So sweet a death as hanging presently.
> *Aaron.* If there be devils, would I were a devil,
> To live and burn in everlasting fire,
> So I might have your company in hell
> But to torment you with my bitter tongue!
>
> (145–50)

Tamora uses of herself the word Lodovico applied to Iago:

> I'll find some cunning *practice* out of hand . . .
>
> (V. ii. 77)

As the antimask to the naïvely noble hero, Aaron is a "practicer" of the inverted criminal heroism of Seneca. He "mounts aloft" in rhetoric that might be Tamburlaine's and talks to his "thick-lipp'd" son, a young Caliban, as if he were parodying Hector:

> I'll make you feed on berries and on roots,
> And feed on curds and whey, and suck the goat,
> And cabin in a cave, and bring you up
> To be a warrior and command a camp.
>
> (IV. ii. 177–80)

His challenge to the sons of the queen, which is worth quoting in full, is a nice example of Machiavellian cunning disguised as heroism:

> 'Tis policy and stratagem must do
> That you affect; and so must you resolve
> That what you cannot as you would achieve
> You must perforce accomplish as you may.
> Take this of me: Lucrece was not more chaste
> Than this Lavinia, Bassianus' love.
> A speedier course than ling'ring languishment
> Must we pursue, and I have found the path.
> My lords, a solemn hunting is in hand;
> There will the lovely Roman ladies troop.
> The forest walks are wide and spacious,
> And many unfrequented plots there are,
> Fitted by kind for rape and villany.
> Single you thither then this dainty doe,
> And strike her home by force, if not by words.
> This way, or not at all, stand you in hope.
> Come, come, our Empress, with her sacred wit
> To villany and vengeance consecrate,
> Will we acquaint with all that we intend;

And she shall file our engines with advice,
That will not suffer you to square yourselves,
But to your wishes' height advance you both.
The Emperor's court is like the House of Fame,
The palace full of tongues, of eyes and ears;
The woods are ruthless, dreadful, deaf, and dull.
There speak and strike, brave boys, and take your turns.

                                        (II. i. 104–29)

This is very cheerful, a lively and imaginative call to "villany,"
ending like a call to battle. The inversion is deliberate: "what you
cannot as you would achieve," by direct heroic action, "you must
perforce accomplish as you may," by indirection. The allusions
with which the speech is strewn are used with wit and originality:
Ovid's Lucrece is an example of seductive chastity; the invitation to
the Virgilian hunt, gay and athletic at the start, is modulated to
"rape and villany" in the "ruthless woods" of Philomel's tragic
story; and the prying, gossipy court is evoked perfectly in language
blending the Virgilian and Ovidian (and perhaps the Chaucerian)
myths of *Fama*. The tone of heroic energy,

> And strike her home by force, if not by words . . .

rouses the sons to reply in kind,

> *Chiron.* Thy counsel, lad, smells of no cowardice.
> *Demetrius. Sit fas aut nefas,* till I find the stream
>   To cool this heat, a charm to calm these fits,
>   *Per Styga, per manes vehor.*
>
>   (132–35)

"*Sit fas aut nefas,*" very like Procne's cry as she launches on her path
of revenge, catches the mood of Ovidian and Senecan abandonment to crime, while a tag adapted from Seneca, "*Per Styga, per
manes vehor,*" Phaedra's passionate declaration that she will follow
Hippolytus in the underworld, is twisted to a wicked meaning:
"Until I can cool this lust, I rush through Stygian streams, through
the shades of the dead"; that is, the Arden editor says, "I am in
hell." The combination in the speech of the infernal and the happily active is altogether in "honest Iago's" vein.

But in *Othello* the audience and the hero come to understand that
Iago is a devil in no laughing sense. Perhaps the lack of any moral
recognition of this kind in *Titus Andronicus* is not a very serious

matter. A stage devil plots monstrous deeds and lets others commit them, stabs a nurse in Grand Guignol style and gets a stage punishment as his reward. If the whole play were written in this manner, we might agree with Dover Wilson to take it as a burlesque. But two difficulties arise, both of them connected with the sources of serious interest in *Titus Andronicus*—the Ovidian and Virgilian myths and styles, the themes of marvellous and monstrous change, of heroic action and martyr-like suffering. The main dramatic question of the play, the exposure of an heroic man to "extreme" wrong, is presented in the earlier scenes as an historical action. But with Scene iii of Act II, heroic history gives way to literal enactment of myth. The first difficulty occurs when the rape of Philomel, the sufferings of Io, the vengeful feasts of Philomel and Procne and Thyestes, are spelled out on the stage. Though neither the rhetorical style nor the horrors can be entirely blamed on the Latin poets, some of the more outrageous passages are like Seneca in their cool use of gory language and even more like Ovid in combining physically painful images with startling metaphors. Ovid's figure of the tongue "twitching . . . like the tail of a snake when cut," *tremens . . . utque salire solet mutilatae cauda colubrae . . . palpitat*, perhaps excuses Shakespeare's "crimson river of warm blood" (II. iv. 22). But the Elizabethan out-Ovids Ovid by adding eight lines of "honied" variations on the theme, plentifully seasoned with tricky conceits and classical allusions. The result is nauseating by any standard, literary or humane. The atmosphere of lusty villainy, and the setting of the action in a mythical past, make the ugliness somewhat more bearable, and it may be that the total effect was thrillingly comic to the original audience. But when narrative is literally and crudely translated into dialogue and stage business, horrors that in reading seem fantastic and remote become revoltingly actual or flatly incredible.

Physical cruelty in speech and action in *Titus Andronicus* raises another difficulty, one less easy to deal with justly. Many speeches of Titus and a number of sequences in which he is the chief actor, and nearly all the scenes in which Lucius figures, might have a place in a Shakespearian tragedy of some merit. Only a moral pedant would exclude one of the later heroes from tragic sympathy because of violence, even of a very repellent sort. Spectators accept with understanding and without moral confusion Brutus' political murder of Caesar, Lear's killing of the "slave" that hanged Cordelia, and Othello's misguided act of "justice." In *Titus Andronicus* Lucius is not least noble at the moment when he is killing his father's murderer. We accept in this play as we do in *King Lear* a world in which an aged man makes a foolish and fatal choice, and in which he suffers monstrous blows that no one could call a just reward.

But the moral and dramatic world of *Titus* goes to pieces as the worlds of *Othello* and *Lear* do not. It is possible to dismiss as historical convention the Roman coldness of Titus' acts against his sons in the early scenes of the play, but it is less easy to put up with his behaviour when he turns into the butcher-baker of the final act. As noble Roman and aged father driven by "extremity of woe," Titus should not join the happy criminal society of Seneca's Clytemnestra and Medea, or of Aaron, Tamora, and her sons. When he does, the play gets badly out of joint, and nothing can save scenes in which Titus' speech style becomes barely distinguishable from Aaron's, and in which his actions outdo the devil-Moor. Why, we ask, is all this so much more intolerable than the mythical actions in Ovid on which the scenes are largely based? Why is Titus' collapse merely revolting or incredible and not, like the transformation of Othello, frightening, pitiable, and tragic?

The answers to both questions are connected. Ovid, for all his brilliance and his amusement in demonstrating that the mythical past was as evil as Augustan Rome, maintains a moral as well as narrative distance from the horrors he relates. He is moral almost in spite of himself, since he speaks with the voice of a civilization that places the mythical event within a context of traditional values. In Ovid's telling of the story of Philomela and Procne Tereus is *barbarus* from the outset, a criminal who slyly takes credit for being *pius*. By contrast, there is the genuine if naïve appeal of Pandion to *pietas*, and the pious tears of his daughter. Ovid's treatment of the sisters when they are caught up in the rage of revenge is utterly different from the amorality of Seneca's *Agamemnon,* where the heroine joyously gives way to crime and where—for all the detachment and highmindedness of the choral odes—there is no assurance of a mind or a society outside the criminal world.

The answer to the question why *Titus Andronicus* offends and confuses where *Othello* does not, is indicated by the answer from

Ovid. In *Othello*, Shakespeare does what he fails to do in the more barbarous scenes of *Titus*, and what Seneca never does: he brings to the stage effective voices outside the universe of hell and night in which Iago acts and by which Othello is gradually corrupted. Desdemona, innocent as she is, detects the symptoms of his fall— the "puddling of his clear mind," and the evil "fury" in his voice; and Emilia with simple honesty names the disease. More decisively, Shakespeare introduces a figure and a reality from beyond Iago's Cyprus, in Lodovico, who comes with news from Venice. It is Lodovico who recalls the audience and Othello's companions to what has happened:

> Is this the noble Moor . . . ?

In the last scene of the play there is also Emilia, heroically protesting and telling the truth, and Othello, who now sees the devil in Iago and the darkness of his own corruption.

In *Othello*, by contrast with the "Romaine Tragedie," the voices of innocence and civility are brought in contact with the voices of barbarism and chaos and—more important—the contact is registered within the consciousness of the hero. Though at the end of *Titus Andronicus* Lucius speaks for order in the state, no dramatic connection is made between political disorder and the disordered mind of Titus or any other character. It would be comic to ask whether Titus recognizes the barbarousness of his actions. Although he has seemed more human when he was "not with himself," there is no suggestion that like Hamlet he has been disturbed by doubts or dismayed by lack of control. At one moment in the final orgy a normal moral sense seems to find expression, through—of all people—Saturninus. When in his ultra-Roman mood Titus kills Lavinia, Saturninus asks, not with much effect,

> What hast thou done, unnatural and unkind?

and when Titus kills the Empress, he shouts,

> Die, frantic wretch, for this accursed deed!
> [*He stabs Titus*]

One would not care to read the soul of young Shakespeare from this or any similar episode in *Titus Andronicus*. The scene is a melodramatic free-for-all in a society of maddened killers, a Senecan runaway in dramatic style and action, ending like the *Agamemnon* in moral disorientation. Seneca's example is worth insisting on, because Seneca had given the Elizabethans an approved classical model too potent to be resisted except by a disciplined and mature mind. (Seneca the philosopher seems to have been unable to resist his own convention of translating myth into Roman rhetoric.) Shakespeare goes astray in *Titus Andronicus* because he does not control dramatic direction or model speech to fit new occasions. No trace of the earlier Titus' voice can be heard in the "unnatural" killer of Act V. (The contrast with Othello and Macbeth is worth noting.) The moral effect, though confusing, does not necessarily indicate, as Eliot would have it, an Elizabethan moral "chaos." It may prove rather that the author had a vision of the nightmare world outside "the law of nature and of nations," to which he could not as yet give expression. Incomplete though *Titus* is as a tragedy, the last speeches of Lucius (and some of his earlier gestures) imply the existence of a civilized order that had gone under in the Senecan–Ovidian extravaganza of the immediately preceding scene. Hence the muddle; if there were nowhere any expression of a different standard, *Titus Andronicus* would offer no problem and little interest to the critic. We could dismiss the play as blood and thunder, or accept it as travesty. But if we think of Titus' soliloquy in Act IV ("Come, Marcus, come"), with its flexibility of moral and emotional tone, or of his demands for justice, or his regret that he had given up his right to be emperor, we shall recognize the presence of a dramatic poet who may in time mould speech-of-character to carry the relevant evaluations.

The remarkable thing about the play is not its badness, but the signs it gives of a Shakespeare who will find a way out of the dramatic and rhetorical conventions of the Roman "tragedies" of the 1580s. The way out will be reached not by relying on any single method or model. We may guess that the encounter in the English Histories with an historical reality relatively more familiar than the vague "history" of *Titus* will prevent Shakespeare from long straying in Ovidian and Senecan melodrama. He will make his way into true tragic drama, through returning to the sources of deeper interest in *Titus*, and through a deeper perception of the logic, moral and dramatic, of the Virgilian and Ovidian example. The development will also depend in part on refashioning the Stoic model of the great self exposed to injustice and suffering, yet still enduring. Growth will come, as *Titus Andronicus* dimly shows, through a union of heroic Roman action and suffering with Ovidian (ultimately Virgilian and Homeric) transformation of nobility under stress into the monstrous and beastly. The new vision will include something further—this too is foreshadowed in Ovid, and more certainly in Virgil—the belief in the persistence of nobility and its possible transformation into a nature more human and more beautiful. In spite of its crudity, *Titus Andronicus* gives a foretaste of how the new and larger unity, with the increased control in moral evaluation, will be gained. In the character of Titus as in the character of Lucrece, some of the great questions are raised: why should the noble man suffer, why are his cries for justice unheard, how is he to act, how is he to "be like himself" in "a wilderness of tigers"? Ugly possibilities are offered: he may go mad, he may suffer even more by rigid adherence to the very qualities that have made him a hero, he may turn into a monster and become indistinguishable from his tormentors. There is even a hint that for the hero, as for Frost's countrywoman, "the best way out is through," that the only victory is to lose himself to find himself. There is evidence too, in *Titus Andronicus*, of a potential ability to dramatize the opposite of violence and disorder, to create representatives of directed heroic action, of civilized life, order and peace. Lucius is the sketch for future expressions of this sort, whether in single characters or within the multiple consciousness of the hero; that is to say, Lucius is prophetic not only of Fortinbras, but of heroic Hamlet. But the literary feat of connecting these contrasting and conflicting kinds of experience is well beyond the author of *Titus Andronicus*. How to fuse in a single dramatic and poetic expression the "tigers" and "high resolved men," reason and the beast? The connection will be realized when Shakespeare can write characterizing speech apt to the moment and the dramatic movement, but also bearing through image, metaphor, and thematic word, the necessary moral and emotional evaluations—language that is proof of his power of grasping the whole drama in a single poetic and dramatic vision, and of realizing it in one unbroken act of expression. There are some glimpses of this achievement in a speech of Titus' we spoke of earlier:

> For now I stand as one upon a rock,
> Environ'd with a wilderness of sea . . .

The "wilderness of sea" is linked with the "wilderness of tigers," of humanity preying on itself, and with the sources and the scene of Titus' and Lavinia's suffering; while the man standing "upon a rock" in a lonely seascape symbolizes an heroic self that can, like Lear's, still make an assertion in "extremity of woe."

Romeo and Juliet: A Formal Dwelling

by James L. Calderwood

"Banished" is the severing word that immediately threatens and finally destroys the communion of love since because of it the lovers are forced to communicate through society by means of the friar's message, and that is precisely what they cannot do. Only in a state of lyric seclusion hermetically sealed off from the plague-stricken world outside can their language retain its expressive purity. But the lovers cannot remain forever in the orchard, much as they would like to, and the poet cannot escape the fact that whereas his art is private, wrought in his own stylistic image and even given that personal signature that Shakespeare laments in Sonnet 76, his linguistic medium itself is intransigently public. As part of the vulgar tongue the words he would adopt are contaminated by ill usage, by an ever-present epidemic of imprecision, banality, lies, false rhetoric, jargon, true rhetoric, sentimentality, and solecisms, and by more localized historical plagues such as Petrarchanism, Euphuism, inkhorn neologisms, television commercials, social scientese, and beat or hippie nonspeak. Like Juliet on first confronting Romeo, the poet wants to compel words to abandon their corrupt public identities and submit to his cleansing rebaptism. Or again, to use another of the play's metaphors, like Romeo words as public identities must die ("He heareth not, he stirreth not, he moveth not," Mercutio says of Romeo; "The ape is dead"—II. i. 15–16) so that they may be reborn within the context of the poem ("Call me but love and I'll be new baptized; /Henceforth I never will be Romeo"—II. ii. 50–51).

This account of things is perhaps unduly metaphoric and a bit confusing as regards Romeo, whose verbal status is rather ambiguous. His Petrarchan style is impure, as underscored by Juliet's stylistic objections, because in the context of the play it comes from that extramural world outside the orchard. That is not to say that the sonnets of Wyatt, Sidney, Spenser, or Petrarch himself exhibit corrupt language. It is to say that the Petrarchan *style* has a public existence outside individual Petrarchan poems and that in Shakespeare's time—and certainly in his own view, as Sonnet 130 makes clear—it stood for a debased literary currency. Paradoxically at least some of this impurity derives from the fact that the Petrarchan style aspires to pure poetry and in so aspiring becomes an airy, hyperbolic, mechanically artificial expression of unfelt and undiscriminating feelings. In this sense it is too pure ("Virtue itself turns vice, being misapplied"—II. iii. 21), and when the too pure becomes too popular it turns impure, an infectious blight on the literary landscape.

From this excessive purity excessively available, Juliet recoils, seeking like Shakespeare a more individual style, a more genuine purity. But neither Juliet nor Shakespeare fully succeeds in the attempt to forge a new and authentic idiom. We are clearly asked to regard the movement from Romeo-Rosaline to Romeo-Juliet as an advance from Petrarchan dotage to true romantic love. And surely in large degree it is—after all, this love seals its bond in marriage and bears it out even to and beyond the edge of doom. Granted, and yet I doubt that either we or Shakespeare can rest fully at ease with the lovers' style. The trouble is that the old Romeo is imperfectly killed off; the ape is not really dead—too much of his Petrarchan manner and language live on in him; and Juliet, despite her anti-Petrarchan bias, too readily quickens to the invitations of his style. Her better speeches are resistance pieces that gain eloquence in the process of denying the power of speech itself, most notably in the balcony scene. She scores well off Romeo's verbal extravagance:

> *Romeo.* Ah Juliet, if the measure of thy joy
>   Be heaped like mine, and that thy skill be more
>   To blazon it, then sweeten with thy breath
>   This neighbour air and let rich music's tongue
>   Unfold the imagined happiness that both
>   Receive in either by this dear encounter.

> *Juliet.* Conceit, more rich in matter than in words,
> Brags of his substance, not of ornament.
> They are but beggars that can count their worth,
> But my true love is grown to such excess
> I cannot sum up sum of half my wealth.
>
> (II. vi. 24–34)

But if the worth of private feeling cannot be assessed in the crude countinghouse of language, Juliet seems not always aware of it. This is most noticeable when on learning that Romeo has killed Tybalt her feelings swing from love to dismay:

> O serpent heart hid with a flowering face!
> Did ever dragon keep so fair a cave?
> Beautiful tyrant! Fiend angelical!
> Dove-feathered raven! Wolvish ravening lamb!
> Despised substance of divinest show!
>
> (III. ii. 73–77)

The distinction in the last line between substance and show invites our recollection of the distinction between substance and ornament in her speech just quoted (II. vi. 30–31) and urges on us the stylistic reversal that has occurred. It is wonderfully fitting that Juliet should register the shock to private feeling by adopting Romeo's Petrarchan oxymorons (cf. I. i. 181–88) at the exact moment when her loyalties turn in the antinominalist direction of "family" (she grieves not for Tybalt the unique but for Tybalt the cousin). She quickly recovers from this style and feeling, as does their love in general, but in the remainder of the scene her style (like Romeo's in III. iii) keeps shrilling upward into a mannered hysteria in which conceit, less rich in matter than in words, brags of its ornament, not its substance. Bathos is now their medium, and their verbal excesses are defended on the authority of unique feeling:

> *Romeo.* Thou canst not speak of that thou dost not feel.
> Wert thou as young as I, Juliet thy love,
> An hour but married, Tybalt murdered,
> Doting like me and like me banished,
> Then mightst thou speak, then mightst thou tear thy hair
> And fall upon the ground as I do now,
> Taking the measure of an unmade grave.
>
> (III. iii. 64–70)

Such claims disarm criticism—ours I suppose as well as that of the friar, who must be wincing at the amount of hypothesis required to

40 *James L. Calderwood*

put him in the position of youth and love. No one denies the validity and intensity of the feeling, but of course a riot of feeling need not necessitate a riot of language and premature measurements of graves that look suspiciously like cribs. Romeo rejects all discipline that originates beyond self, whether moral, social, or stylistic. In effect he repudiates the world, and so hastens logically on to the notion of suicide. When Friar Laurence, harried back and forth across the room by the banging of the world at his door and the blubbering of a Romeo who would dissolve all connections with the world, cries in exasperation, "What simpleness is this!" (III. iii. 77) his choice of the noun is perfect, for in the unblended simpleness of Romeo the man of unique feelings there is indeed at this point great silliness. However, Romeo is not altogether as pure in his simpleness as he would like, and radical purgation is called for:

> O tell me, friar, tell me
> In what vile part of this anatomy
> Doth my name lodge? Tell me, that I may sack
> The hateful mansion.
>
> (III. iii. 105–8)

To become pure "Romeo" and extirpate his connections with everything beyond self he would destroy "Montague," the "vile part" of him in which the world has staked its claim. But as the friar points out, the dagger that pierces Montague pierces Romeo as well:

> Why rail'st thou on thy birth, the heaven, and earth?
> Since birth and heaven and earth all three do meet
> In thee at once, which thou at once wouldst lose.
>
> (III. iii. 119–21)

So far as I can see there is small evidence that Romeo absorbs much of the friar's lesson. For him there remains no world beyond the walls of Juliet's garden, where the lovers still strive to meet with all the nominalistic singularity of their Edenic forebears. Their lamentations in III. ii and III. iii are only a more strident stylistic version of their speech in III. v. In this the last scene in which they engage in genuine dialogue before the destructive force of the word "banished" takes its full toll, we see the lyric imagination desperately seeking to impose its own truth on the world of fact and sunrise:

> *Juliet.* Wilt thou be gone? It is not yet near day.
> It was the nightingale and not the lark
> That pierced the fearful hollow of thine ear.
> Nightly she sings on yond pomegranate tree.
> Believe me, love, it was the nightingale.
> (III. v. 1–5)

And again:

> *Juliet.* Yond light is not daylight, I know it, I—
> It is some meteor that the sun exhales
> To be to thee this night a torchbearer
> And light thee on thy way to Mantua.
> (III. v. 12–15)

In line with her nominalistic "A rose by any other word" Juliet would rebaptize Nature, transforming lark and daylight into nightingale and meteor to the end that time stand still. Romeo allows himself to be persuaded that "it is not day," but as soon as he does so Juliet's lyric preoccupation is gone: "It is, it is! Hie hence, be gone, away!" (III. v. 25–26). As it operates in the wide world, language may be less pure than the lovers would wish, but it stands for a view of reality that neither lover nor poet can safely ignore. Time, light, larks, and the usual terms for them remain intransigently themselves, answerable to their public definitions. The lover who withdraws entirely from the world into an autistic domain of feeling must pay for his pleasure with his life, as Romeo would were he to remain in the orchard. By the same token the poet who reshapes language in the exclusive light of his own designs, turning his back on his audience and creating not a truly individual but merely a unique style, must pay for his eccentric pleasures with his poetic life. There is no great danger of that here since the trouble with the lovers' style is not eccentricity but conventionality. The purity it aspires to, like that of the Petrarchanism to which it is uncomfortably akin, is too easily come by. And judging their language this way, I should be quick to add—that is, grading it down for poetic diction and a superabundance of rhetorical figures—is not to impose on the play a modern bias against rhetoric but to accept the implications of the play itself and to honor Shakespeare's own standards, which are implicit in his gradual estrangement over the years from an enameled, repetitive, lyrical style in favor of one that is concentrated, complex, and dramatic.

It would seem then that in *Romeo and Juliet* Shakespeare has encountered but by no means resolved the poet's dilemma. No doubt he must often have known perfectly well where he wanted poetically to go and yet could not get there, and knew that too. On the authority of the play's structure we can assume that he wanted to get from Rosaline to Juliet, from pure poetry to a viable poetic purity, but that he did not complete the journey in satisfactory style. That he realized this seems evident from the care he has taken to protectively enclose the lovers' poetic purity. Robert Penn Warren has shrewdly argued that the "impure poetry" of Mercutio and the nurse—poetry, that is, that reflects the impurity of life itself by means of wit, irony, logical contradictions, jagged rhythms, unpoetic diction, and so forth—provides a stylistic context in which we can more readily accept the too pure poetry of the lovers.[1] Warren assumes in other words that the impure poetry in the play functions much as William Empson claims comic subplots function, as lightning rods to divert the audience's potentially dyslogistic reactions away from the vulnerable high seriousness of the main plot (main style).[2] The implication is that Shakespeare is trying to have it both ways at once, that like Juliet asking for an "unnamed naming" in the balcony scene he asks us to accept the authenticity of a style that he himself knows is too pure and therefore needful of protection. From this perspective one sees that in stacking the literary deck against the lovers—by providing the stylistic opposition of Mercutio and the nurse and the environmental opposition of the feuding families, of fate, coincidences, and mistimings—Shakespeare has actually stacked it in their favor. The obvious contrast is with *Antony and Cleopatra*, and we might note that whereas the impure poetry of Enobarbus functions like that of Mercutio and the nurse, by that time Shakespeare has mastered his own stylistic problems and can imbue those lovers' language with an impurity of its own. If the later technique risks more, it stands to gain more too, and as we all know does.

[1] In his famous article "Pure and Impure Poetry," originally printed in the *Kenyon Review* 5 (Spring 1943):228–54, and since reprinted in many collections of critical essays.

[2] Empson's remarks on subplots appear in *Some Versions of Pastoral*, pp. 25–84 of the New Directions paperback edition (New York, 1960).

The argument made here in terms of style can be extended to character and genre also, for the lovers themselves, no less than their style, are too pure and they acquire in the minds of too many readers an unearned tragic stature. Even though the play rejects uniqueness Shakespeare has nominalistically bleached from Romeo and Juliet most of the impurities that rub off on man by virtue of his public contacts. They simply have no public contacts. Despite the importance of family, they are essentially unrelated, meeting as isolated individuals rather than (like Antony and Cleopatra) as complex human beings with social, political, religious, and even national allegiances and responsibilities to contend with. Insufficiently endowed with complexity, with the self-division that complexity makes possible, and with the self-perceptiveness that such division makes possible, they become a study in victimage and sacrifice, not tragedy. Their experience portrays not the erosion within but the clash without, and the plot harries them toward lamentation instead of vision. One of the major ironies of the final scene in the tomb is that for all its imagery of radiance the illumination is entirely outside Romeo, kindled by torches and Juliet's beauty, not by a self-reflective consciousness. On the stylistic failure as it relates to tragedy Maynard Mack says, "Comic overstatement aims at being preposterous. Until it becomes so, it remains flat. Tragic overstatement, on the other hand, aspires to be believed, and unless in some sense it is so, remains bombast."[3]

In Shakespeare's protection of the lovers Mercutio plays a crucial role, for although Juliet rejects the false purity of Romeo's Petrarchan style she never has to encounter the rich impurity of Mercutio's speech. And it is Mercutio who seems the genuine threat. The nurse's style is abundantly impure, but that is all it is, whereas Mercutio can deliver pure poetry impurely. In his much-admired, much-maligned Queen Mab speech, which looks so suspiciously and conspicuously irrelevant to the main issues of the play, Mercutio turns pure poetry back on itself. Even while presenting a lengthy illustration of pure poetry he defines it as a product of fancy and foolishness airily roaming like Queen Mab herself

---

[3] Maynard Mack, "The Jacobean Shakespeare: Some Observations on the Construction of the Tragedies," in *Jacobean Theatre*, vol. I of Stratford-upon-Avon Studies, ed. John Russell Brown and Bernard Harris (New York, 1960), p. 15.

through dreaming minds, to which it offers substitute gratifications that have no direct bearing on reality—on real courtiers' real curtsies and suits, on lawyers' stunning fees, ladies' kisses, parsons' benefices, soldiers' battles. "Peace, Mercutio, peace!" Romeo cries. "Thou talk'st of nothing." But because Mercutio can talk of something as well as nothing, because he can deal in both pure and impure styles, he is given a tough and enduring eloquence that makes the nurse, mired in the language of sensual expedience, seem gross and Romeo callow. (Romeo to be sure can vie with Mercutio in the lubricities of street speech, but Romeo-with-Juliet is another man altogether; Shakespeare keeps the two scrupulously discrete.)

Entering the orchard where felt experience is sovereign, Romeo can dismiss Mercutio's extramural ribaldry about Rosaline with a famous line—"He jests at scars that never felt a wound" (II. ii. 1). When the wound is in the other chest though, Romeo must play straight man to more famous lines:

> *Romeo.* Courage, man, the hurt cannot be much.
> *Mercutio.* No, 'tis not so deep as a well nor so wide as a
> church door, but 'tis enough, 'twill serve.
> (III. i. 98–100)

This asks to be compared to the lovers' style. They repeatedly claim that language is too shallow a thing to reach into the deeps of private feeling, but their own verbal practice is hardly consistent with such a claim. Whenever their feelings are touched, torrents follow. Hence the bristling oxymorons of the stricken Romeo in I. i.:

> Why then O brawling love! O loving hate!
> O anything, of nothing first create!
> O heavy lightness, serious vanity,
> Misshapen chaos of well-seeming forms!
> Feather of lead, bright smoke, cold fire, sick health!
> Still-waking sleep that is not what it is!
> This love feel I, that feel no love in this.
> (I. i. 182–88)

Hence the same oxymorons from Juliet's lips in III. ii. ("Beautiful tyrant! fiend angelical!" etc.) and the bathos of Romeo in III. iii., for example:

> Heaven is here
> Where Juliet lives, and every cat and dog
> And little mouse, every unworthy thing,
> Live here in heaven and may look on her,
> But Romeo may not.
>
> (III. iii. 29–33)

It is in this context of grotesque verbal posturing, where convulsions of speech coalesce with tantrums of feeling, that Mercutio's words on death acquire a quiet and sustained eloquence. It is those words ironically that best fulfill the stylistic requirements of Juliet's early nominalism. The uniquely felt inner "hurt" Mercutio does not try directly to define, thus avoiding the risks of hyperbole and general verbal inflation that prey on the speech of the lovers when they reflect on *their* wounds. The private feeling that's past the size of speech is suggested only obliquely, in terms of the size of the physical "hurt," and even then by saying not what it is but what it is not. Here in the plain style is functional language, language that like the wound itself is content to be "enough," to "serve" rather than run riot. In general then it is the mixed tones of Mercutio's speech that the lovers most need to incorporate into their own style. But Shakespeare has kept Mercutio permanently stationed on the outer side of the orchard wall, as oblivious of the existence of their love as they are to him.

The public world is too crass and bellicose to assimilate the private truth of love, and Mercutio is a good instance of the fact that there are public truths that the lovers cannot assimilate. Given two such disjunctive languages, only mutual injury remains possible. The lovers' language fails when it seeks to make its way by means of Father John through the plague-ridden world beyond the orchard. Love's feelings hold constant, but during the reunion in the tomb the dialogue of love dissolves into lyric monologues heard only by the speaker. One further step remains. The purity of their love (figured after Romeo's departure in Juliet's resistance to marrying Paris) is reasserted in a second marriage ceremony that is even more private than the first:

> *Romeo.* Arms, take your last embrace. And lips, O you
> The doors of breath, seal with a righteous kiss
> A dateless bargain to engrossing death!
>
> (V. iii. 113–15)

In this final contract the breath of lyric speech and the breath of life are simultaneously expended to seal an endless bond with silence. So too with Juliet, who retreats into a remoter stillness as the noise of the outside world rushes toward her:

> Yea, noise? Then I'll be brief. O happy dagger!
> This is thy sheath. There rest and let me die.
> (V. iii. 169–70)

As the *Liebestod* stressed by Denis de Rougemont and others, Romeo and Juliet's love has been a flight from the frustrations of life toward the consummations of the grave. Similarly, as *Liebestille* their linguistic style has been a flight from noise toward a silence beyond speech. The silence is at last achieved and with it an expressiveness that extends their own bond of feeling outward. For embraced in and by death their still figures bespeak the truth of their love to the wondering representatives of the social order gathered in the tomb, and do so with such persuasiveness that it transforms those random and rancorous individuals into a genuine community united in sorrow and sympathy. The cost, however, runs high. What is purchased is in the Prince's apt phrase a "glooming peace"—peace as public amity has been bought by the sacrifice of the lovers to the peace of an enduring but eloquent stillness. . . .

Shakespeare's success in *Romeo and Juliet* is impressive by comparison with past failures but by no means total. His concentration on, almost celebration of, dramatic form imparts to the play a highly rigid structure based on the division between Montagues and Capulets and between lovers and society. As Sigurd Burckhardt has observed, the play has "a symmetry which, even though it is a symmetry of conflict, is comforting."[4] For despite the family feud the social order is in no real danger of collapse. What turbulence there is gets expressed within a stabilizing framework formed by the Prince and the friar, the one devoted to civil order, the other all reason and moderation. The virulence of the conflict between families is mitigated by the principals themselves, the spindle-shanked and slippered old men who allow the feud to continue less from rancor than from apathy. And the lovers are themselves

[4] In "The King's Language: Shakespeare's Drama as Social Discovery," *Antioch Review* 21 (1961): 369–87.

untainted by the enmities abroad; they are not at odds with an antagonistic society so much as they are simply apart from it—hurt by ricochet rather than direct intent, by a secret that always could be made public but never is. Hence there is a strong sense of the arbitrary about the play and the lovers' fate, which with all its dependence on accident, coincidence, and sheer mistiming seems imposed and gratuitous. Finally at the end there is a too easy resolution both of the social problem of uniting the families and of the dramatic dilemma of finding a style in which the private and public dimensions of language are happily joined.

For the dramatic or more precisely linguistic dilemma is resolved at the end not stylistically but symbolically, by means of the emblematic statues in which Shakespeare has sought to comprise both private and public values. If the lovers' nominalistic conception of speech implies a verbal purity bordering on nonspeech, here in the silence of the statues is that stillness; and if their love has aspired to a lyric stasis, here too in the fixity of plastic form is that stillness. But by being publicly available—representing the lovers and their value but representing them for the Veronese audience—the statues surpass the aspirations and expressive aims of the lovers. The communicative gap between the private secret love and the social order oblivious of the existence of that love is bridged—and this seems the major significance of the statues—by *artistic form*. Cast in such form, the worth of unique experience is popularized without being cheapened. By shifting from a verbal to a visually symbolic plane Shakespeare ingeniously makes the most of his stylistic liabilities while acknowledging silently that the too pure language of the lovers could not in itself effect such a union. For the dual stillness of the statues, their silence and motionlessness, reflects not merely the poetic tendencies of the lovers but in a large sense the formal properties of Shakespeare's play. The statues materialize at the conclusion, that is, precisely at the point at which the play as temporal experience materializes into spatial form for its audience, the point at which form completes itself on stage and crystallizes in our memories. If language has not linked the public and private worlds, then form does. And seen in the perspective of dramatic form, the division between lovers and social order is not divisive because the principle of division itself, the playing off of the two worlds in opposition, gives rise to the

form of *Romeo and Juliet.* The paradox of form is like that of love in
"The Phoenix and the Turtle":

> Two distincts, division none:
> Number there in love was slain.

So the most fruitful coalescence of divided worlds is not to be
found in the verbal paradoxes of the oxymoron but in the dramatic
paradoxes of the play as shaped entity. As symbols of that shaping
the statues of the closing scene reflexively comment on Romeo's
oxymorons of the opening scene (I. i. 181ff). Those oxymorons
clashingly connect the two divided spheres of the opening scene,
the public quarrel in the streets and Romeo's private dotage on
Rosaline. Hence they are uttered just at the moment when Romeo
and Benvolio, who have been talking of Romeo's private problems
in love, arrive at the place where the street violence occurred. The
"airy word" that bred the "civil brawls" (I. i. 96) now expresses in
the discordance of Romeo's oxymorons the inner brawling of
Petrarchan dotage and unites the two spheres of experience, public
and private, as versions of a kind of linguistic noise. In both areas
the word has gone bad. Though somewhat redeemed by the speech
of the lovers later on, the word never gets placed in public circula-
tion. It is left for the statues to symbolize in form an ideal but
dramatically unrealized social and verbal union. "Fain would I
dwell on form," Juliet told Romeo; but it is really Shakespeare who
has dwelt on form in this play, and by doing so has enabled Romeo
and Juliet to dwell permanently *in* form.

One final point. I spoke earlier about the nominalistic impulse
behind Shakespeare's creation of lovers from whom all family or
universal relationships have been deleted—nominalistic because we
are asked to confront the lovers as unique particulars. The fact,
however, that the lovers are less singular in language and character
than we might wish suggests that this deletion of universals is actually antinominalistic, less Aristotelian or Scotist than Platonic.
Uniqueness, Shakespeare seems to have realized by the end of this
play, is not the condition of being free from universal ties and
tendencies; it is not a kind of pure essence left behind after we have
burned off all accidental impurities. Distillation of that sort, in fact,
leaves us with something very like Platonic universals themselves.
But this seems to have been the process by which the lovers were

created—a purification by dramatic fiat, giving us a Platonic conception of pure love cast in the role of particulars. At the end of the play, however, Shakespeare seems to sense that with men as with poems uniqueness resides in the form or contextual organization of nonunique qualities—a form sufficiently complex in its internal relations to defy reductive abstraction. Is this not part of the meaning of the statues also? Only by destroying the formal context of the statues can one commercialize the gold of which they are made. Detached though they are from their fictional surroundings, Romeo and Juliet, like the gold in the statues, are permanently embedded in the context of *Romeo and Juliet,* where presumably not even the critic's chisels can get at their priceless worth.

On *Julius Caesar*

by Nicholas Brooke

The Tudor dream was fading, and the obtruding sense of reality was decidedly less splendid. It became correspondingly more difficult to fulfil a tragic pattern, for in tragedy the idea of splendour must ultimately dominate all that can be thrown against it. The bestiality and evil of *Titus* or of *Richard III* work in a context of heroic and divine possibility; a framework of orderly affirmation sustains the plays; they are rhetorical in structure as well as language. So is *Julius Caesar*; but here rhetoric is brought more sharply in question than ever, and though it unquestionably has a rhetorical structure still, that too is much less easily accepted.

There is more certain evidence for dating *Julius Caesar* than for most of Shakespeare's plays. It was not in Meres' list in 1598, but in the Autumn of 1599 Thomas Platter, the Swiss traveller, described a performance of it at the Globe; and there are several literary allusions to it in the next two years. Even if these points are not individually conclusive, we should expect to date it around 1599, for such a date makes sense of what seems to me its peculiar kind of unsatisfactoriness. For all its brilliance, and its success, it has an uncertainty of tone, structure, and total statement which seems to me in some ways like the uncertainty of *All's Well*; although (witness its popularity) *Julius Caesar* "comes off" in a sense in which *All's Well* does not, its basic equilibrium is not really much greater.

Yet if we should not expect to date it before the end of the 1590s, we should also not expect it to be much later; for behind the "new" elements which I have been indicating there is a familiar shape to be recognized, a Senecan shape, of revenge tragedy. The play is firmly based on the Greatness of Caesar, and the ritual crime of his murder, which is preceded by an elaborate display of portents, storms, and portentous rhetoric; Antony fills the role of faithful (and not very hesitant) revenger; Caesar's ghost sustains the portentous atmosphere, and the revenge is finally accomplished.

All this suggests a form and significance for the play remote from the portrait gallery of "characters" which every schoolboy knows, and seemingly equally remote from the concern with men as men which I have been postulating. Hence it is important to stress first that it *is* the play's structure, establishing a simple pattern elaborated by a stress on supernatural forces and blood imagery very like what we have already seen in *Richard II*. Antony's speech over Caesar's body seem to roll *Titus*, *The Spanish Tragedy*, and *Richard II* all up in one:

> O, pardon me, thou bleeding piece of earth,
> That I am meek and gentle with these butchers.
> Thou art the ruins of the noblest man
> That ever lived in the tide of times.
> Woe to the hand that shed this costly blood!
> Over thy wounds now do I prophesy
> (Which like dumb mouths do ope their ruby lips,
> To beg the voice and utterance of my tongue),
> A curse shall light upon the limbs of men;
> Domestic fury and fierce civil strife
> Shall cumber all the parts of Italy;
> Blood and destruction shall be so in use,
> And dreadful objects so familiar,
> That mothers shall but smile when they behold
> Their infants quartered with the hands of war,
> All pity chok'd with custom of fell deeds;
> And Caesar's spirit, ranging for revenge,
> With Ate by his side come hot from hell,
> Shall in these confines with a monarch's voice
> Cry havoc and let slip the dogs of war,
> That this foul deed shall smell above the earth
> With carrion men, groaning for burial.
>   (III. i. 254–75)

In general form, this speech is close to the prophetic handling of sap and blood images in the first two acts of *Richard II*; in ornate detail it goes further back, with the ruby lips of the bleeding

wounds, to Marcuis' speech at the end of Act II of *Titus*; and
Caesar's Senecan spirit with Ate by his side substitutes the classical
figures of *The Spanish Tragedy* for the biblical Cain that haunted
Richard. For a famous, but rather curious, moment towards the
end the "monarch's voice" seems close to Henry V with "Cry havoc
and let slip the dogs of war"; Antony's rallying cry is unexpected
before he returns to carrion men groaning for burial, but it is not
here that his rhetoric is called in question. What he utters here is,
very powerfully, an emblematic summary of the play. In this it is an
extension of the tremendous elaboration of cosmic disturbance in
the storm that shatters Roman peace in Act II.

But here there is a strong point of difference from earlier plays:
the emblematic commentary on *Titus* was not questioned; that on
Richard II hardly could be, since the supernatural powers invoked
were so explicitly biblical. But here belief in cosmic portents
(although apparently confirmed by the whole play—the storm precedes Caesar's death, and the ghost Brutus') is frequently described
as mere superstition, and Caesar's scepticism is debated:

> But it is doubtful yet
> Whether Caesar will come forth to-day or no;
> For he is superstitious grown of late,
> Quite from the main opinion he held once
> Of fantasy, of dreams, and ceremonies.
> It may be these apparent prodigies,
> The unaccustom'd terror of this night,
> And the persuasion of his augurers,
> May hold him from the Capitol to-day.
>
> (II. i. 193–201)

If Shakespeare did not make this up, he certainly amplified it, for it
is not in Plutarch. It produces an odd effect, for Caesar's credulity,
identified with his ageing megalomania, discredits all credulity,
discredits in fact the structure of portents on which I have said the
play is constructed; or at least questions it, for the result is
ambivalent. This ambivalence casts a similarly indefinite shadow on
the play in other ways: the great Caesar is also absurd in his Mar-
lowan self-assertion; Antony, with all his devotion and skill, is
offensive; a similar irony reveals in Cassius (but only occasionally) a
crude jealousy, and it calls Brutus' high-mindedness into question.
The play seems to have equal and opposite tendencies towards the

nobility of tragedy on the one hand, and a world of dust and ashes on the other. There is also a perplexing hovering on the edge of comedy which is sometimes explicit (as, for instance, with Casca's description of Caesar in comic prose in I. ii), but sometimes not at all clear: there are many passages which seem at least to invite a sense of the ridiculous without being decisively "meant" to be funny.

This sense of absurdity is involved in the gap I have indicated between the play's portentous magniloquence, and its insistent concern with men as men; its interest in demagogy, and in "characters." But this is not quite such a simple matter as it has been made out. Certain differences from earlier plays are obvious: even the most formal speeches here do not reach the conclusive ending in couplets, and the utterance has very often a decidedly "naturalistic" tone close to prose, as well as sometimes actually being prose. In this way the stress is laid more directly than in earlier plays on how men actually behave. We are made to feel this very clearly in the first scene between the tribunes and the populace, a trivial dialogue mostly in prose, with only one adventure in rhetoric, the lament for Pompey.

Thus far we are certainly directed to men as men; and the same insistent naturalism emerges in the carefully interposed glimpses of Brutus' home life: we are to feel that these men are like ourselves at least as much as that, being Roman, they are very different. Roman society lacked a divine sanction, or at least it seemed to the Christian tradition to have done so; it was therefore a fit ground in which to explore the political behaviour of men empirically, freed from the assumption of a providence shaping their ends. To push this attitude too far in considering English history or politics was ideologically dangerous, and this may account for the succession of Roman plays that succeeded the earlier spate of English history plays: *Julius Caesar*, Jonson's *Sejanus* and *Catiline*, Chapman's *Caesar and Pompey*, *Coriolanus*, all have a common interest in politics as an autonomous activity. The political interest in *Titus Andronicus* cast the Roman empery in a mould only marginally different from Tudor despotism; but in *Julius Caesar* the danger of monarchy is the basis of the conflict.

In this way the character interest subserves a function in the play; but when (for instance) T. S. Dorsch devotes nearly all of his critical discussion of the play to an analysis of characters we soon become aware not only that this is old familiar ground, but that it is distorting it fatally.[1] "The character of Decius Brutus is clearly established in half a dozen speeches" (lvii) provokes me to retort that Decius Brutus has no defined character at all, he has only a function; actors of widely different characteristics can play him equally satisfactorily: he may be fat or thin, honest or dishonest, what you will: what he *does*, in the play, is to bring out Caesar's proneness to flattery. But this kind of attention is no less absurd when applied to major figures:

> We have good-humouredly accepted arrogance of this kind in recent English leaders who have served us conspicuously; why not in Shakespeare's Caesar? . . . Casca's account of the scene in the marketplace, with its scarcely veiled hostility to Caesar, must not, for what it can tell us of Caesar's character, be taken any more seriously than Cassius's tirade.
>
> (xxxi–xxxii)

This proposes a kind of historical inquiry into the character of Caesar, using the play as a document from which to make deductions—and discounting anything that casts doubt on the image of a "noble" Caesar (or Churchill). But this is a play: words cannot be judged in the same way as in a historical document; though the motives of the speaker may qualify the judgement on his words, they cannot simply be "rejected" unless we cut the play. We are not trying Caesar in a court of law where some witnesses will be deemed "unreliable": all the figures and all their utterances are part of the structure which we are to regard.

It becomes clear, I think, that the central issue of the play is not "what is the character of Caesar"—the more obviously because he is dead half-way through. The stress on men as men is vitally important as modifying the structure of pattern and emblem evident in earlier plays: modifying, not replacing. Caesar's arrogance and weakness are part of an insistent naturalism set against another order governed by storm and blood. The relationship between them can only be understood in the process of the play. . . .

The opening scenes [of the play] direct our attention on to the political business of men, with the stress on valuation: what *is*

[1] *Julius Caesar*, 1955, pp. xxvi–lx.

human greatness? And the effect is ambivalent. We recognize nobility as something that is there, but we see also the sham, the mere bullying bodies, the ludicrous. The dual vision is insisted on in the structure, keeping the big ceremonial scene offstage and finally relating it in comic prose; and in the utterance, rhetorical or prosaic verse; heroic idea or physical image. These are comments on men as men which are general in their application as well as specific, and it is clearly limiting their relevance to refer them only to the "characters" of, say, Caesar and Cassius. In *Titus Andronicus* the contrast of Imperial splendour and human bestiality ("his limbs are lopp'd") was a generic one; the development is both more subtle and infinitely more complex here, but it is not wholly unlike in kind. But whereas in *Titus* the ceremony of Imperial election was staged, while the ritual murder took place off-stage, here that situation is reversed, and the ritual murder is to be the play's central scene.

There is a further structural likeness to *Titus* to be noted before I drop a parallel which may easily be overpressed. In that play the second act is unified by the pastoral emblems of the hunt; what I take to be the second movement here (I. iii to II. iv : no interval is implied between the acts and the division seems to be arbitrary) is entirely dominated by the great storm. The stress is shifted to forces outside men. But whereas the overall movement in the first scenes seemed clear, I have less confidence in this second movement. However obviously ironic Caesar's repudiation of the soothsayer might be, we have generally been led firmly towards a critical and sceptical outlook which inevitably complicates our response to the storm. If it is to be taken simply as an image of the civil strife of Rome, it is bound to seem overdone. If, on the other hand, it symbolizes a natural or supernatural order beyond human control, the difficulty is to credit it. I do not, of course, mean that such a symbol cannot be used for dramatic purposes unless we literally believe in it; by no means; but where the play itself so clearly invokes scepticism the suspension of disbelief is more difficult. The required ambivalence is easier to recognize than to imagine.

The storm, of course, is naturally as well as supernaturally terrifying: pedestrians are killed in the streets of Rome. It is insisted on in the original stage directions (*Thunder and Lightning; Thunder still; Thunder and Lightning,* and so on) and continually in the dialogue, whether as an expression of fear, courage, superstition, or scepticism. The only intermission is provided by the scene in Brutus' orchard where the contrasting calm is very effective. And that serves to emphasize the symbolic significance of the storm. Brutus stands and talks outside the world of Rome, the human whirligig of storm, and his orchard, like a May garden, is similarly withdrawn; a position of physical and mental calm from which he can view the tempest as a distant firework display in the city.

But the idyllic withdrawal is not of course possible; or at least is not possible without a complete surrender of power and responsibility. Within the dialogue of the conspirators the storm image is replaced by its equivalent in the little world of man, the image of blood. Brutus strains the security of his position by continually forcing distinctions on the blood-lust of others:

> No, not an oath . . .
>
> (II. i. 114)

> Swear priests and cowards, and men cautelous,
> Old feeble carrions, and such suffering souls
> That welcome wrongs; unto bad causes swear
> Such creatures as men doubt; but do not stain
> The even virtue of our enterprise,
> Nor th' insuppressive mettle of our spirits,
> To think that or our cause or our performance
> Did need an oath; when every drop of blood
> That every Roman bears, and nobly bears,
> Is guilty of a several bastardy,
> If he do break the smallest particle
> Of any promise that hath pass'd from him. (129–40)

The concept of honour which is thus rooted in blood has manifest dangers, for blood cannot be dissociated from its other senses (as we feel here). This is even more striking a few lines later:

> Let's be sacrificers, but not butchers, Caius.
> We all stand up against the spirit of Caesar,
> And in the spirit of men there is no blood.
> O, that we then could come by Caesar's spirit,
> And not dismember Caesar! But, alas,
> Caesar must bleed for it. And, gentle friends,

> Let's kill him boldly, but not wrathfully;
> Let's carve him as a dish fit for the gods,
> Not hew him as a carcass fit for hounds.
>
> (166–74)

One could fairly say that the whole tragic conception of the play is concentrated in that last astonishing image. Brutus is trying to sustain the distinction I noted in I. ii., between spirits and bodies, magnanimity and mere physical domination; and as Cassius walks boldly in the storm while Brutus worries apart in his orchard, so Brutus wants to kill a spirit without a drop of blood while Cassius is content (or realistic enough) to be a butcher. Like Titus before him and Othello after, Brutus would justify a murder by ritualistic dedication: "Let's be sacrificers, but not butchers." Thus there is something preposterous about "carve him as a dish fit for the gods," which is surely not a failure in the symbolic organization, but a positive indictment of the fatuous distinction. Men *are* bodies, Caesar's blood *must* flow, and Brutus must leave the orchard to be destroyed in the storm. Brutus' much vaunted nobility comes in question here: in one sense it is real enough—we do not doubt his moral superiority to Cassius; but it is quite unreal in another sense, for its valuation of men, ignoring their brute nature, is inevitably false. Brutus' utterance stands in direct contrast to Cassius' tale of the swimming match; but it reveals a confusion of values no less radical. ´

Thus the correspondence is established between the distinguishable aspects of this part of the play: between the symbolic storm and the orchard, between the contrasting images of flesh and spirit, and between Brutus' conspiracy and Cassius'. And they are all linked by an uncertainty of outlook: the storm is portentous of a force superior to man, or else it is a vulgar superstition to regard it as a portent at all, it is "just a storm"; and the conspiracy is either a necessary and inevitable action (an "enterprise"), or else it is a vulgar deed of jealous underlings. The ambivalence persists, and it is the vitally interesting thing about the play; but it is not altogether satisfactory. It seems, as I have suggested, over-insisted on, and therefore a trifle absurd when our attention is so often directed away from symbols on to men as they are, a naturalism that appears here in the brief glimpses of Brutus' domestic life (so different from Caesar's just afterwards). The storm is part of the intricate structure of the play as I see it, but it is also outgrowing that, generalizing and simplifying into the obvious Senecan pattern that I propounded initially. In later plays, *Pericles* or *The Tempest*, the storm symbol is virtually the extent of our knowledge of a tragic experience for which we have little dramatic equivalent; but here we are concerned with the dramatic equivalent, and the symbol seems less than the thing, not more (as the storm which opens Act II of Othello seems excessive for its symbolic function). The emblem patterns of *Titus* or of *Richard II* grew into their own structures; but here the emblems and the action do not co-exist so easily, the symbols need to grow out of the action more organically, as the image of grotesque flesh in Act I does. The difference, of course, is that although in *Richard II* a distinction is established between divine order and human competence, there they do not become radical alternatives, whereas here they are set in conflict as modes of thought. The same is, I think, true of *Hamlet,* and creates acute problems there; but the system of belief involved in a Christian cosmology is more readily established than one in Roman augury which is distanced from the start.

Likeness [to] and difference from *Hamlet* can be seen in the handling of dawn at the end of this scene compared with Horatio's famous lines concluding the opening of the later play. Here there is a slightly comic maladroitness in the debate between the conspirators as to where the dawn *is*: it neatly suggests their lack of direction at the same time as moving the play on to the day that follows the night of storm; but it is more than a little absurd. So also is the emblem of the Roman matrons' nobility when Portia displays her self-inflicted wound: this may represent the physical brutality of the society, and does contrast oddly (but not at all clearly) with Brutus' wish not to shed blood, but chiefly it seems to be a striking incident in Plutarch for which Shakespeare has not discovered a sufficiently explicit relevance.

Act II, scene ii, returns to the storm and the portents, with Calphurnia's dreams and her fears, and Caesar's reiterated "Caesar shall go forth" which is variously courageous and idiotic. In the last scene Brutus was struggling for coherence of values amid the conspirators on whom the comment was clear, not because Brutus ever made it, but precisely because he did not, because of the difference between his utterance and theirs. Here Caesar also, in a different way, is concerned with value:

> Caesar should be a beast without a heart
> If he should stay at home to-day for fear.
> (II. ii. 42–43)

Caesar is a lion with a heart—in Calphurnia's dream "an hundred spouts did run pure blood"—and this directly negates Brutus' ambition to destroy a spirit without blood. The lion is the king of beasts; but with Caesar we do not forget that he *is* a beast, an animal of blood. So, when we reach Caesar's clearest statement of *his* value—"The cause is in my will: I will not come" (71)—we recognize this "will" as being, however splendid, "blood-ruled" in the Elizabethan sense. Value is, and is not, here. Just as Brutus' values are false because men are *not* spirits, but *men*, filled with blood; so Caesar's value is only an outgrowth of the blood-ruled beast, and there follows immediately a demonstration of his will succumbing to flattery.

The dramatic core of this is clearly concerned with value: should men be regarded as noble, or as beastly? Different men and different values are juxtaposed such that none can clearly triumph: we are in a way brought close to the debates on "will" and "value" in *Troilus and Cressida*, where a similarly dusty answer is returned, with clearer definition. The obvious comment on Caesar is in the Trojan debate on Helen:

> *Troilus.*   What's aught but as 'tis valued?
> *Hector.* But value dwells not in particular will.
> (II. ii. 52–53)

There the image of the ageing flirt Helen makes the point very clear: here we have an ageing, blustering Caesar, not so clearly valueless, but his value cannot lie in his "particular will." That irony is enforced here in a way that is not repeated in *Troilus*, by the structure that is larger than any man, the world of storms, of dreams, and predicted spouts of blood. . . .

This part of the play [Act III] ends, then, like the first with prose comedy; but this scene has a sharper and a far more brutal edge than Casca's account of Caesar's fit. The general movement of the play is away from the noble image towards the ignobility of man. This is continued in Act IV in the unpleasant scenes between Antony, Octavius, and Lepidus, as well as less obviously but even more damagingly, in the quarrel scene between Cassius and Brutus, which implicates even Brutus' personal honour. His anger emerges in a rhetorical recounting of the honourable murder of Caesar, which keeps echoing Caesar's own utterance, as well as lapsing into Cassius':

> *Cassius.* O ye gods, ye gods! Must I endure all this?
> *Brutus.* All this? ay, more: fret till your proud heart break;
>   Go show your slaves how choleric you are,
>   And make your bondmen tremble. Must I budge?
>   Must I observe you? Must I stand and crouch
>   Under your testy humour? By the gods,
>   You shall digest the venom of your spleen,
>   Though it do split you; for, from this day forth,
>   I'll use you for my mirth, yea, for my laughter,
>   When you are waspish.
> *Cassius.*   Is it come to this?
> *Brutus.* You say you are a better soldier:
>   Let it appear so; make your vaunting true,
>   And it shall please me well. For mine own part,
>   I shall be glad to learn of noble men.
>
>   (IV. iii. 41–54)

Brutus' rage is expressed in physical images like Cassius' in Act I, and he arrives at a patent physical jealousy. Before long he has reached out to gods, thunderbolts, and high Olympus. The mother-child images in which their reconciliation is effected are hardly impressive, any more than the farcical little scene with the poet just afterwards. But these may be as much weaknesses in Shakespeare's writing as in his creatures. And there is another side to this: compared with Cassius' petty dishonesty, Brutus' anger can fairly approach the heroic tone, and the subsequent demonstrations of his stoicism on hearing of Portia's death seem to reinforce this reconstructing of the heroic figure. But in the images, and the echoes of absurdity, and in our knowledge of the insufficiency of honour there are curious undercurrents: the play is being turned into heroic tragedy, but the process is rather clumsy, and in the diminishing echoes of critical attitudes, apparently unwilling. It is difficult to respond to this rhetoric when rhetoric, and the ideas of value, honour, and so on which it conveys, have been so carefully exposed earlier.

None the less, this seems to be what the play demands. Caesar's ghost drives Brutus to the recognition:

> O Julius Caesar, thou art mighty yet!
> Thy spirit walks abroad, and turns our swords
> In our own proper entrails.
>
> (V. iii. 94–96)

But all this is slightly confused as a new and simpler set of values emerge to endorse the tragic conclusion. It is true that it is not altogether simple: Cassius dies by error, and there is emblematic amplification of the error:

> *Messala.* Mistrust of good success hath done this deed.
> O hateful Error, Melancholy's child,
> Why dost thou show to the apt thoughts of men
> The things that are not?
>
> (V. iii. 66–69)

Such an end is apt enough for Cassius, but it seems to put even him into a framework of heroic error, so that Brutus can speak a noble epitaph over him and Titinius:

> Are yet two Romans living such as these?
> The last of all the Romans, fare thee well!
>
> (98–99)

They are not the last of course, for Brutus' death is yet to come. The idea of the noble Roman dominates unchallenged at the end, even in Cassius. Brutus' suicide is overdone, as everyone coyly declines to kill him, but it is certainly not deliberate farce, and Antony can affirm Brutus' value without question:

> This was the noblest Roman of them all.
> All the conspirators save only he
> Did that they did in envy of great Caesar;
> He only, in a general honest thought
> And common good to all, made one of them.
> His life was gentle, and the elements
> So mix'd in him, that Nature might stand up
> And say to all the world, "This was a man!"
>
> (V. v. 68–75)

This is, of course, magnificent; and it goes without question in the text. But in our minds questions must arise, if not at once while under its immediate spell, then shortly afterwards. The play has indeed been concerned with noble Romans, but we have been taught by it to see that nobility ambivalently; and even more have we learnt to question "great Caesar."

In other words, Brutus' tragedy, of noble error, in which Cassius has fat enough to participate, has been a part of the play; but never till now was it the whole. The questioning of values, the contrasting of the blood-free spirit of man with the grotesque image of his clumsy body, the inclination to see Roman nobility as comically or farcically degraded— all these things have been strong in the play, but they find no place in this noble finale. It is inevitable, I think, that their absence should be felt as a criticism of the end. The parts of the play have not grown consistently into a whole, and it is therefore a fragile tragic value that is built up here, one which cannot survive criticism.

Hence my suggestion of a likeness to *All's Well*: a process of probing and questioning of value joined to a final assertion of rectitude, where the two do not stand in a clear relation. *All's Well* has a false and cheap happy ending; and in a sense the end of *Julius Caesar*, though far more powerful, is equally "happy": it is reassuring—all's well, when such a glow of assured values can be accepted. But the play as I have seen it implied something less reassuring, something more like *Troilus and Cressida* where no tragedy is allowed and the end shows life simply going on, Troilus to more futile wars, and Pandarus groaning at his diseases. Here again *Julius Caesar* is like *All's Well*, in its stress on physical decrepitude; but *Julius Caesar* is not venereal, the canker'd rose is not involved as yet. That is part of the profounder disturbance in *Hamlet*. And in *Hamlet* there is something of the same problem, of a tragic ending not fully responsive to the play; but it is a far more complex situation. In *Hamlet* there is also a conflict of different dramatic worlds: a Senecan play of Ghost and Revenge, and a sceptical one which gives such things no credence. This duality I remarked in *Julius Caesar*, and in the end the ghost has the better of it. Considering how long it has been read as a gallery of characters and played as a political commentary in modern dress, it is worth reiterating that there is at least as much blood, both on the stage and in the words, in this play as in *Titus Andronicus*.

In short, I find a quality in the play that exceeds its simple framework, and is not reconciled with it. Splendid as it is, Antony's last speech is a tour-de-force, the use of rhetorical poetry to overwhelm our doubts. And it is ironical that this should occur in a play which almost more than any other sharpens its audience's critical awareness of language, and especially of the power of rhetoric to deceive: for *Julius Caesar* is a brilliantly written play, a climax to the developing sensitivity to varying modes of utterance with which Shakespeare experimented in his earliest work.

Hamlet

by Kenneth Muir

high and excellent Tragedie, *that openeth the greatest wounds, and sheweth forth the* Vlcers *that are covered with* Tissue . . .[1]

(SIR PHILIP SIDNEY)

It was, perhaps, Sidney's account of tragedy that led Shakespeare to use as one of the iterative images of *Hamlet* that of the hidden ulcer. The sickness imagery has been explained in various ways—as reflecting the disease of Hamlet himself, as proliferating from the Ghost's description of the effect of Claudius's poison, as indicating the rottenness of the state of Denmark—but, if the images are considered in context, it becomes apparent that only the last of these explanations has any validity. The images, with only one exception, refer either to the rottenness of the court, to the sin of Claudius and Gertrude, or to the King's guilty fear of his nephew.

There does not seem to have been any mystery about the play, or about the character of the hero, until the end of the eighteenth century. Then Romantic critics and their successors concentrated their attention on the character of the hero, in which they found the explanation of his postponement of revenge until it had involved the death of Polonius and his two children, of Gertrude, Rosencrantz and Guildenstern and of Hamlet himself. They diagnosed the case in a variety of ways, from Goethe's parable of the

[1] *The Defence of Poesie* (1595), Sig. E4ᵛ.

oak-tree planted in a costly vase and Coleridge's idea that Hamlet
thought so much that he "lost the power of action in the energy of
resolve" to Schopenhauer's "weakness of will," Bradley's stress on
the traumatic shock of Gertrude's remarriage and Freud's Oedipus
complex. These conflicting views led C. S. Lewis to argue that
critics depicted only themselves when they thought they were
depicting Hamlet and they did this because he was in fact Every-
man, tainted with original sin. Professor Lewis invited the retort
that as an amateur theologian, particularly interested in original
sin, he was as likely to hold this view of Hamlet as Freud was to
diagnose Oedipus Complex. "I have a smack of Hamlet myself, if I
may say so," Coleridge admitted.[2] But the tendency of critics to
draw self-portraits does not necessarily mean that Hamlet is
characterless: it may mean rather that the methods we employ for
ascertaining his character are inappropriate.

Side by side with those critics who seek for the reasons for
Hamlet's delay in his psychology are those who emphasise the fact
that Shakespeare's play was based on an earlier one, possibly by
Kyd, and that in the finished product there are traces of the more
primitive original. Shakespeare did not quite succeed in effecting a
complete transformation of the old play. He retained incidents and
motivations proper to a primitive revenge play, but incompatible
with the sophisticated hero of his own. The character who medi-
tates on suicide is unlike the one who spares Claudius at his prayers
because he wants to be sure of damning his soul, who speaks of
Polonius's corpse as "the guts," or who sends Rosencrantz and
Guildenstern to their deaths, "not shriving time allowed," without
pity or remorse. The play, therefore, is deeply flawed by Shakespeare's attempt to pour new wine into old bottles.

Against this view must be set the fact that Shakespeare seems to
have taken exceptional pains with the play. The second quarto
version is so long that it cannot have been accommodated in the
two-hour traffic of the stage, and it may never have been per-
formed without substantial cuts. This would seem to suggest that
Shakespeare wrote for his own satisfaction and that, if he retained
"primitive" elements from the old play, he did so deliberately. Nor
is it difficult to guess why. By putting a sensitive and sophisticated

[2] S. T. Coleridge, *Table Talk*, June 15, 1827.

Renaissance prince—scholar, soldier, courtier—in a situation that requires only a primitive avenger to set the world to rights, he provides a tragic contrast fraught with irony. For in such a situation a man's virtues may become liabilities.

In recent years, however, much more stress has been laid on Hamlet's defects. Wilson Knight in *The Wheel of Fire* spoke of him as morbid and neurotic, less healthy than his uncle.[3] Madariaga, who assumed that he had seduced Ophelia, ascribed the cause of his procrastination to his egotism:[4]

> Hamlet, in spirit and intention, does not avenge his father; he avenges himself. . . . Hamlet could not pour himself into action because he was too egotistic for that. All action—even crime— requires freedom from egotism.

Whatever we may think of this view of Hamlet's character, the last remark is manifestly false: we can all think of criminal egotists. Professor L. C. Knights is another critic who has a low opinion of Hamlet's character.[5] We were told that "the desire to escape from the complexities of adult living is central" to his character, and that "his attitudes of hatred, revulsion, self-complacency and self-reproach" are "forms of escape from the difficult process of complex adjustment which normal living demands." Professor Knights appears to exaggerate the normality of Hamlet's position. To have an adulterous mother, to have one's father murdered, and to lose one's kingdom to the murderer can happily still be regarded as abnormal. In his later study of *Hamlet* he argues that the Ghost's commands should have been disregarded:[6]

> The Ghost is tempting Hamlet to gaze with fascinated horror at an abyss of evil. . . . Hamlet does not merely see the evil about him, does not merely react to it with loathing and rejection, he allows his vision to activate something within himself—say, if you like, his own feeling of corruption—and so to produce that state of near paralysis that so perplexes him.

Hamlet, Professor Knights thinks, is a sterile intellectual whose disgust with himself is used to shock and damage others. He seems

[3] *The Wheel of Fire* (1949), chap. II.

[4] *On "Hamlet"* (1948), pp. 103,105.

[5] *Explorations* (1946), pp. 66 ff.

[6] *An Approach to "Hamlet"* (1960), p. 47.

not to realise that some of his own actions are sinful. He is fascinated by the lust he condemns in his mother. He indulges in self-
dramatisation, dramatising both his melancholy and his grief at
Ophelia's death.

This bare summary does not do justice to the persuasiveness of
Professor Knights' argument. But even though we may allow that
Hamlet is infected by the evil of the world of Elsinore and partially
corrupted by the task he has to do—what I have elsewhere called
the occupational disease of avengers—the self-dramatisation of
which Professor Knights complains can better be explained as
Shakespeare's own dramatisation of Hamlet's feelings.

Are we to accept the view that the Ghost is tempting Hamlet to
evil? Professor Eleanor Prosser in a well-argued book agrees with
Professor Knights. She starts from the condemnation of revenge by
Elizabethan moralists and theologians and claims that virtuous
characters in Shakespeare's plays "faced with the wanton murder"
of their kin either forgive or leave their cause to heaven. But she
plays down the element of personal vengeance in Macduff's determination to kill the murderer of his wife and children. She has
some more effective arguments in her discussion of the Ghost's
appearances. It departs, apparently offended, when Horatio
invokes heaven. On its second appearance, it vanishes on the crow-
ing of the cock, starting "like a guilty thing upon a fearful summons," though only erring spirits are compelled to depart at
cockcrow. When Hamlet confronts the Ghost he is not certain
whether it brings "airs from heaven or blasts from hell." The Ghost
does not appeal "to Hamlet's love of virtue; it is not arousing his
determination to serve the justice of God." It follows that the Ghost
cannot be a penitent soul come from purgatory, acknowledging the
justice of his punishment. Here Professor Prosser is surely mis-
taken for the Ghost laments that he was sent to his account,

> Unhous'led, disappointed, unanel'd,

and confesses that he is

> confin'd to fast in fires,
> Till the foul crimes done in my days of nature
> Are burnt and purg'd away.

She is on stronger ground in her interpretation of the cellarage
scene, in which the Ghost speaks from beneath the stage, "the

familiar abode in Elizabethan drama of demons, furies and damned souls." The Ghost acts like a devil, Professor Prosser thinks, because it is a devil. This leads her to argue that the Ghost intervenes in the closet scene, not to protect Gertrude, but to prevent her from repenting. This interpretation is impossible to accept since the Ghost's words indicate a loving concern for Gertrude; and if the Ghost were a devil in disguise he would not have warned Hamlet not to contrive anything against her but to leave her to the stings of conscience.

Professor Prosser makes one damaging admission. When Hamlet says that if Claudius does not reveal his guilt during the performance of "The Murder of Gonzago,"

> It is a damned ghost that we have seen.

Professor Prosser comments:[7]

> There is no hint that a damned ghost might have told the truth. . . . Admittedly, the argument of this study would be strengthened immeasurably if Horatio countered with the warning that the instruments of darkness can tell us truths in order to betray us.

It would indeed: and the fact that Horatio does nothing of the kind must make one sceptical of Professor Prosser's main theory. There are other objections too (e.g. Hamlet does not decide in the "To be or not to be" soliloquy to reject coward conscience). But the fundamental objection both to Professor Prosser and to Professor Knights is that Claudius is an unpunished murderer and usurper; and whether the Ghost is a spirit of health or goblin damned, it is Hamlet's bounden duty, after checking the truth of the story, to execute justice on his uncle. Hamlet is not just a private avenger; and, although we may deplore his hatred and the errors that spring from it, we cannot believe, in the world of the play, that he ought to have accepted the situation and done nothing about it. As the author of *The Hystorie of Hamblet* put it, after warning his readers not to conspire against their lawful sovereign:[8]

> If vengeance ever seem to have any shew of justice, it is then, when piety and affection constraineth us to remember our fathers unjustly

---

[7] *Hamlet and Revenge* (1967), p. 178.

[8] I. Gollancz, *The Sources of "Hamlet"* (1926), p. 197.

murdered . . . and which seeke the means not to leave treason and
murder unpunished.

Even the pious and prolific William Perkins admitted that it was
sometimes legitimate to take the law into one's own hands:[9]

when violence is offered, and the Magistrate absent; either for a
time, and his stay be dangerous; or altogether, so as no helpe can be
had of him, nor any hope of his comming. In this case, God puts the
sword into the private mans hands.

In the state of Denmark there was no hope of the Magistrate's
coming.

There remains the problem raised by Professor Prosser: why
does the Ghost behave like a stage devil? This is sometimes
explained as a survival from the pre-Shakespearian *Hamlet,* or as a
device used by Hamlet and the Ghost to put Horatio and Marcellus
off the scent. It may be suggested, too, that a devil who wished to
convince a man that he was his father's spirit would hardly fall into
the mistake of behaving like a stage devil. All the Ghost does is to
demand that Hamlet's companions should swear to keep the secret
of his appearance—it is Hamlet himself who treats the Ghost as a
stage devil. The men swear by grace and heaven, a vow which
would not please a devil, but which apparently gives rest to the
perturbed spirit.

Apart from this it was necessary for the action of the play that
there should be some doubt about the nature and provenance of
the Ghost. When Hamlet is first informed of the haunting, he
speaks as though it were an evil spirit in the shape of his father:

If it assume my noble father's person,
I'll speak to it, though hell itself should gape
And bid me hold my peace.

(I. ii. 243–45)

When he first confronts the Ghost he prays for the protection of
angels and ministers of grace; but he is convinced by the Ghost's
tale that it is "honest"—not a devil in disguise. Professor Prosser
assures us that ghosts from purgatory would be full of joy and
tranquillity and would not be vindictive. But it is not certain that
Shakespeare was aware of this; or that, even if he was, he would

---

[9] Cited Fredson Bowers, *Elizabethan Revenge Tragedy* (1940), p. 36.

necessarily conform to it in writing a play. Banquo's ghost is not particularly tranquil, nor are the ghosts who appear on the eve of Bosworth Field. In *Hamlet* it seems that Christian teaching about the after-life is contaminated with memories of the Classics, and perhaps of folklore.[10]

Hamlet himself is well aware of the dangers he runs in conversing with spirits. Horatio speaks of the physical dangers, but Hamlet asks:

> And for my soul, what can it do to that
> Being a thing immortal as itself?

Later on, "lapsed in time and passion," he confesses that there may well be a danger to his soul:

> The spirit that I have seen
> May be a devil; and the devil hath power
> T'assume a pleasing shape; yea, and perhaps
> Out of my weakness and my melancholy,
> As he is very potent with such spirits,
> Abuses me to damn me.
>
> (II. ii. 594–99)

It is precisely because he is aware of the danger of damnation that he arranges to catch the conscience of the King by a performance of a play; and the King's reactions to the performance convince both Hamlet and Horatio that the Ghost's story was true. Shakespeare has already let the audience into the secret in the previous scene, when Claudius reveals his guilt in an aside (III. i. 50). After that, no member of an audience, however expert in demonology, is likely to believe that the Ghost is a devil in disguise.

We must start, therefore, from the assumption that Hamlet is charged with the duty of killing Claudius.

Hamlet is not the sole avenger of the play. Laertes, Fortinbras and Pyrrhus all have injuries to avenge: Laertes, the deaths of Polonius and Ophelia; Fortinbras, the death of his father and loss of some territory; Pyrrhus, the death of his father. All three are contrasted with Hamlet. The Dido play—which seems to be an oblique compliment to Marlowe's—provides Hamlet with a num-

---

[10] J. C. Maxwell, "The Ghost from the Grave," *Durham University Journal* 17 (1956), pp. 55–59.

ber of reminders of his own situation. The mobled Queen, weeping for Priam, is contrasted with Gertrude, whose tears for her husband had soon been dried. Pyrrhus, the avenger, is depicted as a figure of evil. His arms are "Black as his purpose"; his appearance is "dread and black"; he is "total gules," covered with the blood "of fathers, mothers, daughters, sons"; he is, finally, "hellish." He is about to kill Priam, when he hears the noise of Ilium's fall.

> For lo! his sword,
> Which was declining on the milky head
> Of reverend Priam, seemed i'th'air to stick.
> So as a painted tyrant Pyrrhus stood,
> And like a neutral to his will and matter
> Did nothing.
>
> (II. ii. 471–76)

After this pause,

> Aroused vengeance sets him new awork,

and he slays the old king, while Hecuba sees him

> make malicious sport
> In mincing with his sword her husband's limbs.

This savage and evil avenger, murdering an aged man who was not guilty of his father's death in battle, contrasts with the more civilised Hamlet who finds it difficult to execute the man who has secretly murdered his father after seducing his mother. The central image of the sword suspended motionless over his enemy is repeated in Act III when Hamlet holds his sword over his kneeling enemy. Hamlet wants to be as ruthless as Pyrrhus, and in the soliloquy after the *Dido* speeches he laments that he is pigeon-livered and lacks "gall / To make oppression bitter." He uses the ability of the actor to weep real tears "But in a fiction, in a dream of passion" as a reproach to himself for being unable to carry out his duty, or as he absurdly puts it, that he "can say nothing." He can say a great deal, but not act.

Fortinbras is praised by Hamlet as "a delicate and tender prince" and he is named by him as his successor. But all the other evidence undercuts these tributes. We hear of him in the first scene as one who has secretly mustered a band of soldiers, who seem little better than brigands, to seize the lands lost by his father. He has

> Shark'd up a list of lawless resolutes,
> For food and diet, to some enterprise
> That hath a stomach in't.

(I. i. 98–100)

Voltemand and Cornelius are dispatched on an embassage to the "impotent and bed-rid" King of Norway, who rebukes Fortinbras but empowers him to use the troops to attack Poland. There is no suggestion that the war is a just one. It is, as one of his captains tells Hamlet, a war of aggression:

> Truly to speak, and with no addition,
> We go to gain a little patch of ground
> That hath in it no profit but the name.
> To pay five ducats, five, I would not farm it;
> Nor will it yield to Norway or the Pole
> A ranker rate should it be sold in fee.
>
> > *Hamlet.* Why, then the Polack never will defend it.
> > *Captain.* Yes, it is already garrison'd.
> > *Hamlet.* Two thousand souls and twenty thousand ducats
> >   Will not debate the question of this straw.
> >   This is th'imposthume of much wealth and peace,
> >   That inward breaks, and shows no cause without
> >   Why the man dies.

(IV. iv. 17–28)

In the soliloquy that follows Hamlet uses the example of Fortinbras' action as a reproach to his own inaction. In the dialogue with the Captain war is thought of as a fatal disease, and the campaign against Poland absurd and irrational; but in the soliloquy Hamlet argues that god-like reason was not given us to fust in us unused, as though the war was the result of a rational decision. Fortinbras is

> a delicate and tender prince,
> Whose spirit with divine ambition puff'd
> Makes mouths at the invisible event,
> Exposing what is mortal and unsure
> To all that fortune, death, and danger dare,
> Even for an egg-shell. Rightly to be great
> Is not to stir without great argument,
> But greatly to find quarrel in a straw
> When honour's at the stake.

(IV. iv. 48–56)

The surface argument is contradicted by the detail. A spirit inflated with ambition—even when qualified with the epithet "divine"—is guilty of the sin by which the angels fell, as Wolsey reminds us. The egg-shell and the straw underline the worthlessness of the prize; and the preceding dialogue makes it clear that honour is not at stake. Hector's speeches in the debate in *Troilus and Cressida* (II. ii. 8–24, 53–60, 163–88) are devoted to showing that honour and justice should not be in opposing scales, and that "fear of bad success in a bad cause" ought to qualify the desire for glory.

Hamlet admires Fortinbras as his opposite, but we are not meant to share his view which springs from despair and self-disgust. It is natural that when he is dying, his mind jogged by the news of the arrival of Fortinbras from his victorious campaign, he should prophesy the election to the throne of Denmark of the barbarous adventurer. His own disastrous failure made him choose as best for his country a man most unlike himself. Fortinbras is thus enabled to avenge his father's death, not merely regaining the territory he forfeited, but acquiring the whole country of Denmark.

The third avenger, Laertes, is even more obviously Hamlet's foil, as Hamlet himself recognises just before the final duel, and as he confesses to Horatio,

> by the image of my cause, I see
> The portraiture of his.

Laertes is not aware of the parallel. He does not know that Hamlet's father had been murdered by his successor, nor that Claudius had seduced Gertrude. He does know that Hamlet had killed Polonius—though it was not a deliberate murder; and he knows that his beloved sister had been driven mad and been drowned as a result of Hamlet's actions, and he thinks that Hamlet had tried to seduce her. They are both brilliant fencers. Here the resemblance ends. In almost every other way the two men are contrasted. In the first scene in which they appear, Hamlet wishes to return to the university at Wittenberg; Laertes wishes to return to Paris for extra-curricular activities. In his warning to Ophelia, Laertes assumes that Hamlet cannot marry her and that therefore his intentions are dishonourable. This view of the case is shown to be wrong when Gertrude, at Ophelia's graveside, mentions that she had hoped the girl would be Hamlet's bride. When Laertes hears of his father's death, he hurries home from Paris and raises a successful rebellion against the King. The ease with which he invades the palace suggests that Hamlet was not prevented from killing Claudius by external obstacles.

Laertes, in accepting his role as avenger, knows that he is violating the moral law:

> To hell, allegiance! vows, to the blackest devil!
> Conscience and grace, to the profoundest pit!
> I dare damnation: to this point I stand,
> That both the worlds I give to negligence,
> Let come what comes; only I'll be reveng'd
> Most throughly for my father.

Here, as elsewhere, Laertes is indulging in stock responses. He is behaving as he thinks other people would expect a bereaved son to behave. In the later scene where Claudius asks him what he would do to show himself his father's son, he answers: "To cut his throat i' th' church." This, as many critics have assumed, is an unconscious comment on Hamlet's conduct when he finds the King at his prayers, and fails to seize the opportunity. The King's reply to Laertes—

> No place indeed should murder sanctuarise—

implies that Hamlet's manslaughter of Polonius was a case of murder, while the murder of Hamlet in church would be a case of justifiable homicide. Later in the same scene Laertes enthusiastically seconds the treacherous scheme to kill Hamlet in a duel by the use of an unbated foil:

> he, being remiss,
> Most generous, and free from all contriving,
> Will not peruse the foils.

This tribute to Hamlet's character from his would-be murderer outweighs the denunciations of certain squeamish modern critics. Laertes agrees to the scheme and adds:

> And, for that purpose, I'll anoint my sword.
> I bought an unction of a mountebank,
> So mortal, that but dip a knife in it,
> Where it draws blood, no cataplasm so rare,
> Collected from all simples that have virtue

Under the moon, can save the thing from death
That is but scratched withal.

(IV. vii. 141–47)

This reveals the full extent of Laertes' depravity—not merely because he is prepared to kill Hamlet treacherously, but because he purchased poison in case he might have occasion to use it.

Laertes appears on two other occasions. His leaping into Ophelia's grave and his ranting—what Hamlet calls "the bravery of his grief"—provoke the confrontation between the two avengers and ensure that Laertes will proceed with his treacherous plan. Just before the duel he promises to receive Hamlet's "offered love, like love" and that he will not wrong it. Some qualms of conscience make him hesitate, but in the end he gives Hamlet the necessary scratch. Hamlet in turn wounds Laertes, and Laertes confesses that he is justly killed with his own treachery, and asks his "noble" opponent to exchange forgiveness, though putting the blame on the King. Harold Jenkins protests against the view that Laertes is "some sort of villain," saying that Hamlet has more than his rank in mind when he calls him "a very noble youth."[11] Of course, Laertes arouses some sympathy when he encounters Ophelia mad or hears of her drowning. But the general impression he makes is of a coarse-grained, insensitive figure, who is put into the play to exhibit the primitive avenger Hamlet is temperamentally unfitted to be.

These three avengers are all foils to Hamlet. They have lost their fathers, two in battle and one by manslaughter. None of them is faced with the task of avenging a brutal murder; nor is any of them spurred on by a supernatural command. Yet none of them is delayed or deterred by an inner conflict or by moral scruples. It is beside these, coarse-fibred as they are, that Shakespeare means us to consider his hero. That Hamlet calls Fortinbras "a delicate and tender prince" and Laertes "a very noble youth" tells us more about Hamlet than about his fellow-avengers, for we have just seen the evil aggression of the one and the treacherous designs of the other. . . .

The parable of the recorders (III. ii.) may be taken as a warning to commentators and critics that they cannot pluck out the heart of

[11] *Hamlet and Ophelia* (1964).

Hamlet's mystery by the use of some simple formula; and, although it is plainly important to consider him in relation to his foils, this evidence is mainly negative. It shows that the two extremes of criticism are both wrong—that we could not really approve either of a Hamlet who avenged his father without hesitation or compunction, or of one who decided to let Claudius remain in possession of the fruits of his crime.

It is, perhaps, misleading to speak of approving or disapproving of one of Shakespeare's heroes. We need, in the greatest tragedies, at least to sympathise; and the kind of criticism that reads like a speech by the public prosecutor, or—still worse—by the Grand Inquisitor, has not proved very rewarding. . . .

By means of the performance of "The Murder of Gonzago" Hamlet convinces himself and Horatio that the Ghost's story was true; but the choice of the play informs Claudius that Hamlet has stumbled on his secret, and Hamlet's insulting behaviour is so reckless that one can only assume that he knows that he will have to kill Claudius soon or be murdered by him. His manic behaviour after the King's departure makes the audience suppose that he is about to sweep to his revenge. But the double message from the Queen, brought first by Rosencrantz and then by Polonius, deflects Hamlet's mind to the other duty imposed on him by the Ghost—to contrive nothing against Gertrude, but rather leave her to heaven and the stings of conscience. Hamlet's soliloquy at the end of the scene begins with the hatred and violence of a conventional avenger. He appears to be working himself up to a state of excitement in which he can kill the King:

> 'Tis now the very witching time of night,
> When churchyards yawn, and hell itself breathes out
> Contagion to this world. Now could I drink hot blood, ,
> And do such bitter business as the day
> Would quake to look on.
>
> (III. ii. 378 ff.)

Then he remembers that he has to visit his mother and cautions himself against the use of violence:

> O heart, lose not thy nature; let not ever
> The soul of Nero enter this firm bosom.

> Let me be cruel, not unnatural:
> I will speak daggers to her, but use none.

Nero did not merely murder Agrippina, he committed incest with her. Hamlet has to caution himself against committing matricide; and the words have been used to support the theory that Hamlet is in love with his mother and jealous of Claudius. But the reference to Nero may have been suggested by the name of Claudius; for the Emperor Claudius, whom Agrippina incestuously married, was murdered by her so that Nero could be Emperor. The story seems to have been in the mind of whichever dramatist was responsible for the renaming of Feng as Claudius.[12]

Immediately afterwards Hamlet is given his first opportunity of avenging his father. The performance of "The Murder of Gonzago" has proved Claudius's guilt; Hamlet has lashed himself into a violent mood; and he stumbles on the King, unguarded and defenceless. Instead of seizing the opportunity, he spares him, ostensibly because a man killed at his prayers would go to heaven instead of to the hell he deserved. Shakespeare reveals that the King, unknown to Hamlet, was unable to pray.

This is one of the crucial episodes in the play and our interpretation of Hamlet's character depends to a considerable extent on the way we interpret Hamlet's speech, "Now might I do it pat."

> Do we take Hamlet's reasons for not killing the King at their face value, and shall we then be as much revolted by them as Johnson was? Or shall we assume, with Coleridge and Bradley, that the wish to send Claudius to hell was an afterthought, offered by Hamlet to excuse his own failure to act? Such critics can point to the tell-tale *might* in the first line or to the "craven scruple" of which Hamlet speaks as he embarks for England. Or shall we suppose that Hamlet has an instinctive revulsion from killing a defenceless man at the foot of an altar—unlike Laertes and Pyrrhus—and then, revolting against his own revulsion, works himself up into a passion of hatred which provides him with a substitute for action? The desire to damn one's enemy, body and soul, is characteristic of the revenge play; but Shakespeare may be using a commonplace for more sophisticated purposes.[13]

Whichever interpretation is followed, we are driven to the conclusion that Hamlet hates the man he has to kill. He cannot kill in

[12] See William Montgomerie, "More an Antique Roman Than a Dane" *The Hibbert Journal* 59 (1960): pp. 67–77

[13] Kenneth Muir, *Shakespeare: Hamlet* (1963), p. 40.

cold blood; but if he kills in rage his action will be the expression of revenge rather than of justice.

In the scene with his mother, Hamlet is able to stab the rat behind the arras, believing it to be the King. No spectator has thought this strange because it is an instinctive and natural reaction. So too is his cool and callous dispatch of Rosencrantz and Guildenstern to their doom—it was their life or his.

It has been argued by some critics that in his upbraiding of his mother Hamlet is

> fascinated by what he condemns. . . . And it is because of the impurity and indiscriminateness of his rejections that, brief moments of friendship and respite apart, he takes refuge in postures.[14]

He is, we are told, complacent and self-righteous, as when he asks Gertrude to forgive him his virtue. Freudians go further and declare:

> It is an unavoidable psychological conclusion that the torrent of erotic pictures which Hamlet hurls at his mother indicate unconscious fantasies on his own part in which he is not only the accusing spectator, but also the active participant.[15]

The self-righteousness apparently shown in some speeches is offset by Hamlet's former condemnation of himself as a miserable sinner crawling between earth and heaven; and the violent attack on his mother's sin is mingled, not surely with incestuous feelings, but with filial affection for the sinner. Hamlet, in accordance with his plan, is speaking daggers to her, so as to arouse her sluggish conscience. This goes beyond the Ghost's injunction of leaving her to heaven and the pricking of conscience. Hamlet's method is to hold up a mirror in which the Queen can see herself and her "inmost part," by describing with brutal realism the significance of her adultery at an age when "the heyday in the blood is tame," and by showing her "The counterfeit presentment of two brothers"—the godlike and the bestial. Hamlet's plan is justified by its success. His words like daggers enter Gertrude's ears and she repents: she sees the black spots in her soul. The Ghost appears at the height of

---

[14] L. C. Knights, *An Approach to "Hamlet"* (1960), p. 65.

[15] E. Jones, *Hamlet and Oedipus* (1949).

Hamlet's denunciation of Claudius, not surely to prevent the Queen's repentance, but to save her from the knowledge that her first husband had been murdered by her second.

But despite his success with his mother, Hamlet is in a desperate position. He has revealed to his uncle that he knows his secret crime; he has passed over the one opportunity he has had of avenging his father; and, by killing Polonius, he has raised up an avenger, driven Ophelia mad, and given Claudius a good excuse for taking strong action against him. It is no wonder that, after the death of Polonius, Hamlet should wonder whether he is God's minister, called upon to execute justice on a sinner who would otherwise escape punishment, or a scourge of God, a wicked man who is used by God to punish sinners, but at the expense of damning himself.[16]

In the soliloquy he speaks just before sailing to England, Hamlet is faced with the complete failure of his mission, and he cannot understand why he has not carried out the Ghost's commands.

> whether it be
> Bestial oblivion or some craven scruple
> Of thinking too precisely on th'event—
> A thought which, quarter'd, hath but one part wisdom
> And ever three parts coward—I do not know
> Why yet I live to say "This thing's to do."
>
> (IV. iv. 39–44)

Oblivion it obviously is not; ordinary cowardice it cannot be; but it may be, as Coleridge thought, that Hamlet thought "too precisely on th'event," or that he was deterred by "some craven scruple." It is a curious paradox that the one intellectual among Shakespeare's tragic heroes should be least able to know why he acts or fails to act.

On the voyage, as we have noted, Hamlet does act, spontaneously, ruthlessly and bravely; and on his return he is greatly changed, meditating gravely but without bitterness on man's mortality, and no longer agonising about his failure to carry out the Ghost's command. The reasons for the change are not revealed until the final scene. His escape from death by means of the forged warrant and the providential attack by the pirates convince him that

[16] Fredson Bowers, "Hamlet as Minister and Scourge," *PMLA* 70 (1950): 740–47.

> Our indiscretion sometime serves us well
> When our deep plots do pall; and that should learn us
> There's a divinity that shapes our ends,
> Rough-hew them how we will.
>
> (V. ii. 8–11)

Then, as Horatio immediately recognises, news would soon arrive
of the execution of Rosencrantz and Guildenstern and therefore if
Hamlet did not act quickly it would be too late. On this Hamlet
remarks calmly, "The interim is mine." But he also has a premonition of his own death and a quiet acceptance of it which differs
considerably from his previous death-wish:

> There is a special providence in the fall of a sparrow. If it be now, 'tis
> not to come; if it be not to come, it will be now; if it be not now, yet it will
> come—the readiness is all.
>
> (V. ii. 212 ff.)

After detailing the sins and crimes of Claudius, culminating in the
attempt on his own life, Hamlet asks Horatio:

> Is't not perfect conscience
> To quit him with this arm? And is't not to be damn'd
> To let this canker of our nature come
> In further evil?
>
> (V. ii. 67–70)

The contraction of the time available, the certainty of the justice of
his cause, and the conviction that providence is watching over him
and that he will be provided with an opportunity for executing the
King, combine in Hamlet's mind—and critics may combine them in
different proportions. What they should not do is to ignore the
hints given by Shakespeare in the text and to misread the tone of
those passages as despair or the resignation of defeat.

As soon as the Queen falls dead and he learns from Laertes that
he himself is dying, Hamlet slays the King without hesitation. Not,
surely, as the Freudians would have it, because he and the King are
no longer rivals; nor because the King, to prevent his own
exposure, has allowed the Queen to drink from the poisoned cup;
nor because Hamlet is the supreme egotist who can avenge himself
but not his father. Some of the reasons for the lifting of the inhibi-
tion that prevents Hamlet from acting have already been discussed—the change of heart apparent since his return to Denmark,

his determination to wait for the right, providential opportunity,
his conviction that he need have no scruple about killing the King,
the knowledge that time is running short. The death of the Queen
and Laertes' accusation of Claudius provide the opportunity for
which Hamlet has been waiting: he can kill the King in such a way
that the action will be seen as just; on the spur of the moment, so
that he will not be able to think too precisely on the event; after
Gertrude's death so that he will not cause her either shame or grief
by the revelation of Claudius's crimes; and, of course, his own
death-wound makes immediate action necessary.

In his last moments Hamlet is concerned for the state of Denmark and gives his vote to Fortinbras—a concern which Dame
Rebecca West, despite her dislike of Hamlet, has brought herself to
applaud.[17] But he is also concerned lest his name should be vilified
by people ignorant of the true facts. He therefore urges Horatio
not to drink the poison:

> Absent thee from felicity awhile,
> And in this harsh world draw thy breath in pain
> To tell my story.

Shakespeare, too, is concerned to defend Hamlet from his detrac-
tors. His repentant killer, Laertes, calls him noble and exchanges
forgiveness. Fortinbras gives him a soldier's funeral and pro-
nounces that he would have made an excellent king. Horatio, to
whom his death makes life intolerable despite his ability to endure
fortune's buffets, gives him a tender valediction:

> Good night, sweet prince,
> And flights of angels sing thee to thy rest!

We are plainly not meant to regard Hamlet with the disapproval
several recent critics have expressed.

Horatio tells us of the woe and wonder—the admiration and
commiseration—that is the appropriate reaction and summarises
the action of the play:

> So shall you hear
> Of carnal, bloody, and unnatural acts;
> Of accidental judgments, casual slaughters;
> Of deaths put on by cunning and forc'd cause;

17 *The Court and the Castle* (1967), p. 31.

> And, in this upshot, purposes mistook
> Fall'n on th'inventors' heads.

It will be apparent what conclusions follow from the line of argument we have been pursuing. As the Ghost was the authentic spirit of Hamlet's father and not the devil in his shape, one must accept the fact that, in the world of the play, it was Hamlet's bounden duty to avenge the murder. In the situation in which he was placed, Hamlet had to establish the honesty of the Ghost; he had to convince others that he was not killing the King because he had been cheated of the throne; and he had to avoid exposing his mother's adultery and incest. But in addition to these practical reasons for delay, there seems little doubt that Hamlet had scruples about the ethics of revenge. In Lascelles Abercrombie's phrase, Hamlet exhibited "the heroism of moral vacillation."[18] If he had refused altogether to execute justice on the King, on the grounds that a Christian should not resist evil, we should feel that he had failed in his duty. If, on the other hand, he had swept to his revenge without hesitation, we should regard him as insensitive and barbarous. Although he never directly questions the morality of revenge, Hamlet's soliloquies would convey to an Elizabethan audience (as Professor Lawlor has cogently argued)[19] that he was being deterred by precisely this. Living in a rotten society he could not be guided by its moral code—he had to construct his own: and on his actions depended the future of his country. His agonised self-communings show how he was wrung by the anguish of choice. The tragedy is caused partly by the situation—the usurpation by an incestuous murderer—and partly by the character of the man called upon to set right the disjointed society. The death of Polonius, Ophelia, Laertes, Rosencrantz, Guildenstern and Gertrude are directly or indirectly due to Hamlet's failure to strike the King at his prayers.

As I have said elsewhere, what Shakespeare did

> was to imagine a "noble" and "sweet" Prince, sensitive, sophisticated
> and intelligent, placed in a situation where his acknowledged duty
> could only be repugnant—as it would be to Hamlet's critics if they

---

[18] *The Idea of Great Poetry* (1925), p. 181.

[19] *The Tragic Sense in Shakespeare* (1960), p. 73.

were unfortunate enough to find themselves in his position—and where his intelligence made his duty all the more difficult.[20]

It is, of course, necessary not to minimise Hamlet's sins and shortcomings. We have to remember that we catch only glimpses of the Prince as he was before the two-fold shock he sustained by the sudden death of his father and the hasty remarriage of his mother to the uncle he disliked. To this double shock which plunged Hamlet into acute melancholia, there were added three more—the knowledge that his father had been murdered, the knowledge that his mother had committed adultery, and the desertion of Ophelia. His consciousness of the evil power of sexual desire colours his outlook so that he believes that reason panders will, that beauty transforms honesty to a bawd, and that mankind is utterly corrupt. He might have used Newman's words: "Since there is a God, the human race is implicated in some terrible aboriginal calamity."

Hamlet is aware in general terms of his own morbidity, and his own sinfulness. But he sometimes seems blind on particular occasions to the evil in himself. It was inevitable that he should hate Claudius, and natural that as a substitute for action he should lash himself into rages against his enemy, but it is a hatred that interferes with the successful accomplishment of his task. It was natural that he should kill Polonius, but wrong that his repentance should be so perfunctory; it was necessary to send Rosencrantz and Guildenstern to their deaths, but wrong to disclaim any scruples about them, and he is bitterly cruel to the woman he loved. He says nothing about his responsibility for Ophelia's death, but Shakespeare may have decided that this would have interfered with the effect he was aiming at in the last act of the play.

Hamlet, then, is by no means an ideal figure. But his faults are largely caused by the situation in which he finds himself and by the distasteful task he is called upon to perform. Like many avengers, he becomes the deed's creature. But he purges himself of some of his morbidity about sex, by disgorging it in the closet scene; and he recovers calm and dignity in the final scene. No audience feels that it was inappropriate of Horatio to pray for flights of angels as his friend dies.

[20] *Shakespeare: Hamlet* (1963), p. 61.

Hamlet and Psychoanalysis

by Meredith Anne Skura

I have been suggesting that despite Shakespeare's discovery about the nature of human motivation in general, we have no basis for psychoanalyzing the characters who are part of its expression. His plays are like Freud's metapsychology and not like case histories; the "reality" of his characters, even though it depends on their being irrational as well as rational beings, does not include the kind of unconscious experience on which an analysis is based. The analyst and the poet are, after all, dealing with different aspects of human nature and different manifestations of the unconscious. The analyst always deals with more of the mind than does either the poet or the theoretician who makes maps of the mind. Like the poet, the analyst asks about a character's unacknowledged motives; but unlike the poet, he traces these back to other thoughts, other experiences, other contexts, which gave rise to motives and give them their only meaning. What is unique about psychoanalysis is that it not simply identifies strange behavior but also locates a source for behavior in something besides current experience—and these two goals are inseparable. By definition, the experiences the analyst deals with are independent of and often alien to current experience. They derive from fixations to periods sometimes so distant that we not only do not remember them but could not recognize a memory of them. These experiences are not responsive to the ongoing realities of life, even though they may find hiding places and even breeding places there.

In fact, the more realistic a character is, in the sense of responding fully and believably to his world, the more problematic it may be to assign an unconscious complex of motives to him—just as it is hard to know how to deal with insights into the unconscious minds of real people whose integrity is otherwise not in question. Even in life, evoking unconscious motives seems unrealistic, because it means invoking explanations which contradict felt experience and which require us to completely readjust our image of ourselves—and of human nature. It means invoking those alien trains of thought and preoccupations whose connections to reality are often illogical; the determining role of these motives in behavior is redundant, at least in "normal" people. What do you do when you find out that your friend's altruism derives from childhood rivalries, or that your surgeon's flawless operations satisfy his otherwise inactive sadistic fantasies from childhood? Any revision of our view of ourselves or other people implied by this new, discontinuous insight usually occurs in a psychoanalyst's office—and for the most part we do not go there unless we find that the self we thought we knew is inconsistent. We wait until the altruism goes sour or the surgeon botches a simple procedure. Even in the analyst's office, there is little room for diagnoses like the ones often offered as psychoanalysis of character—a psychoanalytic tag offered as explanation, as though the name made the behavior any more explicable—like J. I. M. Stewart's diagnosis of Leontes as homosexual.[1] There is no place for such wild analyses[2] or diagnostic cataloging, but only for the slow unraveling of all the disowned ideas and experiences leading from the forgotten past to present behavior. Yoking a hidden, otherwise invisible, motive from something called the unconscious to the surface is not enough. If purely unconscious motives *are* there, they are hard to locate: Is Brutus unconsciously killing his father when he kills Caesar? There is no room for these motives in the fully explained world of the play; or rather, there is room for too many of them. In actuality, almost nothing is abso-

[1] J. I. M. Stewart, *Character and Motive in Shakespeare: Some Recent Appraisals Examined* (London: Longmans, Green, 1949), pp. 30–37.

[2] See Sigmund Freud, "Wild Psychoanalysis" (1910), in *Standard Edition of the Complete Psychological Works of Sigmund Freud* (hereafter *SE*) (London: The Hogarth Press, 1953), vol. 11, pp. 221–27.

lutely "unconscious" in this way; the unconscious motive is always present in some form, however bizarre or disowned, and always provides the analyst with cues to its presence.

In Shakespeare's plays, however, there are no such cues, nothing that demands to be understood in terms other than the ones introduced by the world of play and the action it contains. His plays make sense of irrational behavior by externalizing it, as we have seen, in an explanatory myth. Even the characters who seem like psychiatrists' textbook cases when taken out of their plays have objective correlatives for their behavior. The play's world explains, even if it does not always justify, what the characters do. The behavior *is* irrational, and the characters *do* participate in the creation of comic or tragic chaos—but the causes of their behavior work on divine, natural, and social levels, as well as on the level of the individual divided will. The explanation lies in the context, not in some additional unseen shaper of the will, and certainly not in offstage, never-mentioned past events.

To invoke unconscious motives in such a fictional world is similar to invoking tragic flaws to explain tragedy—blaming a comfortably flawed agent who does not fit in with his environment instead of realizing that the agent is an essential part of it. To blame Hamlet's tragic flaw for his fate is to leave our sense of his world undisturbed; it allows us to overlook the painful contradictions in a flawed world, which is the only world we have, and to locate them in one easily identified part of one character's mind. In an even more reductive way, it hides the paradox that Hamlet's greatness is inseparable from his flaw. The homosexual label moves the flaw to the less visible unconscious level, but it nonetheless lodges the problem in a specific deviation. It comforts the audience by isolating Leontes from them, just as it isolates his flaw from his own heterosexual self; but it ignores the fact that Leontes' "homosexual" jealousy is inevitable in any world which is to know the value of passion at all. The cause of his jealousy is not found in an eccentric accident outside the current situation in Leontes' unique history, but forms an essential paradox within it. A crude diagnostic label which turns tragic experience into mere pathology is obviously inappropriate for Leontes, as it is for real people. But for characters enmeshed in their fictional worlds, even the most sensitive and carefully descriptive psychoanalysis is out of place, though it would not be in life. My expectations about a man next door who acted like Leontes would be very different from my expectations about Leontes in *The Winter's Tale*. For the man next door I would be more inclined to accept Stewart's diagnosis of homosexuality, at least as a starting point for investigation. My conventions for analyzing behavior in life include the assumptions that behavior has psychological determinants, often unconscious, and that certain clusters of visible traits in one person may well spring from the same source as in another. In *The Winter's Tale*, however, the clusters of traits can only mean what they mean in the play itself, just as Othello's blackness means only what it means in his play, not what it would mean in the world at large. One cannot follow Philip Roth's autobiographical hero, who reflected upon his own migraines "in the same supramedical way that I might consider the illness of a Milly Theale or a Hans Castorp,"[3] because those illnesses belong not to the characters alone but to whole worlds.

Hamlet may seem an exception to this rule, which is perhaps one reason why it continues to invite diagnosis and analysis. We are especially tempted to talk about Hamlet's childhood fixations, because he not only seems driven—with his compulsive humor, his obsessive use of sexual imagery, his sudden veerings from intensity to abstraction—but is thoroughly entangled with his parents. However, while a real man with an Oedipus complex is entangled with childish memories of his parents, Hamlet must cope with two live human beings who are actually provoking his strange behavior by their own. Hamlet's whole world justifies his supposedly oedipal behavior, and everything he feels—excess and all—makes perfect sense in a rotten world like Denmark. We can blame him only for his idealism and his adolescent visions of what Denmark—and a father—might be like; but even there Shakespeare gives him some support by evoking for our mind's eye the old Hamlet and Denmark as it used to be.

Hamlet is sensitive but not neurotic when he recoils from his father's death, his mother's marriage to a boorish substitute, his betrayal by two old school friends, his desertion by Ophelia and, worst of all, his failure to live up to his own expectations and become a perfect courtier or a revenge-play hero. The objective

[3] Philip Roth, *My Life as a Man* (New York: Holt, Rinehart and Winston, 1970), p. 55.

correlative for his behavior is a world fallen in his idealistic eyes; and Shakespeare makes it clear that neither the ideals nor the fall are particular to Hamlet. He is coming of age in a tragic world, feeling the thousand natural shocks that flesh is heir to; it is no wonder he is sick of action, sick of sexuality, sick of everything that means becoming an adult in such a world. There may be a suggestion that his idealism is not pure, just as Brutus's rationalizations for sacrificing Caesar are not pure; but there are impurities enough in what we see of the world and of Hamlet's current motives without our having to invoke unconscious motives from a past world. Idealism always comes at the cost of more pragmatic and social virtues; one sometimes adopts idealism precisely because it precludes the less attractive necessities of life, as well as because one believes in it. But no matter how costly, idealism is not necessarily neurotic.

Shakespeare's plays explain and make sense of behavior by creating a context for it in just this way, even when the explanations are not so direct or explicit as in Hamlet's case. Nothing literally causes Leontes' jealousy or justifies Othello's in the way that Denmark causes Hamlet's melancholy, but Shakespeare gives us enough information to make sense of their jealousy nonetheless. Othello may be wrong about Desdemona, but he is right about Bianca; he lives in a world where women do sell themselves. In Leontes' case, the mere suddenness and irrationality of his jealousy is explanation enough. We know everything when we hear that he has seen the "spider in the cup"; his motiveless malignancy is a fact about his world, a human mystery as inexplicable as the suddenness of bear attacks or storms at sea. We must look to the human condition for an explanation of his behavior, not to an eccentricity in Leontes. . . .

I do not wish to dismiss psychoanalytic commentary completely, however. It is easy enough to dispel the ghost of an Oedipus complex from Hamlet's mind, but not so easy to dismiss the sense that the drama that Freud describes is implicated in Shakespeare's. The two *are* connected, but not through character analysis: the evidence that argues against Hamlet's having an Oedipus complex simultaneously suggests another role for the oedipal material in the play. Precisely because Hamlet's world justifies his responses, it also makes real the fantasies of a typical oedipal-stage child. An adoles-

cent may have all of Hamlet's feelings, but he has no justification
for them, except in his own fantasies. Such fantasies, of course,
never include the subject's own inappropriate desires and certainly
do not include oedipal complexes. They always create, instead, an
external scene which makes sense of the adolescent hero's feelings,
just as Freud's patients invented seduction scenes to rationalize
their own desires: "My father made me do it." The fantasy, by its
very nature, cannot be symptomatic unless the figure at its center is
free from symptoms. The paranoiac never thinks that anything is
wrong with him; and in his fantasies, nothing is. The young woman
who dreams that her mother fell onto the railroad tracks is indig-
nant when the analyst asks, "Why did you want to see your mother
dead?" "It wasn't my fault!" the woman says. "I tried to save her but
she wouldn't listen."[4]

In the play *Hamlet*—more than in any of the other major tragedies—the hero is not at fault. Whatever is wrong is wrong with
Hamlet's entire world, a world that recreates every adolescent's
fantasies about growing up. Not everyone is a prince in the midst of
such parental decay, but everyone feels as if he were. All parents
have been involved in mysterious, dirty crimes, which are to be
hesitantly guessed at and reluctantly believed, though they compel
the imagination and leave the child feeling foolish and left out.
Every son's father, now degenerated into a bloated satire of himself, was a hero; and every mother shares Gertrude's blindness to
his faults. Every son believes he has the best of reasons to tell his
mother to stay out of his father's bed and the best, most externally
imposed reasons for murdering his father. The difference is that,
for Hamlet, this is all *true*. There is a fundamental difference
between the fantasizer as he represents himself in his fantasy and
as he really is; *Hamlet* recreates the fantasy, not the fantasizer.

. . . Take the oedipal stories themselves. Where Freud saw only
differences in the degree of repression, we can see different
aspects of human nature. For Freud, both Sophocles' *Oedipus Rex*
and Shakespeare's *Hamlet* present the same Oedipus complex; they
are different only in how openly they do so. Sophocles gives the

---

[4] Cited by Jacob Spanjaard in "The Manifest Dream Content and Its Significance in
The Interpretation of Dreams," *International Journal of Psychoanalysis* 50 (1969): 227 ff.

more straightforward presentation, because Oedipus actually fulfills every child's wishes by murdering his father and marrying his mother. By Shakespeare's time, however, the "secular progress of repression among mankind"[5] had left us incapable of Sophocles' honesty. Hamlet can hardly bring himself to act at all, and when he does kill Claudius, he kills himself as well; Gertrude he never touches.

Yet when today we think of the oedipal child, caught in a triangle of intense, vaguely defined jealousies and attractions, a frustrated outsider mystified by adults, then *Hamlet* comes much closer to a straightforward presentation of his experience than does *Oedipus Rex.* If Sophocles presents anything we might recognize as an oedipal complex, it is not apparent in Oedipus's past crimes but in his triangular confrontation with Creon and Jocasta: first, when he arrived at Thebes after answering the Sphinx and found it ruled by Queen Jocasta and her brother; and second, on stage, when Creon and Jocasta question his present rashness and his authority. These scenes give us something of the feeling of what it is like to be an oedipal child, but they are transformed; here Oedipus is in charge, as the child never is. As for the two deeds themselves, the very identification of two such well-defined heroic acts distorts the child's experience of a diffuse guilt and an unlocated evil—an experience that much more closely resembles Hamlet's in Denmark. Such identification is closer to metapsychology than to an open case history: Freud transforms the immediacy and confusion of oedipal experience into abstract terms ("our first sexual impulse and our first hatred"),[6] while Sophocles transforms them into concrete dramatic acts (murder at the crossroads and marriage at the gates of Thebes), but both transformations distance the acts. Sophocles' handling of the oedipal experience is not so much an open wish fulfillment as a kind of repression. He projects not only the impulse but these deeds themselves, so that these deeds take place offstage and in the past; they are facts to be discovered and discussed, not lived through. They are acts rather than feelings and ideas. Psychology has been transformed into history, phenomenology into cosmology.

---

[5] Freud, *The Interpretation of Dreams* (1900), *SE*, vol. 4, p. 264.
[6] *Ibid.*, p. 262.

Hamlet, by contrast, presents the phenomenological experience of an oedipal situation: the intense longings barely disguised as appropriate emotions, the jealousy though justified, the good intentions, and, perhaps most of all, the sense of being only a child in someone else's world. When Oedipus arrived at Thebes, Creon and Jocasta made way for him as king; when Hamlet returns to Denmark for "th' election," he is still only a prince in his uncle's world. While Oedipus's agony is shown as a conflict between present and disowned past, Hamlet's is vividly portrayed as a present conflict occurring completely within his own mind. Shakespeare gives outward justification for the conflict, but unlike the conflict in *Oedipus Rex,* it is an internal one. . . .

Fantasy's role cannot be predicted; it crops up wherever it can, taking over or slipping out like a taboo subject in polite conversation, and it affects not only the story or plot but the character configurations, the landscape, the props, the imagery, and the language. The presence of fantasy is anything but a mere substitution of a hidden story for an open one. Fantasy is present in the proliferation of scenes arising from different elements of the text, sometimes more, sometimes less directly and obviously; it is sometimes literally part of the text and sometimes only a distant echo.

The best evidence for the presence of an oedipal fantasy in *Hamlet,* for example, is not in the single analogy between the play's plot and an oedipal fantasy but rather in the sheer multitude of oedipally suggestive scenes, images, and configurations which emerge whole or in pieces from the ongoing action. The central oedipal images of unnatural murder and unnatural sex proliferate and become inseparable, first as a double aspect of Claudius's parental, secret crime and then as aspects of Hamlet's own voyeuristic and retaliatory desires. Finally, it becomes impossible to tell who is doing what to whom, as the identities of criminal and victim merge and switch in the primitive fantasies provoked by the play's language and action. Claudius poisons both sword and cup; he pours poison into the King's ear and drops poison into the Queen's cup; murder and incest on the rational level become the single crime of destructive sexuality in the fantasy. And this crime spreads to "poison the ear of Denmark" and taint all human communication, as people "take," "beg," or "assault" each others' ears throughout the dialogue. It is in this context that Hamlet makes his own gestures toward sexuality and murder, and we begin to see the several oedipal triangles generated around the paternal apex as different men take the role of Hamlet's "father." The fact that Polonius the father spies on Hamlet's interview with his beloved Ophelia links this scene to the later one when Polonius (now actually taken for Hamlet's father) spies on Hamlet's interview with his beloved mother. As in all primitive fantasies, it is hard to tell whether the son is taking his father's place and repeating his crime, or whether he is punishing his father and *un*doing his crime. Is Hamlet taking Hamlet senior's place and repeating Claudius's crime, or is he punishing Claudius and undoing Claudius's crime? Is a brother (Claudius) pouring poison into his brother's (the older Hamlet's) ear, as in the play-within-a-play? Or is a nephew (Hamlet) pouring poison into his uncle's (Claudius's) ear, as in the dumb show? Or is the son pouring poison in his father's ear, if we short-circuit the two actions?

It is also hard to determine whether Hamlet is attacking his father murderously or attacking his mother sexually. He goes to Gertrude's room "speak[ing] daggers," and though he had vowed to use none, Gertrude finds soon enough that his words "like daggers enter in mine ears." Is Hamlet here imitating his father/uncle's incestuous attack on Gertrude? Or is he attacking that father by attacking his mother? "Father and mother are one flesh," as Hamlet explains when he calls Claudius "my loving mother," and Hamlet's attacks on his mother in the bedroom scene harm the images of Claudius, not Gertrude: first a picture of Claudius as a "mildew'd ear" and then a stand-in for Claudius, dead behind the arras where he was trying to "overhear." The confusion between murderous and sexual attacks is further complicated by a confusion between attack and suicide. In the last scene, Hamlet's revenge literally destroys him; elsewhere he is hoist with his own verbal petards, as when he admiringly calls up the image of a bloody young murderer: no sooner does he tell how Pyrrhus is about to murder Priam, than the citadel of Troy collapses and "takes prisoner Pyrrhus' ear."

The foregoing is just evidence of the *presence* of oedipal fantasy material in the play: I am not suggesting that these fantastic reversals and equivalences replace the more rational distinctions which "really" make up the action but that they enrich and complicate an already ambiguous world. Fantasy material is always present; it is, according to one investigator, the "baseline of [mental] activity,"[7] even on the higher preconscious level, and it dominates all unconscious thought. What makes literature special, however, is the way it draws on fantasies and yet escapes from the chaos of pure fantasy; the way it forms hierarchies so we can separate what is really going on from what might be going on and can distinguish the theme from the variation. What makes literature unique is neither the presence of nor the eradication of fantasy, but the play between kaleidoscopic patterns of fantasies on the one hand and, on the other, the impression we get of a stabler action which emerges from it. Sometimes the network of fantasy variations merely resonates with the stable manifest story, in the way I have described earlier. But most often there is a more concrete connection, and we can spot the crisis in the manifest story which has opened a path into the fantasy level. Things fall apart in Hamlet's world where love and murder ought to be separated, and we descend into a nightmare where they are inseparable, where echoes are the truth, ghosts are real, and the King is a liar. But the play, unlike a true nightmare, always maintains the distinction between fantasy and reality, however revealing—and accurate—the threat of their merger may be.

---

[7] Eric Klinger, *Structure and Functions of Fantasy* (New York: Wiley-Interscience, 1971), p. 348.

Othello: The Problematics of Love

by Rosalie L. Colie

By the time he came to write *Othello*, Shakespeare had learned to cope with some of the problems still open in *Romeo and Juliet*, and could do so without losing any advantages of his working out in the earlier play a wonderfully heightened language of love. *Othello* is a remarkably integrated play, its action compressed, its imagery consistent, its language profoundly connected with the personalities of the various characters, as well as subservient to the needs of plot, action, and theme. In *Othello*, it seems, the different aspects of the play have been deeply driven into one another, to be separated by some narrow critic only at grave danger to the play as a whole. I know that this is so, and since my way of working in this exercise necessarily stresses certain elements at the expense of others, I shall try to strike my subject as lightly as I can and, wherever possible, to indicate the connection of my stress-points to other parts of the play.

Othello is a play about love and its relation to the rest of life. *Antony and Cleopatra* aside, it is difficult to find another major English Renaissance tragedy in which love is so frankly central, so stripped and so exposed. In this play, the lovers are not star-crossed, but crossed by their own personalities, by their own natures, so excellently fine, and by the peculiarities of the small, intimate society in which they carry on their lives. Like *Romeo and Juliet*, this play makes use of a situation and of characters habitually associated with the classical comic tradition.[1] From a slightly dif-

[1] Robert A. Watts, "The Comic Scenes in *Othello*," *SQ* 18 (1967): 349–54; Barbara H. C. de Mondonça, "*Othello*: A Tragedy Built on Comic Structure," *SS* 21 (1968): 31–38.

ferent perspective, the play's elements can be seen to be those of the city comedy. An elderly man, a blackamoor even, marries a young wife and is jealous of his young assistant. We do not commonly think of *Othello* as a tale of January and May, though Iago and Othello are quick enough to accept such an interpretation of the situation. Actually, Shakespeare has turned that triangle of *senex, puella*, and *adulescens* upside down. Desdemona loves the *senex* with unqualified devotion, and though Cassio certainly admires Desdemona, and his language to and about her is in the classic courtly tradition, his affections are clearly occupied elsewhere. Othello fears that he is mocked by the public for being a January deceived by May; in fact, the public admires him the more for his achievement of so lovely a wife. The stock characters in the play are not at all what we might expect, either: the prostitute Bianca, for instance, stationed on an island where transient military and naval men are always ready for her favors, turns out to love Cassio "really," far beyond her rights as a stock figure.

With the major characters Shakespeare performs splendid tricks. Othello is a Moor, by stage convention expected to be both lecherous and violent, as well as servile; so Moors appear on the English stage, one of them, Aaron, cast by Shakespeare himself as a typical eastern villain.[2] What has happened in this play is that at the outset the Moor is introduced to the audience in terms of such extraordinary nobility as to erase the stereotype from the audience's mind. Later we are forced to discover that it is just the stereotyped qualities of emotionalism, volatility, and gullibility from which Shakespeare finally derives Othello's tragic breaking— after he has bred us away from expecting them in such a hero. By these means, as so often elsewhere, Shakespeare gets it both ways: he breaks the traditional presentation and exploits it at its most conventional points, after having quite cleaned the situation of stereotypical implications. Othello *is* noble, but in his nature reside those qualities of which he is most afraid, exactly the violence, the trickery, the gullibility of the stock-Moor. As was his custom in the

---

See also the important remarks by K. M. Lea in *Italian Popular Comedy*, vol. 2, pp. 378–79; and Allan Gilbert, *The Principles and Practice of Criticism* (Detroit, 1959), pp. 27–45. For material on this subject, I am indebted to June Fellows.

[2] Eldred Jones, *Othello's Countrymen* (Oxford, 1965).

great tragedies, Shakespeare chose heroes of startling eccentricity—Hamlet, a thoughtful prince cast as revenger; Lear, an old madman, conspicuously foolish and unjust; Macbeth, corrupted early in the play, whose corruption plays itself out during the action; Antony, proud, careless, and sensual, linked to a cheating, trivial, sensual partner both with him and against him; Coriolanus, cold, proud, passionate, and unreasonable. Not the least daring was Othello, a Moor in Venice, a warrior turned lover, a primitive more civilized than the super-subtle Venetians.

In *Othello* there is much unmetaphoring, largely in relation to medieval and Renaissance romance and lyric traditions; I want to deal especially, though not exclusively, with Shakespeare's use in this play of the sonnet tradition. First of all, the appearance of hero and heroine: traditionally, the lady-love is fair, both in coloring and in spirit; golden hair and white skin are so typical for the role of beloved that Sidney made the point that his individuated Stella's eyes were black, and Shakespeare could appear original in loving a brunette. Desdemona is fair, within and without. The less fair, less spiritually refined qualities attributed to the standard courtly lover-poet have in fact been written into Othello's background and appearance. He *is* black, and, when pressed, the Venetians remind him of it. Though we are led to expect the opposite, Othello's external blackness turns out to match one segment of his inner life, as well of course as his external behavior to his wife. By taking literally conventional fairness and darkness, Shakespeare has given a new dimension to an artificial arrangement so trite as to appear meaningless: part of the shock involved in this marriage relies upon literary as well as upon social conventions. The relations of lover and beloved conventional in romance and lyric—she morally superior to him—have also been deepened to mean in this play something more than a traditional compliment to a lady. Mere *compliment* is indeed irrelevant: in *Othello* the conventions have been translated into consequential moral fact.

As in *Romeo and Juliet*, in *Othello* much is made of the difference between light and dark, between night and day, here tightly connected to the emblematic fairness and darkness of heroine and hero. As in *Romeo and Juliet*, crucial scenes in *Othello* are night-pieces. The abrupt and brilliant beginning, when Othello's bridal

night is interrupted by the news of the Turk; a second interrupted
bridal night on Cyprus; the sacrificial murder—each has its language of light and dark reinforcing the conjunction of fair heroine
and dark hero, of moral clarity and psychological darkness. Other
kinds of contrast occur, one of which has not received its notice
due—the more remarkable because it is so obvious. Recently, much
has been made of "Venice" as a way of life, in this play as in *The
Merchant of Venice*.[3] We know, perhaps even better than the Elizabethan audience did, how appropriate Venice is as the setting for
this sort of scene. We know why the merit system worked to
Othello's benefit and to Iago's annoyance, why strangers were in
Venice at all, and why strangers, however favored, had difficulty in
coming to terms with their difference in the city. We know the
social exclusiveness of the class from which Desdemona came, and
why Venetian patricians were willing to pay so much to keep war at
a distance from their lives ("Why this is Venice; my house is not a
grange"). Othello's usefulness to the state, in protecting it from
warfare on its shores, was sufficient to override even a patrician's
rights in his daughter's marriage. The source aside, which made
clear that the story was a Venetian one, Shakespeare made excellent use of his locus, contrasting the comfort and materialism of the
great trading city with the intangible values of Othello's courage
and Desdemona's purity.

Another way of saying all this is that Shakespeare contrasted
materialist Venetian ways with those of love—or, to take love's most
obvious location, Venetian with Cyprian ways. In spite of its distance from Venice, the island of Cyprus was, like Rhodes, crucial to
the strategic defense of the city against the Turk. In realistic terms,
Cyprus was a familiar name on the Venetian tongue. Othello and
Iago had seen action there before the events of the play began; the
Venetians murmur about Cyprus and Rhodes before the danger is
made "certain then for Cyprus." Once Othello and Desdemona
arrive on the island, all the action of the play takes place there, and

---

[3] See Alvin Kernan, "Introduction,"*Othello* (New York: Signet, 1963), pp. xxv–xxx;
Allan Bloom, "Cosmopolitan Man and the Political Community: An Interpretation of
Othello," *ASPR* 54 (1960): 139–58; with Sigurd Burckhardt's rejoinder, *ibid.*, pp.
158–66; and the further discussions by these authors (*ibid.*, pp. 457–64, 465–71,
474–93).

appropriately, when we consider that the rites of Venus, with actual and metaphorical sacrifices, were centered on the island. For Cassio, Cyprus is "this worthy isle"; for Iago, "this warlike isle," and "this fair island." It is peopled by "generous islanders," for whom on their deliverance and his wedding night Othello is glad to proclaim holiday. Cinthio's story had established Cyprus as the site of the complicated murder of a Venetian wife by a Moor and a machiavel, but Cinthio made no particular reference to the symbolism implicit in the site. Shakespeare deepens the references to Cyprus, drawing out the island's latent power as the primary locus of love, the island to which, after her birth from the sea-foam, Aphrodite was wafted on her pearly shell. In Cassio's approach to Desdemona coming ashore on the island, the significance of the place is made plain: his heralding of her, "our great captain's captain," turns into a welcoming benediction of the lady, "The divine Desdemona" (II. i. 73), coming like the goddess from the sea. *O dea certe:*

> O, behold,
> The riches of the ship is come ashore!
> Ye men of Cyprus, let her have your knees:
> Hail to thee, lady! and the grace of heaven,
> Before, behind thee, and on every hand,
> Enwheel thee round!
>
> (II. i. 82–87)

That the island is sacred to love, Cassio had made clear a few lines earlier in his invocation for Othello's protection at sea:

> Great Jove, Othello guard,
> And swell his sail with thine own powerful breath,
> That he may bless this bay with his tall ship,
> And swiftly come to Desdemona's arms,
> Give renew'd fire to our extinct spirits,
> And bring all Cyprus comfort. . . .
>
> (II. i. 77–82)

Quite without Iago's suggestiveness, Cassio simply celebrates the ritual love proper to the occasion, the characters, and the island; in his turn, Othello disembarks with love's rites on his mind, speaking to his wife in a speech of marvelous hyperbole, interrupted by his memory of his duty as commander, and by his courteous greeting of his "old acquaintance of the isle."

Love is rarely simple, and only at first blush does Aphrodite appear to provide uncomplicated satisfactions. The island dedicated to her is not, as the play makes clear, so well-fortified as Rhodes; Othello, we are told, knew "the fortitude of the place" from his stays on the island earlier. Actually, in its metaphoric sense, "the fortitude of the place" is what Othello did *not* know—the enormous secret strength of Aphrodite was what overthrew him, his sexual jealousy (in the existence of which he could not believe) coming to dominate his mind and finally his personality. All the references to Cyprus—and there are many more, some of Iago's with considerable *double-entendre*—make perfectly good superficial sense within the literal arrangements of the play; taken with their undertone of symbolic reference, their meaning is even more deeply sunk into the central preoccupation of *Othello*, the problematics of what is called "real" love. . . .

Other themes in Othello's last speeches offer commentary on the customary languages of literary love. Traditionally, ladies are "cold," as diamonds, as the springs of Helicon, as snow, as ice. Beatrice and Laura were both chilly; even Ronsard's willing ladies were occasionally "froides." Desdemona, we know, was not cold in her lifetime, but only in her death:

> cold, cold, my girl,
> Even like thy chastity.
>
> (V. ii. 276–77)

Once more, the metaphor is made real, thrust back into brutal actuality: Desdemona is at last made "cold."

The imagery of light and dark, playing in many contexts, comes to its climax in the great speech before Desdemona's murder. By her marriage, Desdemona had evidently come to terms with Othello's blackness, as her explanation of her unfilial behavior makes plain. But Othello, it turns out, had not, whatever he may have thought. As Iago's insinuations bore into him, Othello seeks reasons why Desdemona should not love him:

> Haply, for I am black,
> And have not those soft parts of conversation
> That chamberers have, or for I am declin'd
> Into the vale of years,
>
> (III. iii. 267–70)

he says, pathetically and ambiguously explaining things to himself. And a bit later, in a rage:

> my name, that was as fresh
> As Dian's visage, is now begrim'd, and black
> As mine own face. . . .

(III. iii. 392–94)

Desdemona had spoken for herself when she said, "I saw Othello's visage in his mind"; but as events turn out, his mind can be "begrim'd" and black as his face.

Robert Heilman and others have studied the ways in which Othello's grandiloquence falls into the extravagant, passionate, fragmentary, derogatory language that shares more and more with Iago's choice of syntax and vocabulary.[4] It is interesting to note that even in this degeneration, there are traces of literary love conventions. Othello ceases to see Desdemona whole: as she loses her integrity for him, he sees her only in parts—and, far more important, his rage is such that he wishes to tear her into bits. It is the passionate rage that strikes us, as it ought, with most force, so that Othello's abusive "Noses, ears, and lips" does not obviously make mock of the catalogue of mistresses' separate features so dear to writers of blasons and sonnets. Such literary elements are by the by, of course: they do not insist upon themselves, and we do not insist upon them. What we are to notice is the realistic use by the playwright of this kind of reference, as the disjunction of the parts of Desdemona's face is seen to match the disruption in Othello's mind and feelings about her.

Believing himself wronged, Othello reverses the light-dark imagery, calling Desdemona "thou black weed"—although her fairness never ceases to move him deeply, even at that terrible moment. As he readies himself to take her life, Othello speaks in an image cluster gathering up all the themes of fairness, coldness, hardness, and death:

> I'll not shed her blood,
> Nor scar that whiter skin of hers than snow,
> And smooth, as monumental alabaster. . . .

(V. ii. 3–5)

---

[4] Robert B. Heilman, *Magic in the Web* (Lexington: University of Kentucky Press, 1956), *passim*; and Matthew N. Proser, *The Heroic Image in Five Shakespearean Tragedies* (Princeton: Princeton University Press, 1965), chapter 3.

The notion of a tomb, made so concrete in *Romeo and Juliet*, is only glanced at here, its power the greater for its obliqueness. A few lines after these, the rose comes in, to make the contrast between cold and warmth, colorlessness and intensity, death and life. A literary parallel might be Petrarca's sonnet 131, where the rose blooms against the snow and, after its brief life, cannot be revived. To hunt among Petrarca's poems for parallels is reliably rewarding, even precisely to the combinations of light and dark that best fit this play. In Laura, of course, light and fairness combine in exceptional radiance; in her imperfect lover, especially imperfect when absent from his lady, darkness prevails—and, one notes, the very darkest sort of darkness, Petrarca tells us: Moroccan or Moorish darkness.

Other love-poets rang changes on Petrarca's oxymora and oppositions, his freezings in fire, his burnings in ice, his poverty in riches, his "*dolce ire*," "*dolcezza amara*," "*dolce errore*," his love that brightens night, darkens day, embitters honey and sweetens vinegar, his peace unfound after armistice, and so on. Oxymoron and contradiction became official figures, expressing in figural shorthand the internal conflicts surfaced by love's intensity. Worked by generations of lyricists, the figure of oxymoron tended to stretch into longer syntactical forms, sentences expressing contradictoriness and paradox. Othello speaks in such contradictions—"O thou black weed, why art so lovely fair?" is his *odi et amo*, a highly condensed version of the conflicting emotions Shakespeare had far more fully worked out in his own sonnets of obsession. Finally, in the soliloquy after Desdemona's death:

> So sweet was ne'er so fatal: I must weep,
> But they are cruel tears; this sorrow's heavenly,
> It strikes when it does love. . . ,
>
> (V. ii. 20–22)

the confusions and contradictions of the language bespeak the degree of his suffering. Paradox takes hold at the end, when Othello is beyond restitution and beyond honor, in an echo from the love poetry, and more poignantly, from his own disembarkation speech: "Then in my sense 'tis happiness to die." This time, "dying" fulfills great crimes and great grief, not the overwhelming happiness he had experienced at reunion with Desdemona. Like

Romeo, Othello himself dies as the sonnet-lover should, upon a kiss:

> I kiss'd thee ere I kill'd thee, no way but this,
> Killing myself, to die upon a kiss.
>
> (V. ii. 359–60)

The metaphor is gone, but its echo remains, to remind us, as it reminds Othello, of what is gone with the loss of that love, with the loss of that lady's life.

What all this language does in *Othello* is what it does in *Romeo and Juliet*: it reminds us of what love lyrics exist to proclaim, that through all the misunderstandings, the violence, the betrayals and self-betrayals, love is at base the most beautiful of human experiences, its satisfactions so great that loss of love can bring incomparable results. It reminds us that in spite of their fictions, poets can be right—that whatever else happens in a man's life, it is his love which most reveals and strips him, which makes his private life sufficiently important to outweigh his public life. In *Romeo and Juliet* the lovers try to live privately, in a social situation that permits no such privacy; their sonnet language is properly self-important and self-referential, overriding all other considerations as long as love can. The lyrical language of that play, beautiful and buoyant, is at the same time a very obvious language, as befits the subject and the energies of a youthful play about youth; the lyrical element in *Othello* is so understated, so absorbed into the whole play that we hardly realize all that it does.

When we do, at last, realize that even the plot of *Othello* is in fact the unmetaphoring of typical sonnet-narrative, it comes both as a surprise and as a revelation. Nonetheless, that is just what it is: the sonnet-sequence plot has been animated into dramatic action. Fair bride and darker lover achieve, after initial difficulties, perfection of happiness, only to have jealousy break in, which in sonnet narratives may indeed result in love's death, but at most a metaphorical death. The lovers in sonnets generally survive, either to achieve a deeper love after the clearing up of misunderstanding, or to free the lover from an unworthy obsession. In life, of course, such endings are rare: real misprision, real jealousy, real irrationality sicken love past revival. In ordinary life, the ends of such affairs, even between great spirits, are not heroic and are rarely tragic, merely wasteful and sad. In this play, one conventional sonnet ending is reached, with the metaphorical death in fact unmetaphored. Love literally dies, then; that act is irreversible, Desdemona and love cannot be revived or recalled. But through all the misunderstanding, a kind of reconciliation is reached: the hero learns that his lady is true and his notion of her false. He recognizes the consistent virtue of his wife, and, by reason of his new understanding, can take the terrible consequences of his error. We accept Othello's heroism in part because of the speed and sureness with which he reaffirms his original judgment of Desdemona and of his love for her; after his praise of her steady goodness, he ends his life as judge and executioner of his own criminal self. It is not life-like, perhaps: but the love-fiction has, at Desdemona's death, come to take its consequences, to move onto another moral plane, to become, as tragedy must be, a fiction of responsibility.

In Othello's psychology, too, the schemata of official romantic love have left their deep mark. Because his view of love was so stereotyped, he could not see his wife as she actually was, but was fooled into taking her at Iago's fictional assessment. She was in fact generous, frank, and devoted, more openly so than the coy mistress of sonnet prescription. Her very deviation from romantic type made it easier for Othello to accept Iago's explanation of her, to accept, then, a familiar literary stereotype in place of the (remarkable, it is true) real person. Part of the extraordinary irony of this play is that in one sense, Othello's acceptance of Iago's story is a version of realism, as the world, or the literary world, sees realism. Desdemona's behavior was so romantic, so ideal, that it could indeed seem very unlikely. Iago's interpretation of the world, cheap and cynical though it is, is the version the world tends to take for real—or, Iago's interpretation most persuasively presents the stereotype of realism. Just as with Edmund, whose bastardy speech makes us at first entertain some sympathy for him, but whose behavior reveals, by his own account too, his fundamental lawlessness, so with Iago: the conventions of cynicism, usually protected by fears of romanticism within us, are ultimately revealed as the shoddy things they are. Altogether, we find the problematics of love—the psychology, the language, the behavior of love and its twinned opposite, jealousy—can ultimately be restudied through its expressive stereotypes.

Stereotypes themselves are a problem, because they are at once shoddy and valuable. Their thinness attenuates meaning; their commonplaceness and cliché reiteration make them seem automatic and trivial. All the same, though, stereotypes are developed in the first place because they answer in some measure fundamental needs, either as a simplified version of reality or to give shape to our deep hope that reality can be reinterpreted in some simple way. Artists and writers working with the stereotypes and schemata of their craft must maneuver delicately through the problem so raised, attempting not to say something everyone knows or expects to hear, and yet to speak in terms that everyone can understand.

Shakespeare managed miraculously to bring off his tragic exercise in dramatic sonnetry: by springing the sonnet plot back into what seems to be reality, he made the effects of love suddenly more patent, more critical, more crucial than they seem to be in their usual habitat, the protected and enclosed garden of love lyrics. By exploiting the self-examination and self-expression of the lyric lover, especially the sonnet lover, he made such private feelings seem suddenly almost heroic. By allowing private to move into public life, the profound inwardness of love to work in heroic personalities and thus to open upon tragic possibilities, he raises a lyric plot to tragic scope. Another way of saying this is that the playwright took the literary love conventions seriously, and by making various literary conventions seem elements in a real situation shows us the power and grievousness of the love they represent.

From literary conventions, he took part of his fable and much of his language. Without the literary conventions at his disposal—and without having practiced them in his own earlier works—Shakespeare would have had a hard time convincing us of the importance, especially the tragic importance, of a story so trivial and so sordid as Cinthio's novella. At this play's heart lies a critique of the artificiality built into stylized language and the behavior which that language permits and even encourages. In *Romeo and Juliet*, there is plenty of criticism of the love language—Mercutio's comments on the numbers that Petrarca and others "flowed in" tell us much—but this criticism never points to the morality beneath the conventions. There, the language points toward emotional condition, but does not reveal its nearly inexpressible complexities. In a fairly standard way, too, the sonnet ethos is affirmed unquestioned. Juliet, with her language more "real" than her lover's, is to be taken as the nobler, or more mature, character of the two—indeed, in the simplifying of his language, we are to read Romeo's growth through his new love. Desdemona's language is even more direct than Juliet's, both in a comparison between the two women's utterances and within the contexts of the two plays. As a result, Desdemona is obviously less rhetorical, even less poetic, than her husband; her verbal directness displays, we think, the plain "truth" of her nature. Othello's language displays something quite other: it shows us that his concepts of love are less grounded in psychological reality, are far more stereotyped, than those of his wife. Othello, after all, wooed an admitted prize among women; Desdemona studied her husband and chose him at considerable expense to herself. Othello's vulnerabilities show in his enormous pride, to warn us, if not him, of the delicate balance of his personality, especially when it is subjected to peculiar and unfamiliar stress. Less fearful of her senses and fearless of appearing sensual, Desdemona finds it easier to behave with absolute loyalty to Othello than he to her—a loyalty rare in what is called real life. She dies, indeed, upon an act of generosity, trying to clear her husband of the imputation of crime. By convention, the lady is of finer stuff than her lover; by convention, her excellence raises his moral level. Desdemona is fair; she has, in Spenser's words, "The trew fayre, that is the gentle wit,/ and vertuous mind . . . ,"[5] and thereby raises the moral level of her lover, at a cost, however, incommensurate with the gain. Love is not a thing to be taken lightly, nor can it be interpreted along conventional lines, even when, as in *Othello*, its conventions turn out to be true. In criticizing the artificiality he at the same time exploits in his play, Shakespeare manages in *Othello* to reassess and to reanimate the moral system and the psychological truths at the core of the literary love tradition, to reveal its problematics and to reaffirm in a fresh and momentous context the beauty of its impossible ideals.

---

[5] *Amoretti*, lxxix.

On *Othello*

by Stanley Cavell

I ask how it is that we are to understand, at the height of *The Winter's Tale*, Hermione's reappearance as a statue. Specifically I ask how it is that we are to understand Leontes's acceptance of the "magic" that returns her to flesh and blood, and hence to him. This is a most specific form of resurrection. Accepting it means accepting the idea that she had been turned to stone; that that was the right fate for her disappearance from life. So I am asking for the source of Leontes's conviction in the rightness of that fate. Giving the question that form, the form of my answer is by now predictable: for her to return to him is for him to recognize her; and for him to recognize her is for him to recognize his relation to her; in particular to recognize what his denial of her has done to her, hence to him. So Leontes recognizes the fate of stone to be the consequence of his particular skepticism. One can see this as the projection of his own sense of numbness, of living death. But then why was this *his* fate? It is a most specific form of remorse or of (self-)punishment.

Its environment is a tale of harrowing by jealousy, and a consequent accusation of adultery, an accusation known by every outsider, everyone but the accuser, to be insanely false. Hence Leontes is inevitably paired with Othello. I call attention to two further ways in which *The Winter's Tale* is a commentary upon *Othello*, and therefore contrariwise. First, both plays involve a harrowing of the power of knowing the existence of another (as chaste, intact, as what the knower knows his other to be). Leontes refuses to believe a true oracle; Othello insists upon believing a false one. Second, in both plays the consequence for the man's refusal of knowledge of his other is an imagination of stone. It is not merely an appetite for beauty that produces Othello's most famous image of his victim, as a piece of cold and carved marble (". . . whiter skin of hers than snow, / And smooth, as monumental alabaster"—V. ii. 4–5). Where does his image come from? . . .

That the integrity of my (human, finite) existence may depend on the fact and on the idea of another being's existence, and on the possibility of *proving* that existence; an existence conceived from my very dependence and incompleteness, hence conceived as perfect, and conceived as producing me "in some sense, in [its] own image"; these are thoughts that take me to a study of *Othello.*

Briefly, to begin with, we have the logic, the emotion, and the scene of skepticism epitomized. The logic: "My life upon her faith" (I. iii. 294) and " . . . when I love thee not / Chaos is come again" (III. iii. 91–92) set up the stake necessary to best cases; the sense I expressed by the imaginary major premise, "If I know anything, I know this." One standing issue about the rhythm of *Othello's* plot is that the progress from the completeness of Othello's love to the perfection of his doubt is too precipitous for the fictional time of the play. But such precipitousness is just the rhythm of skepticism; all that is necessary is the stake. The emotion: Here I mean not Othello's emotion toward Desdemona, call it jealousy; but the structure of his emotion as he is hauled back and forth across the keel of his love. Othello's enactment, or sufferance, of that torture is the most extraordinary representation known to me of the "astonishment" in skeptical doubt. In Descartes's first Meditation: "I realize so clearly that there are no conclusive indications by which waking life can be distinguished from sleep that I am quite astonished, and my bewilderment is such that it is almost able to convince me that I am sleeping." (It does not follow that one is *convinced* that one is awake.) When Othello loses consciousness ("Is't possible? —Confess? —Handkerchief? —O devil!"— IV. i. 42–43), it is not from conviction in a piece of knowledge but in an effort to stave the knowledge off. The scene: Here I have in mind the pervasive air of the language and the action of this play as one in which Othello's mind continuously outstrips reality, dissolves it in trance or dream or in the beauty or ugliness of his incantatory imagination; in which he visualizes possibilities that reason, unaided, cannot rule out. Why is he beyond aid? Why are the ear and the eye in him disjoined? We know that by the time he formulates his condition this way:

> By the world,
> I think my wife be honest, and think she is not,
> I think that thou are just, and think thou are not;
> I'll have some proof . . .
>
> (III. iii. 389–92)

he is lost. Two dozen lines earlier he had demanded of Iago "the ocular proof," a demand that was no purer a threat than it was a command, as if he does indeed wish for this outcome, as if he has a use for Iago's suspicions, hence a use for Iago that reciprocates Iago's use of him. Nothing I claim about the play here will depend on an understanding of the relation between Iago and Othello, so I will simply assert what is suggested by what I have just said, that such a question as "Why does Othello believe Iago?" is badly formed. It is not conceivable that Othello believes Iago and *not* Desdemona. Iago, we might say, offers Othello an opportunity to believe something, something to oppose to something else he knows. What does he know? Why does it require opposition? What do we know?

We have known (say since G. Wilson Knight's "The *Othello* Music") that Othello's language, call it his imagination, is at once his, and the play's, glory, and his shame, the source of his power and of his impotence; or we should have known (since Bradley's *Shakespearean Tragedy*) that Othello is the most romantic of Shakespeare's heroes, which may be a way of summarizing the same facts. And we ought to attend to the perception that Othello is the most Christian of the tragic heroes (expressed in Norman Rabkin's *Shakespeare and the Common Understanding*). Nor is there any longer any argument against our knowledge that Othello is black; and there can be no argument with the fact that he has just married, nor with the description, compared with the cases of Shakespeare's other tragedies, that this one is not political but domestic.

We know more specifically, I take it, that Othello's blackness means something. But what specifically does it mean? Mean, I mean, to him—for otherwise it is not Othello's color that we are

interested in but some generalized blackness, meaning perhaps
"sooty" or "filthy," as elsewhere in the play. This difference may
show in the way one takes Desdemona's early statement: "I saw
Othello's visage in his mind" (I. iii. 252). I think it is commonly felt
that she means she overlooked his blackness in favor of his inner
brilliance; and perhaps further felt that this is a piece of deception,
at least of herself. But what the line more naturally says is that she
saw his visage as he sees it, that she understands his blackness as he
understands it, as the expression (or in his word, his manifestation)
of his mind—which is not overlooking it. Then how does he understand it?

As the color of a romantic hero. For he, as he was and is, manifested by his parts, his title, and his "perfect soul" (I. ii. 31), is the
hero of the tales of romance he tells, some ones of which he wooed
and won Desdemona with, others of which he will die upon. It is
accordingly the color of one of enchanted powers and of magical
protection, but above all it is the color of one of purity, of a perfect
soul. Desdemona, in entering his life, hence in entering his story of
his life, enters as a fit companion for such a hero; his perfection is
now opened toward hers. His absolute stake in his purity, and its
confirmation in hers, is shown in what he feels he has lost in losing
Desdemona's confirmation:

> . . . my name, that was as fresh
> As Dian's visage, is now begrim'd, and black
> As mine own face. . . .
>
> (III. iii. 392–94)

Diana's is a name for the visage Desdemona saw to be in Othello's
mind. He loses its application to his own name, his charmed self,
when he no longer sees his visage in Desdemona's mind but in
Iago's, say in the world's capacity for rumor. To say he loses
Desdemona's power to confirm his image of himself is to say that he
loses his old power of imagination. And this is to say that he loses
his grasp of his own nature; he no longer has the same voice in his
history. So then the question becomes: How has he come to dis-
place Desdemona's imagination by Iago's? However terrible the
exchange, it must be less terrible than some other. Then we need to
ask not so much how Iago gained his power as how Desdemona lost
hers.

We know—do we not?—that Desdemona has lost her virginity, the protection of Diana, by the time she appears to us. And surely Othello knows this! But this change in her condition, while a big enough fact to hatch millennia of plots, is not what Othello accuses her of. (Though would that accusation have been much more unfair than the unfaithfulness he does accuse her of?) I emphasize that I am assuming in Othello's mind the theme and condition of virginity to carry their full weight within a romantic universe. Here is some recent Northrop Frye on the subject:

> Deep within the stock convention of virgin-baiting is a vision of human integrity imprisoned in a world it is in but not of, often forced by weakness into all kinds of ruses and stratagems, yet always managing to avoid the one fate which really is worse than death, the annihilation of one's identity. . . . What is symbolized as a virgin is actually a human conviction, however expressed, that there is something at the core of one's infinitely fragile being which is not only immortal but has discovered the secret of invulnerability that eludes the tragic hero.[1]

Now let us consolidate what we know on this sketch so far. We have to think in this play not merely about marriage but about the marriage of a romantic hero and of a Christian man; one whose imagination has to incorporate the idea of two becoming one in marriage and the idea that it is better to marry than to burn. It is a play, though it is thought of as domestic, in which not a marriage but an idea of marriage, or let us say an imagination of marriage, is worked out. "Why did I marry?" is the first question Othello asks himself to express his first raid of suspicion (III. iii. 246). The question has never been from his mind. Iago's first question to him is "Are you fast married?" and Othello's first set speech ends with something less than an answer: "But that I love the gentle Desdemona, / I would not my unhoused free condition / Put into circumscription and confine / For the sea's worth." Love is at most a necessary not a sufficient condition for marrying. And for some minds, a certain idea of love may compromise as much as validate the idea of marriage. It may be better, but it is not perfect to marry, as Saint Paul implies.

We have, further, to think in this play not merely generally of marriage but specifically of the wedding night. It is with this that

[1] *The Secular Scripture*, p. 86.

the play opens. The central of the facts we know is that the whole
beginning scene takes place while Othello and Desdemona are in
their bridal bed. The simultaneity is marked: "Even now, very now,
an old black ram / Is tupping your white ewe . . . " (I. i. 88). And
the scene is one of treachery, alarms, of shouts, of armed men
running through a sleeping city. The conjunction of the bridal
chamber with a scene of emergency is again insisted on by Othello's
reappearance from his bedroom to stop a brawl with his single
presence; a reappearance repeated the first night in Cyprus. As
though an appearance from his place of sex and dreams is what
gives him the power to stop an armed fight with a word and a
gesture. Or is this more than we know? Perhaps the conjunction is
to imply that their "hour of love" (I. iii. 298–99), or their two hours,
have each been interrupted. There is reason to believe that the
marriage has not been consummated, anyway reason to believe that
Iago does not know whether it has. What is Iago's "Are you fast
married?" asking? Whether a public, legal ceremony has taken
place or whether a private act; or whether the public and the private have ratified one another? Othello answers by speaking of his
nobility and his love. But apart from anything else this seems to
assume that Iago's "you" was singular, not plural. And what does
Othello mean in Cyprus by these apparently public words?

> . . . come, my dear love,
> The purchase made, the fruits are to ensue,
> The profit's yet to come 'twixt me and you.
>   (II. iii. 8–10)

What is the purchase and what the fruits or profit? Othello has just
had proclaimed a general celebration at once of the perdition of
the Turkish fleet and of his nuptials (II. ii.). If the fruits and profit
are the resumption of their privacy then the purchase was the
successful discharge of his public office and his entry into Cyprus.
But this success was not his doing; it was provided by a tempest. Is
the purchase their (public) marriage? Then the fruits and profit
are their conjugal love. Then he is saying that this is yet to come. It
seems to me possible that the purchase, or price, was her virginity,
and the fruits or profit their pleasure. There could hardly be
greater emphasis on their having had just one shortened night
together, isolated from this second night by a tempest (always in

these matters symbolic, perhaps here of a memory, perhaps of an anticipation). Or is it, quite simply, that this is something he wishes to *say* publicly, whatever the truth between them? (How we imagine Desdemona's reaction to this would then become all important.)

I do not think that we must, nor that we can, choose among these possibilities in Othello's mind. On the contrary, I think Othello cannot choose among them. My guiding hypothesis about the structure of the play is that the thing *denied our sight* throughout the opening scene; the thing, the scene, that Iago takes Othello back to again and again, retouching it for Othello's enchafed imagination; is what we are shown in the final scene, the scene of murder. This becomes our ocular proof of Othello's understanding of his two nights of married love. (It has been felt from Thomas Rymer to G. B. Shaw that the play obeys the rhythm of farce, not of tragedy. One might say that in beginning with a sexual scene denied our sight, this play opens exactly as a normal comedy closes, as if turning comedy inside out.) I will follow out this hypothesis here only to the extent of commenting on that final scene.

However one seeks to interpret the meaning of the great entering speech of the scene ("It is the cause, it is the cause, my soul. . . . Put out the light, and then put out the light . . . "), I cannot take its mysteries, its privacies, its magniloquence, as separate from some massive denial to which these must be in service. Othello must mean that he is acting impersonally, but the words are those of a man in a trance, in a dream-state, fighting not to awaken; willing for anything but light. By "denial" I do not initially mean something requiring psychoanalytical, or any other, theory. I mean merely to ask that we not, conventionally but insufferably, assume that we know this woman better than this man knows her—making Othello some kind of exotic, gorgeous, superstitious lunkhead; which is about what Iago thinks. However much Othello deserves each of these titles, however far he believes Iago's tidings, he cannot just believe them; somewhere he also *knows* them to be false. This is registered in the rapidity with which he is brought to the truth, with no further real evidence, with only a counter-story (about the handkerchief) that bursts over him, or from him, as the truth. Shall we say he recognizes the truth too late? The fact is, he recognizes it when he is ready to, as one alone can; in this case, when its burden is dead. I am not claiming that he is trying not to believe Iago, or wants not to believe what Iago has told him. (This might describe someone who, say, had a good opinion of Desdemona, not someone whose life is staked upon hers.) I am claiming that we must understand Othello, on the contrary, to want to believe Iago, to be trying, against his knowledge, to believe him. Othello's eager insistence on Iago's honesty, his eager slaking of his thirst for knowledge with that poison, is not a sign of his stupidity in the presence of poison but of his devouring need of it. I do not quite say that he could not have accepted slander about Desdemona so quickly, to the quick, unless he already believed it; but rather that it is a thing he would rather believe than something yet more terrible to his mind; that the idea of Desdemona as an adulterous whore is more convenient to him than the idea of her as chaste. But what could be more terrible than Desdemona's faithlessness? Evidently her faithfulness. But how?

Note that in taking Othello's entering speech as part of a ritual of denial, in the context of taking the murder scene as a whole to be a dream-enactment of the invisible opening of the play, we have an answer implied to our original question about this play, concerning Othello's turning of Desdemona to stone. His image denies that he scarred her and shed her blood. It is a denial at once that he has taken her virginity and that she has died of him. (But it is at the same time evidence that in suffering the replacement of the problem of God by the problem of the other this man has turned both objects into stone, so that we might at this moment understand his self-interpretation to be that of an idolater, hence religiously as well as socially to be cast out.) The whole scene of murder is built on the concept of sexual intercourse or orgasm as a dying. There is a dangerously explicit quibble to this effect in the exchange,

> *Othello.* Thou art on thy death bed.
> *Desdemona.* Ay, but not yet to die.
>
> (V. ii. 51–52)

The possible quibble only heightens the already heartbreaking poignance of the wish to die in her marriage bed after a long life.

Though Desdemona no more understands Othello's accusation of her than, in his darkness to himself, he does, she obediently shares his sense that this is their final night and that it is to be some dream-like recapitulation of their former two nights. This shows in her premonitions of death (the Willow Song, and the request that one of the wedding sheets be her shroud) and in her mysterious request to Emilia, " . . . tonight / Lay on my bed our wedding sheets" (IV. ii. 106–7), as if knowing, and faithful to, Othello's private dream of her, herself preparing the scene of her death as Othello, utilizing Iago's stage directions, imagines it must happen ("Do it not with poison, strangle her in her bed, even the bed she hath contaminated." "Good, good, the justice of it pleases, very good"—IV. i. 203–5); as if knowing that only with these sheets on their bed can his dream of her be contested. The dream is of contamination. The fact the dream works upon is the act of deflowering. Othello is reasonably literal about this, as reasonable as a man in a trance can be:

> . . . when I have pluck'd the rose,
> I cannot give it vital growth again,
> It must needs wither; I'll smell it on the tree,
> A balmy breath, that doth almost persuade
> Justice herself to break her sword: once more:
> Be thus, when thou art dead, and I will kill thee,
> And love thee after. . . .
>
>   (V. ii. 13–19)

(Necrophilia is an apt fate for a mind whose reason is suffocating in its sumptuous capacity for figuration, and which takes the dying into love literally to entail killing. "That death's unnatural, that kills for loving"—V. ii. 41—or that turns its object to live stone. It is apt as well that Desdemona sense death, or the figure of death, as the impending cause of death. And at the very end, facing himself, he will not recover from this. "I kissed thee ere I killed thee." And after too. And not just now when you died from me, but on our previous nights as well.)

The exhibition of wedding sheets in this romantic, superstitious, conventional environment, can only refer to the practice of proving purity by staining.—I mention in passing that this provides a satisfactory weight for the importance Othello attaches to his charmed (or farcical) handkerchief, the fact that it is spotted, spotted with strawberries.

Well, were the sheets stained or not? Was she a virgin or not? The answers seem as ambiguous as to our earlier question whether they are fast married. Is the final, fatal·reenactment of their wedding night a clear denial of what really happened, so that we can just read off, by negation, what really happened? Or is it a straight reenactment, without negation, and the flower was still on the tree, as far as he knew? In that case, who was reluctant to see it plucked, he or she? On such issues, farce and tragedy are separated by the thickness of a membrane.

We of course have no answer to such questions. But what matters is that Othello has no answer; or rather he can give none, for any answer to the questions, granted that I am right in taking the questions to be his, is intolerable. The torture of logic in his mind we might represent as follows: Either I shed her blood and scarred her or I did not. If I did not then she was not a virgin and this is a stain upon me. If I did then she is no longer a virgin and this is a stain upon me. Either way I am contaminated. (I do not say that the sides of this dilemma are of equal significance for Othello.)

But this much logic anyone but a lunkhead might have mastered apart from actually getting married. (He himself may say as much when he asks himself, too late, why he married.) Then what quickens this logic for him? Call whatever it is Iago. What is Iago?

He is everything, we know, Othello is not. Critical and witty, for example, where Othello is commanding and eloquent; retentive where the other is lavish; concealed where the other is open; cynical where the other is romantic; conventional where the other is original; imagines flesh where the other imagines spirit; the imaginer and manager of the human guise; the bottom end of the world. And so on. A Christian has to call him devil. The single fact between Othello and Iago I focus on here is that Othello fails twice at the end to kill Iago, knowing he cannot kill him. This all but all-powerful chieftain is stopped at this nobody. It is the point of his impotence, and the meaning of it. Iago is everything Othello must deny, and which, denied, is not killed but works on, like poison, like Furies.

In speaking of the point and meaning of Othello's impotence, I do not think of Othello as having been in an everyday sense impotent with Desdemona. I think of him, rather, as having been surprised by her, at what he has elicited from her; at, so to speak, a success rather than a failure. It is the dimension of her that shows itself in that difficult and dirty banter between her and Iago as they await Othello on Cyprus. Rather than imagine himself to have elicited that, or solicited it, Othello would imagine it elicited by anyone and everyone else.—Surprised, let me say, to find that she is flesh and blood. It was the one thing he could not imagine for himself. For if she is flesh and blood then, since they are one, so is he. But then although his potency of imagination can command the imagination of this child who is everything he is not, so that she sees his visage in his mind, she also sees that he is not identical with his mind, he is more than his imagination, black with desire, which she desires. Iago knows it, and Othello cannot bear what Iago knows, so he cannot outface the way in which he knows it, or knows anything. He cannot forgive Desdemona for existing, for being separate from him, outside, beyond command, commanding, her captain's captain.

It is an unstable frame of mind that compounds figurative with literal dying in love; and Othello unstably projects upon her, as he blames her:

> O perjur'd woman, thou dost stone thy heart
> And makest me call what I intend to do
> A murder, which I thought a sacrifice.
>   (V. ii. 64–66)

As he is the one who gives out lies about her, so he is the one who will give her a stone heart for her stone body, as if in his words of stone which confound the figurative and the literal there is the confounding of the incantations of poetry and of magic. He makes of her the thing he feels (" . . . my heart is turned to stone"—IV. i. 178), but covers the ugliness of his thought with the beauty of his imagery—a debasement of himself and of his art of words. But what produces the idea of sacrifice? How did he manage the thought of her death as a sacrifice? To what was he to sacrifice her? To his image of himself and of her, to keep his image intact, uncontaminated; as if *this* were his protection from slander's image of him, say from a conventional view of his blackness. So he becomes conventional, sacrificing love to convention. But this was unstable; it could not be said. Yet better thought than the truth, which was that the central sacrifice of romance has already been made by them: her virginity, her intactness, her perfection, had been gladly forgone by her for him, for the sake of their union, for the seaming of it. It is the sacrifice he could not accept, for then he was not himself perfect. It must be displaced. The scar is the mark of finitude, of separateness; it must be borne whatever one's anatomical condition, or color. It is the sin or the sign of refusing imperfection that produces, or justifies, the visions and torments of devils that inhabit the region of this play.

If such a man as Othello is rendered impotent and murderous by aroused, or by having aroused, female sexuality; or let us say: if this man is horrified by human sexuality, in himself and in others; then no human being is free of this possibility. What I have wished to bring out is the nature of this possibility, or the possibility of this nature, the way human sexuality is the field in which the fantasy of finitude, of its acceptance and its repetitious overcoming, is worked out; the way human separateness is turned equally toward splendor and toward horror, mixing beauty and ugliness; turned toward before and after; toward flesh and blood.

—But Othello certainly knows that Desdemona exists! So what has his more or less interesting condition to do with skepticism?—[I knew you were still there. This is the last time we can meet like this.] In what spirit do you ask that question? I too am raising it. I wish to keep suspicion cast on what it is we take to express skepticism, and here especially by casting suspicion on whether we know what it means to know that another exists. Nothing could be more certain to Othello than that Desdemona exists; is flesh and blood; is separate from him; other. This is precisely the possibility that tortures him. The content of his torture *is* the premonition of the existence of another, hence of his own, his own as dependent, as partial. According to me further, his profession of skepticism over her faithfulness is a cover story for a deeper conviction; a terrible doubt covering a yet more terrible certainty, an unstatable certainty. But then this is what I have throughout kept arriving at as the cause of skepticism—the attempt to convert the human condition, the condition of humanity, into an intellectual difficulty, a riddle. . . .

Tragedy is the place we are not allowed to escape the consequences, or price, of this cover: that the failure to acknowledge a best case of the other is a denial of that other, presaging the death of the other, say by stoning, or by hanging; and the death of our capacity to acknowledge as such, the turning of our hearts to stone, or their bursting. The necessary reflexiveness of spiritual torture.

—But at any rate Othello is hardly in doubt that he can ever know whether Desdemona is, for example, in pain (perhaps suffering heartache), and for that reason in doubt that she exists; so again his problem cannot match the skeptical one.—But I ask again: Do we know what it is to be in such a doubt? and know this better than we know how to think of Othello's doubt? Moreover, is it even clear what it would mean to say that Othello does not doubt matters of Desdemona's consciousness such as that she has, or may have, some easily describable pain? If what he imagines is that she is stone, then *can* he imagine that she is in pain? . . .

Is the cover of skepticism—the conversion of metaphysical finitude into intellectual lack—a denial of the human or an expression of it? For of course there are those for whom the denial of the human *is* the human. . . . Call this the Christian view. It would be why Nietzsche undertook to identify the task of overcoming the human with the task of overcoming the denial of the human; which implies overcoming the human not through mortification but through joy, say ecstasy. If the former can be thought of as the denial of the body then the latter may be thought of as the affirmation of the body. Then those who are pushed, in attempting to counter a dualistic view of mind and body, to assert the identity of body and mind, are again skipping or converting the problem. For suppose my identity with my body is something that exists only in my affirmation of my body (as friendship may exist only in loyalty to it). Then the question is: What would the body *become* under affirmation? What would become of *me?* Perhaps I would know myself as, take myself for, a kind of machine; perhaps as a universe.

I conclude with two thoughts, or perspectives, from which to survey one's space of conviction in the reading I have started of *Othello*, and from which perhaps to guide it further.

First, what you might call the philosophy or the moral of the play seems all but contained in the essay Montaigne entitles "On some verses of Virgil," in such a remark as: "What a monstrous animal to be a horror to himself, to be burdened by his pleasures, to regard himself as a misfortune!" The essay concerns the compatibility of sex with marriage, of sex with age; it remarks upon, and upon the relations among, jealousy, chastity, imagination, doubts about virginity; upon the strength of language and the honesty of language;

and includes mention of a Turk and of certain instances of necrophilia. One just about runs through the topics of *Othello* if to this
essay one adds Montaigne's early essay "Of the power of imagination," which contains a Moor and speaks of a king of Egypt who,
finding himself impotent with his bride threatened to kill her,
thinking it was some sort of sorcery. The moral would be what
might have been contained in Othello's " . . . one that lov'd not
wisely, but too well," that all these topics should be food for
thought and moderation, not for torture and murder; as fit for rue
and laughter as for pity and terror; that they are not tragic unless
one makes them so, takes them so; that we are tragic in what we
take to be tragic; that one must take one's imperfections with a "gay
and sociable wisdom" (in "Of experience," Montaigne's final essay)
not with a somber and isolating eloquence. It is advice to accept
one's humanity, and one can almost see Iago as the slanderer of
human nature (this would be his diabolism) braced with Othello as
the enacter of the slander—the one thinking to escape human
nature from below, the other from above. But to whom is the
advice usable? And how do we understand why it cannot be taken
by those in directest need of it? The urging of moderation is valuable only to the extent that it results from a knowledge of the
human possibilities beyond its urging. Is Montaigne's attitude fully
earned, itself without a tint of the wish for exemption from the
human? Or is Shakespeare's topic of the sheets and the handkerchief understandable as a rebuke to Montaigne, for refusing a
further nook of honesty? A bizarre question, I suppose; but meant
only to indicate how one might, and why one should, test whether
my emphasis on the stain is necessary to give sufficient weight to
one's experience of the horror and the darkness of these words and
actions, or whether it is imposed.

My second concluding thought is more purely speculative, and
arises in response to my having spoken just now of "the refusal of
imperfection" as producing "the visions and torments of devils that
inhabit the region of this play." I do not wish to dispute the evidence marshalled by Bernard Spivack in his *Shakespeare and the
Allegory of Evil* showing Iago to be a descendent of the late morality
figure of the Vice. I mean rather to help explain further the
appearance of that figure in this particular play, and, I guess, to
suggest its humanizing, or human splitting off (the sort of inter-

pretation Spivack's book seems to deplore). It is against the tradition of the morality play that I now go on to call attention—I cannot think I am the first to say it out loud—to the hell and the demon staring out of the names of Othello and Desdemona. I mention this curiosity to prepare something meant as a nearly pure conjecture, wishing others to prove it one way or another, namely that underlying and shaping the events of this play are certain events of witch trials. Phrases such as "the ocular proof" and " . . . cords, or knives / Poison, or fire, or suffocating streams . . ." (III. iii. 394–95) seem to me to call for location in a setting of judicial torture. And I confess to finding myself thinking of Desdemona's haunting characterization of a certain conception of her as "a moth of peace" when I read, from an 1834 study called *Folk-lore of the NE of Scotland*, "In some parts of Scotland moths are called 'witches' " (quoted in Kittredge, *Witchcraft in Old and New England*). But what prompts my thought primarily is the crazed logic Othello's rage for proof and for "satisfaction" seems to require (like testing for a woman's witchcraft by seeing whether she will drown, declaring that if she does she was innocent but if she does not she is to be put to death for a witch): What happened on our wedding night is that I killed her; but she is not dead; therefore she is not human; therefore she must die. ("Yet she must die, else she'll betray more men"—V. ii. 6.) Again he claims not to be acting personally, but by authority; here he has delivered a sentence. I recall that the biblical justification for the trial of witches was familiar from the punishments in *Exodus:* "Thou shalt not suffer a witch to live." Othello seems to be babbling the crazed logic as he falls into his explicit faint or trance: "First, to be hanged, and then to confess; I tremble at it" (IV. i. 38–39), not knowing whether he is torturer or victim.

I introduced the idea of the trial for witchcraft as a conjecture, meaning immediately that it is not meant as a hypothisis: I do not *require* it for any interpretative alignment of my senses with the world of this play. It is enough, without supposing Shakespeare to have used literal subtexts of this sort, that the play opens with a public accusation of witchcraft, and an abbreviated trial, and is then succeeded with punctuating thoughts of hell and by fatal scenes of psychological torture, and concludes with death as the proof of mortality, that is, of innocence (cf. "If that thou be'st a devil, I cannot kill thee"—V. ii. 283). Enough, I mean, to stir the same depths of superstition—of a horror that proposes our lack of certain access to other minds—that under prompting institutions caused trials for witchcraft. *Othello* is at once, as we would expect of what we call Shakespeare's humanity, an examination of the madness and bewitchment of inquisitors, as well as of the tortures of love; of those tortures of which both victim and torturer are victims.

So they are there, on their bridal and death sheets. A statue, a stone, is something whose existence is fundamentally open to the ocular proof. A human being is not. The two bodies lying together form an emblem of this fact, the truth of skepticism. What this man lacked was not certainty. He knew everything, but he could not yield to what he knew, be commanded by it. He found out too much for his mind, not too little. Their differences from each other—the one everything the other is not—form an emblem of human separation, which can be accepted, and granted, or not. Like the separation from God; everything we are not.

So we are here, knowing they are "gone to burning hell," she with a lie on her lips, protecting him, he with her blood on him. Perhaps Blake has what he calls songs to win them back with, to make room for hell in a juster city. But can philosophy accept them back at the hands of poetry? Certainly not so long as philosophy continues, as it has from the first, to demand the banishment of poetry from its republic. Perhaps it could if it could itself become literature. But can philosophy become literature and still know itself?

On *Macbeth*

by Norman Rabkin

As one watches the birth of Shakespearean tragedy in *Richard III*, it is hard not to fancy that one sees the early expression of the same understanding of human behavior that makes the mature tragedies possible. For the play's energy, its power to arouse energetic responses in us, comes from Richard's joy in the familial crimes he engineers with such gusto. These crimes are singularly lacking in the conventional motivation Shakespeare's revisers need to supply. Neither ambition nor the more modern explanation of Richard's behavior as his response to his physical deformity carries adequate conviction. The pleasure of Richard's crimes lies in the acting out of deep intrapsychic motives, in the annihilation of the hero's family and his world. So far has Shakespeare come at the very beginning of his theatrical career.

Only Richard's pleasure and Shakespeare's not yet fully realized power differentiate Richard essentially from Macbeth. Like Richard, Macbeth fools himself and us into thinking that it is the golden round that drives him to regicide. As in *Richard III*, so in *Macbeth* one can point to no single moment when the hero seems able to enjoy the sweet fruition of an earthly crown. But in *Macbeth*, more clearly than in *Richard III*, the regicide's lack of pleasure in his accomplishments is presented not moralistically, as a judgment on evil deeds, but as a defining fact of the deeds themselves. For if Richard at least enjoys the process of manipulation and murder by which he gets where he finally does not want to be, Macbeth's response to his own action is constantly one of horror. As has repeatedly been noticed, he does what he does, not as his wife would do it, willingly in a clear cause, but as if he must do what he does not want to do, and for causes he cannot enunciate. As said earlier, it is Lady Macbeth, never her husband, who speaks of the "golden round" (I. v. 28). It is she, not he, who claims that he wants to have what he esteems "the ornament of life." Macbeth, in response, suggests that his own concern is rather with what "may become a man" and with the knowledge that to do what she suggests is to deny or to destroy his own manhood (I. vii. 41–47). With singular consistency, in fact, Shakespeare denies Macbeth even a single line that indicates ambition as the spring of his action.[1]

As with the other adaptations . . . Davenant's 1674 redaction of *Macbeth* unwittingly constitutes an astute piece of criticism. Davenant did everything he could to make sense, sensibly (and of course lethally to Shakespeare's play) making Macduff the hero Shakespeare had failed to make of him, conversely turning Macbeth into

---

[1] Oddly, Macbeth's letter to Lady Macbeth telling her of the witches' prophecy speaks only "of what greatness is promis'd *thee*" (I. vi. 12–13). Lady Macbeth, to be sure, speaks at several points of her husband's ambition:

> Thou wouldst be great,
> Art not without ambition. . . .
> What thou wouldst highly,
> That wouldst thou holily; wouldst not play false,
> And yet wouldst wrongly win. Thou'ldst have, great Glamis,
> That which cries, "Thus thou must do," if thou have it . . . ."   (I. v. 18–23)

On the eve of the murder she reminds him of "the hope . . . Wherein you dress'd yourself," suggests that he would "have that / Which thou esteem'st the ornament of life," and reminds him that he did "break this enterprise to me" (I. vii. 35–48). But all of this language, like "the golden round," is hers, and Shakespeare gives us no opportunity to see Macbeth in a moment of unequivocal ambition. He mentions ambition once, when in soliloquy he anticipates the inevitable consequences of the murder and admits that the only "spur / To prick the sides of [his] intent" is "Vaulting ambition, which o'erleaps itself, / And falls on th'other—" (I. vii. 25–27). Imaging ambition as a horse, he sees it as rising only to fall, as self-destructive and doomed to failure. This is hardly like what one normally thinks of as the ambition that incites men to political crime. Even Macbeth's first assertion of a desire for the crown, "the swelling act / Of the imperial theme" (I. iii. 128–29), is extraordinarily vague, scarcely focused on the pleasures of being king, and it is followed immediately by lines that seem to express premature remorse for an evil deed not yet even fully imagined. Macbeth mentions the crown again during the "show of Eight Kings and Banquo last," and once again his words suggest guilt and fear rather than an interest in royal power for himself and his descendants: "Thou art too like the spirit of Banquo. Down! / Thy crown does sear mine eyeballs" (IV. i. 112–13).

an uncomplicated villain whom audiences might simply and successfully judge. But Davenant revised not only to simplify the moral response of the audience. He wanted not only to make us despise a man who is obviously wicked, but also to help us understand why Macbeth does such wicked things; and he recognized, as his revisions tell us, that Shakespeare had left that crucial matter obscure. In Davenant's version, as not in Shakespeare, Macbeth's motivation is just what one would expect: ambition.

A bell rings, and Shakespeare's Macbeth goes to do what cannot be undone:

> Hear it not, Duncan, for it is a knell
> That summons thee to heaven or to hell.
>
> (II. i. 62–63)

These are the last lines we shall hear Macbeth speak until he emerges with bloody hands, and as always they convey only the anguish he feels at what he must do. But Davenant's Macbeth feels and speaks otherwise:

> O Duncan, hear it not, for 'tis a bell
> That rings my Coronation, and thy Knell.[2]

Ambition is ever his concern. He must choose first between it and virtue, later, as he hears of his wife's distress, between it and love. Thus he shows none of the difficulty Shakespeare's protagonist has, after his encounter with the witches, in formulating the explicit decision to kill Duncan; and afterwards, when Lady Macbeth suggests that he can escape his troubles by resigning his crown, he demonstrates more openly than Shakespeare's hero ever does his desire to be king. What Shakespeare achieved with so much delicacy, the delineation of an evil man as tragic hero through the exploration of his inner process and the demonstration of his purposeless subjection to drives he does not understand and goals he does not want, Davenant has consistently eliminated. No longer must the audience see the tragedy from Macbeth's point of view as well as Duncan's. The hero is Macduff, selflessly concerned with Scotland and rejecting any temptation to ambition. Macbeth is simply the villain of the piece.

---

[2] William Davenant, *Macbeth*, II. i. 49–50. My text of the 1674 adaptation is Spencer, *Five Restoration Adaptations of Shakespeare*.

Furthermore, Davenant depoliticizes *Macbeth* as successfully as Otway does *Julius Caesar*. The first prerequisite of a healthy polity is the fusion in its central authority of grace, legitimacy, and power. Here as elsewhere Shakespeare suggests the ultimate unattainability of such a polity by splitting the characteristics of the necessary leader, giving to Duncan inner gentleness and divinely sanctioned legitimacy, but to Macbeth the driving force it takes to impose one's will on history. On its political level Shakespeare's play is the tragedy of what happens when these qualities are opposed to one another; it is thus an exploration of precisely the same issue [that is] the heart of the problem in *Henry V*. But in Davenant's play that issue has disappeared. Macduff is every inch a king, Macbeth simply an unsound intruder into a self-sufficient world. Like Tate's *Lear*, the new tragedy is most notable not for its simple and explicit moral but for its efficient elimination of a design that made such a moral so trivial as to be almost irrelevant to what the play was all about.

Just so David Garrick's acting version, which did so much to restore the tragedy to what Shakespeare rather than Davenant intended, needs the explanation of Macbeth's lust for power. Thus Garrick gave to the dying hero a speech that Shakespeare had failed to provide, in which Macbeth can pass judgment on himself and sum up his villainy just as Cibber's Richard had done:

> 'Tis done! the scene of life will quickly close.
> Ambition's vain delusive dreams are fled,
> And now I wake to darkness, guilt and horror.[3]

Perverse though they are, Garrick's lines are steeped in Shakespeare. The "'Tis done" with which they begin echoes the very words Macbeth first speaks as he enters with Duncan's blood on his hands: "I have done the deed." But those words, and everything else Macbeth says in the moments surrounding the murder, tell us that there will be no need, three acts later, to "wake to darkness, guilt and horror": they are the very substance of his act, and he is enticed by no "vain delusive dreams." It is the supreme greatness of Shakespeare's conception that his killer of king and kinsman and self is driven by something darker, something deeper and more terrifying, than golden fantasies of royal power.

[3] Cited in Furness, *Variorum Macbeth* (1873), p. 295.

What then does motivate Macbeth to a chain of murder that leads inevitably to his own inward and worldly destruction? The key, I suggest, is in Lady Macbeth's mysterious explanation for her own surprising sudden inability to kill Duncan: "Had he not resembled / My father as he slept, I had done't," followed immediately by Macbeth's "I have done the deed." Lady Macbeth's compunction, so apparently out of character, acknowledges an unconscious recognition that the killing of a king—of such a king as Duncan, of a kinsman, of the king in such a social structure as that of Scotland—is a form of parricide. And that is what Macbeth knows, and what impels him to his deed.

Only once before the murder does Macbeth allow himself to imagine it with full conceiving of the deed itself. Earlier, confronting the witches, his very syntax is so obscure as to imply his inability to visualize what he is already unconsciously formulating:

> why do I yield to that suggestion
> Whose horrid image doth unfix my hair
> And make my seated heart knock at my ribs? . . .
> My thought, whose murther yet is but fantastical,
> Shakes so my single state of man that function
> Is smother'd in surmise, and nothing is
> But what is not.
>
> (I. iii. 134–42)

Suggestions come in as if from outside, with horrid and unspecified images; thoughts (but not Macbeth) have murders, but they are "fantastical." Only at Forres, in the actual presence of the gracious King, does Macbeth speak more honestly and explicitly with himself:

> Stars, hide your fires,
> Let not light see my black and deep desires;
> The eye wink at the hand; yet let that be
> Which the eye fears, when it is done, to see.
>
> (I. iv. 50–53)

But why now? What has changed? In this ceremonial scene, more than anywhere else, Macbeth plays the role of ideal filial subject—"our duties / Are to your throne and state children and servants"—spelling out what would be a moving credo of monarchical ideology were it not entirely ironic. What enables Macbeth, almost as he enunciates the familial ideal which underlies the structure of the state, to admit to himself at last his readiness to strike down the head and center of that state?

Only one thing happens in this scene: Duncan ritualistically announces that Malcolm will be his heir. Playing the part of loving son to his symbolic father and real kinsman, Macbeth hears Duncan convey his blessings to another son. Interestingly, though there is no suggestion in the play that Duncan's act is anything but proper, Shakespeare's source told him that the King's historical prototype illegally invoked the rule of primogeniture in a Scotland governed otherwise, thus at least partially justifying the rebellion against him.[4] (Similarly in *Julius Caesar*, while shading Brutus's murder of Caesar with emotions generally recognized as parricidal, Shakespeare suppresses his source's suggestion that Brutus was, or at any rate thought himself, Caesar's natural son.) Significantly Shakespeare omits any hint that Duncan's act is illegal, and "Macbeth's ambition," in the words of Geoffrey Bullough, "therefore becomes wilder and less well-founded." For Macbeth it is the very act of treating Malcolm as a favorite son that triggers a murderous impulse, providing the context for the explicit resolve noted above.

> The Prince of Cumberland! that is a step
> On which I must fall down, or else o'er leap,
> For in my way it lies. Stars, hide your fires. . . .

Since, as Bullough observes, "the reasons why the nomination of Malcolm as heir would so disturb him are not brought out . . . Macbeth's claims to the throne by his own birth and through his wife are not mentioned,"[5] one must infer irrational motives. It is as if Macbeth decides to kill Duncan out of the rage of a disappointed sibling. Not that the succession or its announcement is the cause of Macbeth's action: he has already felt the attraction of the deed; rather that this moment defines and crystallizes a parricidal emotion that resides already in his deepest being.

Is it not this unconscious hatred of a father that motivates Macbeth? Is not the terror of the play the fact that its hero, morally as aware as any character in his world, better at judging himself than any of those who witness his crimes, is driven so inexorably to a

---

[4] See Geoffrey Bullough, *Narrative and Dramatic Sources of Shakespeare* (London: Routledge and Kegan Paul, 1973), vol. 7, pp. 431–32.

[5] *Ibid.*, pp. 448–49.

deed he does not want but feels compelled to commit? As Traversi brilliantly argued, Macbeth strikes out to destroy what he above all others recognizes as "the source of all the benefits which flow from his person to those who surround him," and he does so while "groping in the bottomless pit of psychological and spiritual darkness," and does so "in a state of hallucination."[6] Drawn forward by the dagger of the mind he sees before him, Macbeth fantasies himself as Murder personified, who

> with his stealthy pace,
> With Tarquin's ravishing [strides], towards his design
> Moves like a ghost.
>
> (II. i. 52–56)

The analogy is multiply apt, of course: a royal crime in a bedroom at night; the aggression of violence against an almost feminine helplessness; an act whose ultimate victim is its perpetrator. But most powerful in the image is the sense of the crime as one of lust: of an act dictated not by the impulse of ambition, which seemed so rational to Shakespeare's redactors in literary periods less able to acknowledge the darker sources of human action, but by a drive as fundamental and as irrational as that of sex.[7] Almost out of control, excitedly describing the murdered King to the sleepers of the house, Macbeth speaks moments after the crime of "th'expedition of my violent love" (II. iii. 110); like much else that he says here, he comes—as his wife's collapse suggests she understands—too close to the truth. The true horror of *Macbeth* is the suggestion that the nihilistic criminality that we normally associate with the pursuit of power and control may stem ultimately not from such relatively positive goals but from the very hatred of that which has given us life.

The psychoanalytic reading to which I have just pointed is, of course, very much a product of our own age. Much of the most invigorating and plausible work on Shakespeare is now being produced by critics with a Freudian orientation who, unlike some of the early psychoanalytic critics, unlike Freud himself, study liter-

---

[6] D. A. Traversi, *An Approach to Shakespeare* (Garden City: Doubleday, 1956, first published 1938), pp. 156–61.

[7] See Dennis Biggins, "Sexuality, Witchcraft, and Violence in *Macbeth*," *Shakespeare Studies* 8 (1975): 255–77.

ature with an awareness of the ways in which their own limited perspective draws strength from and illuminates a comprehensive view based on a variety of techniques and modes of perception. Such critics have been demonstrating how richly susceptible Shakespeare's understanding of character is to psychoanalytic exploration, and therefore how much Shakespeare seems to have anticipated of modern psychological discovery. The work of these critics is as valuable as any now being done, and it seems only at the beginning of its long march. I do not want, therefore, to suggest any dissatisfaction with it.

On the other hand, it can all too easily be charged that such a claim as, no doubt inspired by the intellectual climate, I have made about Macbeth's motivation is a new reduction invented to replace an old one. Let me confess to the charge. What I have said about Macbeth seems to me unmistakably there to be found. But it was put there not by a twentieth-century author trained in the discipline of Freudian psychology, but by a seventeenth-century dramatist who could not have found any equivalent of that discipline in his culture. What we find in *Macbeth*, therefore, is not the confident demonstration of a familiar syndrome, but rather an obscure hinting of motivations that lie buried too deeply to be susceptible of seventeenth-century explanation. To be sure, Shakespeare's psychological canniness reveals him as one of the great inventors of human self-understanding. Observing personality in life and books, he may have come to certain conclusions about what we might describe as the nature and etiology of psychosis, but as a playwright he does not set out to teach lessons in psychology. He seems to have been unable to imagine a character, and particularly a protagonist created during the period of the great tragedies, without imagining him fully, embodying in him his shrewdest perceptions about human motivation. As the author of *Macbeth*, however, rather than simply as the creator of Macbeth, he has aims that are artistic as well as psychological.

The primary fact about *Macbeth* that Davenant's redaction can teach us is not that Macbeth is oedipal rather than ambitious, but that his behavior is based on unconscious motives which he is incapable of knowing. What an audience takes away is not a lesson in psychopathology but a demonstration of the inscrutability of human behavior. And that is suggested, in *Macbeth* as in *Richard III*, by the fact that the psychological explanation does not explain everything. It does not explain the witches, seen by Banquo as well as by Macbeth, or the truth of prophecies; it does not explain why Richard III was born with his teeth, or why the owl shrieked at his birth and "hideous tempest shook down trees" (*3 Henry VI*, V. vi. 46). I am tempted to believe that if Shakespeare had had access to a fully worked out psychoanalytic theory of human behavior, he would have employed it theatrically with as much skepticism as he seems to give to other explanatory paradigms. The understanding of character suggested by *Macbeth* is only secondarily psychoanalytic; more important is the implication that ultimate motivation is often crucially obscure, and that it can work, in the world as seen with a tragic vision, through a mysterious but definitive complicity with a metaphysical universe. In the worlds of *Macbeth* and *Richard III*, in the universe of Shakespearean tragedy, human behavior is governed by unknown and unknowable forces from within and without; it is no more reducible to the exclusive formulations of modern psychoanalysis than it is to those of seventeenth-century theology. If we may learn from Shakespeare's redactors that the unconscious figures more in his view of character than they want to acknowledge, we must also learn that the ultimate ineffability of human motivation is close to the meaning of Shakespearean tragedy. . . .

The adaptations and imitations we have examined have suggested some insights into Shakespeare's tragedies. I should like to point to some further implications of the group taken as a whole.

The first is a suggestion about the nature of tragedy, particularly as Shakespeare practiced and refined that art. As much modern theorizing about painting and music has demonstrated, conflict between the elements of which it is built is virtually a defining quality of the work of art. In a verbal art the conflicting elements are often, though never exclusively, conceptual, so that literary critics, New or not, have agreed for some time that tension, paradox, ambiguity, and irony—all of them special forms of conceptual conflict expressed in aesthetic forms—are essential elements of authentic literary art. I have called the most characteristic and central kind of conflict in Shakespeare's work "complementarity," an approach to experience in which, as I have suggested here in discussing a few of the plays, radically opposed and equally total commitments to the meaning of life coexist in a single harmonious vision.[8] Shakespeare's complementarity is not restricted to his tragedies, but is rather a crucial feature of almost all his work, both dramatic and nondramatic, and I have suggested that something like complementarity figures in much of the greatest literature of our entire tradition. (The word itself is borrowed from the physicists Bohr and Oppenheimer, who see complementarity as a widespread and fundamental element in human thought.)

But I suspect that it is tragedy, of all literary forms, which most depends on complementarity for its meaning and effectiveness. For though much literature is based on or draws its energy from the play between mutually exclusive points of view, tragedy produces in its audience the most threatening and moving apprehension of the perception that life essentially demands a choice between alternatives while making that choice impossible. The difference between tragedy and other forms is in part one of kind: unlike comedy, for example, it is not concerned with escape or reconciliation, and unlike melodrama, as Heilman notes, it achieves its "total view" by seeing, without taking sides, "the diversity of claims and urgencies that divide humanity,"[9] of the imperatives that constitute the nature of man. But the difference is at least as much one of degree: the intensity of tragedy demands that audiences experience pain in their encounter with a subject matter that is in itself not radically different from that of other forms. Shakespeare's tragedies define the genre for us; whatever successes his redactors achieved they achieved by making the plays into something other than tragedy, something more reducible to rational equation.

The second implication is historical. In a fine little poem about Thomas Hobbes's return to Cromwell's England, John Hollander suggests the postcataclysmic weariness of a country not yet past its troubles but already headed toward the stability—ironically not that of Cromwell's order—which would soon be transforming its institutions and its life:

[8] See my *Shakespeare and the Common Understanding* (New York and London: Macmillan, 1967), pp. 11–28.

[9] Robert B. Heilman, *Tragedy and Melodrama* (Seattle: University of Washington Press, 1968), p. 16.

When I returned at last from Paris hoofbeats pounded
  Over the harsh and unrelenting road;
It was cold, the snow high; I was old, and the winter
  Sharp, and the dead mid-century sped by
In ominous, blurred streaks as, brutish, the wind moaned
  Among black branches. I rode through a kind
Of graceless winter nature, bled of what looked like life.
  My vexing horse threw me. If it was not safe
In England yet, or ever, that nowhere beneath the grey
  Sky would be much safer seemed very plain.[10]

The Stuart restoration nine years after Hobbes's return signals an end as well as a beginning. Not, certainly, an end to partisan strife, class warfare, political and theological disputation; but a closing of the deep divisions that had culminated inevitably in a civil war such as England has not experienced since.

Once dominated by wishful assumptions about the stability of the Elizabethan establishment, our understanding of the political, intellectual, and religious life of England has increasingly encompassed an awareness that the civil war was the result of considerably more than half a century of social breakdown on every level. In this kind of crisis the opposed ideas which normally coexist more or less comfortably in society and the individual become critical issues, the people of all sorts find themselves driven to absolutism of one kind or another: revolution and counterrevolution are, after all, only the ultimate expression of radical reductions. In Shakespeare's day conflicts that had been voiced throughout much of the sixteenth century tended increasingly to polarize those who favored one side or the other. As long as such conflicts raged within the limits of a society still relatively stable, they made tragedy possible. When they grew too strong for society to be able to contain them, tragedy was one of the first casualties of what ensued.

Every aspect of Renaissance thought and life is more deeply conflicted than its counterpart after the watershed. Sixteenth- and early seventeenth-century men and women were constrained to endure fundamental contradictions masked only superficially and with less success as the actual eruption of armed conflict drew near: contradictions between monarchical absolutism and antimonarchical iconoclasm in politics, between fideism and atheism and radical

---

[10] John Hollander, "Hobbes, 1651," in *Movie-Going, and Other Poems* (New York: Atheneum, 1962).

reformism in religion, between the irreconcilable interests of classes, between free will and Calvinistic determinism, between conceptions of heroism—that is, of ideal humanity—as proudly individualistic and as humbly selfless, between reason and intuitive process. Paradox is more than a matter of style in Renaissance literature. Whatever their ultimate commitments, Donne and Milton and Herbert, Chapman and Webster, all, like Shakespeare, built their achievements on the acknowledgment of the impossible simultaneity of contradictory realities. In the greatest works of the period, most profoundly perhaps in *Paradise Lost*, those realities are made to cohere in a vision in which everything has its place and a single point of view reconciles apparent differences, but the tentativeness of the solution, the heroic effort it took to create and maintain it, is evinced both by the complexity of our response to, say, Milton's Satan or Marlowe's Faustus or Shakespeare's Coriolanus, and by the unceasing disagreements of critics as to their authors' real attitudes toward their creations.

The animating contradictions of Renaissance literature may reflect the kind of ferment that precedes the scientific revolution described by Thomas Kuhn, when the intellectual life of a period consists in trying to reconcile disruptive new knowledge with established overviews which no longer comprehend it but cannot yet be abandoned.[11] It might further be argued that in the politics of the later seventeenth century, as in post-Newtonian science, a new gestalt offered a satisfactory point of view from which the old conflicts could be seen as resolvable. This hypothesis might help to explain why in Dryden and Otway, for example, the contest between reason and passion is so much more clearly formulated than it was in the plays they imitated, and why it is so foregone a conclusion. As the new understanding of life leads to well-made and well-meaning plays, the new picture of man leads to a confident definition of character, succinctly expressed by Dryden: "A character . . . is a composition of qualities which are not contrary to one another in the same person."[12] This rubric cannot accommodate the self-destructiveness Davenant has helped us see in Mac-

[11] Thomas S. Kuhn, *The Structure of Scientific Revolutions* (Chicago: University of Chicago Press, 1962).

[12] *"Preface to Troilus and Cressida"* in *Literary Criticism of John Dryden*, ed. Arthur C. Kirsch (Lincoln: University of Nebraska Press, 1966), p. 135.

beth; it keeps out more of Shakespeare's great characters than it admits.

The third implication of our examination is about audiences. Considering the successes of both Shakespeare and Tate, one could hardly fail to draw the inference that people go to the theater at different times for different reasons; and one might legitimately hope that by analyzing the characteristic drama of a period one might infer much about the psychology of those who applauded it. The evidence provided by plays themselves suggests that the audience of Shakespearean tragedy went to the theater to find ways of relieving the cultural pressures under which it lived, while the audience of Restoration tragedy could scarcely have found its experience in the theater so personally important. If Shakespearean theater reflects spiritual crisis in both artist and audience, Restoration theater suggests the inner comfort of a less essentially conflicted period.

Such tentative conclusions are hypothetical, and certainly beyond the scope of the present study to prove or even to press. Whether or not they are valid, however, it is an undeniable fact that Shakespearean tragedy, as understood from the perspective of the Restoration, constitutes an extraordinary balancing act in which the theater explores the most mystifying contradictions in human experience; and, unlike later attempts by dramatists and literary critics alike to explain away the mysteries, it has come down to us not only as our heritage but as our contemporary.

Macbeth: The Murderer as Victim

by E.A.J. Honigmann

Although there are signs of a new "movement" in literary anddramatic criticism, it has not so far made much progress. More and more books now touch on the reader's or theatre-goer's response, yet even those who believe that we should pursue this new critical interest draw back, all too often, when they consider the dangers. If they wish to examine the response to Shakespeare, whose response should it be? An Elizabethan one (impossible)—or a modern one? If a modern one, ought it to be that of the most experienced Man of the Theatre, or of the most learned scholar— or their very own? We could only speak authoritatively about our own; and yet it's not easy to report accurately

> With shabby equipment always deteriorating
> In the general mess of imprecision of feeling.

And other dangers abound. The enthusiast who undertakes to record how he reacts to a play must know when his response is ripe, and ready for collecting. During a performance, immediately after it, a little later, or much later? Indeed, can he respond and observe his own response both at once?

An inward-looking approach leads inevitably to charges of subjectivism or crude egoismus ("All my I," as Coleridge so unkindly said of Fichte's ego-centred philosophy). We need not, however, give up in despair. We can proceed along different lines: instead of merely fingering our own pulses in the theatre, or plugging ourselves into a private galvanometer, we can study the dramatist's technical skills in guiding audience response. As an audience watches a play it "responds" from the first word to the last, and an experienced dramatist knows this and leaves as little as possible to chance: he adjusts his plotting, and much else besides, to ensure that the audience will respond as he wants. His manipulation of response is therefore one of the dramatist's basic skills, no less important than plotting, characterisation, use of imagery or ideas, and the like: and we can observe how it operates exactly as we come to grips with other points of craftsmanship, by studying the text.

I am not arguing that its "response problems" are the only or necessarily the best avenue of approach to a tragedy: I merely urge that criticism ignores them at its peril, intimately intertwined as they are with a play's every other component. Shakespeare's earlier commentators lost their bearings partly because they were not sufficiently interested in these very problems, and, if we follow them, we may still go wrong today. "The character of Iago is so conducted," said Dr. Johnson, "that he is from the first scene to the last hated and despised." "Lady Macbeth," he said, again, "is merely detested; and though the courage of Macbeth preserves some esteem, yet every reader rejoices at his fall." Does such a summing up tally with our experience of Shakespeare's complex characters? I find it unacceptable, if only because Johnson assumed our response to character to be static, "from the first scene to the last," and ignored the fluctuations of feeling that we expect from great drama. With few exceptions, Johnson's successors offered similar reductive statements, or, if they acknowledged that response changes as a play develops, failed to ask themselves how it was done.

The fluidity of response can be illustrated, very simply, from our response to a repeated word. "Nuncle" in *King Lear* (I. iv. 103 ff.) may be "contracted from *mine uncle*, the customary appellation of the licensed fool to his superiors," as editors assure us, but, used as it is by the Fool in his first scene, always preluding a piece of acid wisdom, it becomes a pin-pricking weapon, the Fool's counterpart to Lear's whip, and is tainted by impudence, and possibly by malice. Thus "nuncle," a term of endearment, soon turns into something very different; and our response must change as we learn to understand the word's function (which differs from its meaning, as glossed by the editors).

"In dramatic composition," Maurice Morgann explained long ago, "the impression is the fact." An audience's response changes as the dramatist adjusts the play's impressions. Each spectator participates creatively: consciously or unconsciously he sifts all impressions, compares them with earlier ones, flashes back and forth to the present, revises his expectations. The spectator, that is, attends not only to the immediate speech or situation but simultaneously and unremittingly reassesses the play as a whole, its style, its shape, its probabilities: he responds in many different ways. Response problems therefore take us beyond character, beyond liking or not liking Hamlet, and require us to investigate the spectator's imaginative engagement with the play. How fully do we enter into Hamlet's point of view? How can we take account of "secret motives," which are shown but not described in so many words, in *Othello*? How clear-cut has Shakespeare made the political issues and personal relationships in *Coriolanus*? These are some of the larger response problems that any general essay on one of the three plays would certainly mention. What is now required, however, is a more sharply focused discussion of the dramatist's control of response, bringing out the extraordinary variety of the problems and also the extraordinary variety of Shakespeare's solutions.

Inevitably, a subjective note will sometimes intrude. But I am chiefly concerned with the dramatist's technical skills, not with one person's response. (If I am told that the two cannot be separated, what is the reply? That when the dramatist pulls us in this direction or that, we may observe the fact that he pulls, and the means employed, without always thinking ourselves obliged to define exactly what we feel.) And Shakespeare exercised his skills, I repeat, as an "impressionist" artist: like Bacon, he understood perfectly "what things are to be laid open, and what to be secreted, and what to be showed at half-lights." There can be no doubt about it that he studied the theatre-audience's engagement—at the very least, as vigilantly as Mark Antony watches and guides his audience in the Forum Scene. In the chapters that follow I try to show how an expert in half-lights nudged or dictated the audience response in his greatest plays.

. . . A victim or a villain? Macbeth seems to be both in the murder scene and, though the mixture differs from moment to moment, throughout the first two acts. This impression partly depends upon the flow of information, which the dramatist can regulate as he chooses. The less an audience understands the more inclined it will be to reserve judgement: in *Macbeth* the opening scenes are so arranged that we never know quite enough about the hero's guilt, and he captures our sympathetic attention as it were under cover of darkness. Commentators who translate surmise into certainty consequently distort the spectator's relationship with the dramatic character: clarifying what the dramatist deliberately left obscure they give us either a villain or a victim, and falsify the very nature of their experience.

A "criminal" hero in particular can benefit from the audience's uncertainties. In the opening scenes of *Macbeth* we are made to wonder about the Weird Sisters, their powers, their connection with Macbeth and Lady Macbeth, and Shakespeare artfully withholds the answers. . . . As the play progresses we learn that Banquo thinks them "the instruments of darkness" (I. iii. 124), and that they acknowledge spirits as their "masters" (IV. i. 63). But their exact status remains undefined, except that they are closely associated with an "unknown power" (IV. i. 69). They may be witches, but we cannot take even this for granted: and at the beginning of the play, when we feel our way into Macbeth's mind, a spectator uncontaminated by criticism must think of them as *sui generis*, a mystery.

The mystery extends to their relationship with Macbeth. Dover Wilson assures us that "Macbeth exercises complete freedom of will from first to last."[1] Another critic wrote, more cautiously, that "Macbeth makes no bargain with the emissaries of the powers of darkness; nor are they bargainable. The knowledge offers itself to him: it is, indeed, as he says, 'a supernatural soliciting.' But he is not solicited to the treachery and murder which he commits."[2]

. True, as long as we can be certain that there is no connection between the Weird Sisters and Lady Macbeth. But if Moelwyn Merchant was correct in saying that "it is surely unnecessary to argue today that Lady Macbeth's invocation of 'the spirits that tend on mortal thoughts' . . . is a formal stage in demonic possession,"[3]

[1] Dover Wilson, ed., *Macbeth*, p. xxi.

[2] J. M. Murry, *Shakespeare* (1948 ed.), p. 326.

[3] W. Moelwyn Merchant, in *Shakespeare Survey* 19 (1966): 75.

then Lady Macbeth solicits her husband on behalf of the Weird Sisters. She does so, it should be observed, by hailing him by his three titles, just like the Sisters:

> Great Glamis! Worthy Cawdor!
> Greater than both, by the all-hail hereafter!

She continues where they left off. The Weird Sisters strike first, then Lady Macbeth assaults him in his imagination, blow after blow, and her words have an even more fearful effect—so that theirs seems a joint attack, master-minded from afar. And even if not formally "possessed," Lady Macbeth appears to be somehow in league with evil and Macbeth its victim, a fly in the spider's web who struggles mightily but cannot escape.

"Somehow in league" may sound vague, but we must beware of asserting more than we can prove where the Weird Sisters are concerned. Somehow they make contact with Macbeth's mind, even before he sees them: his very first words, "So foul and fair a day I have not seen," suggest their influence, since he unconsciously echoes their earlier chant. And as they somehow give Banquo "cursed thoughts" in his dreams (II. i. 8), and can invade the sleeping mind, what are we to make of the dagger that seems to marshal Macbeth to Duncan's chamber a mere thirteen lines later? Another cursed thought, planted in Macbeth's mind to draw him to the murder? All of these impressions work together, suggesting that the Weird Sisters have access to the human mind (Lady Macbeth, Banquo, Macbeth), and can attack Macbeth's directly and indirectly.

Yet these impressions never harden into certitude. Neither the very first scene, which was dropped by Tyrone Guthrie because he mistakenly thought it assigned a "governing influence"[4] to the Weird Sisters, nor any other scene proves beyond doubt that Macbeth is just a victim. The dramatic perspective merely inclines us to fear for him. Shakespeare stimulates an anxiety for the hero, before the murder, similar to the audience's protective anxiety for Othello, even though Macbeth's intentions are more straightforwardly criminal than the Moor's. A single passage may illustrate the dramatic advantages—Lady Macbeth's allusion to an earlier meet-

[4] Carol J. Carlisle, *Shakespeare from the Greenroom* (Chapel Hill: University of North Carolina Press, 1969), p. 346.

ing when her husband broke "this enterprise to me" (I. vii. 47 ff.).
On the strength of this passage some editors have postulated lost
scenes or an earlier version of the play. Had the audience actually
witnessed a scene where "the husband and wife had explicitly discussed the idea of murdering Duncan at some favourable opportunity,"[5] we must reply, Shakespeare would not have been able to
arouse the required response, the sense that Lady Macbeth exag-
gerates her husband's guilt. Such a discussion would have left no
room for doubt, whereas Lady Macbeth's oblique reference to a
previous meeting, in a speech that begins so oddly, exists only to
beget doubt:

> What *beast* was't then
> That made you break this enterprise to me?
> When you durst do it, *then you were a man* . . .

The tendency to overstatement and emotionalism is as marked as,
after the murder, her understatement and emotional deadness.
Accordingly, though we believe in a previous meeting, we cannot
trust her account of it. She *says* that he broke the enterprise to her
and swore to carry out the murder, but we have seen how she puts
her ideas into his mind ("Hie thee hither / That I may pour my
spirits in thine ear") and, though Macbeth lets her words pass
unchallenged, we distrust all that she asserts. Her speech, in effect,
makes Macbeth not more but less guilty; we hear her say that he
proposed the murder but, not knowing what really happened, we
overreact to her emotionalism and think him the more likely to be
innocent.

Much depends on the actor's intonation and by-play. He can
slant his performance to make Macbeth more or less a victim (or
villain), and, as theatrical records amply demonstrate, great actors
often chose to clarify these uncertainties. Irving stressed Macbeth's
guilt from the beginning, as we see from his note beside "Stay, you
imperfect speaaers . . ." (I. iii. 70): "Burning in desire." One crucial
line lent itself to three very different interpretations:

> To Lady Macbeth's question, "When does Duncan go hence?" Mr.
> Kemble replies indifferently, "Tomorrow as he purposes." With Mr.
> Kean it assumes a very different aspect. In an emphatic tone, and
> with a hesitating look . . . he half divulges the secret of his breast—

---

[5] A. C. Bradley, *Shakespearean Tragedy* (1904), p. 480.

"To-morrow as he . . . purposes!" . . . [Kean] gave the impression that the idea of murdering Duncan at Dunsinane had already occurred to him. From then on he appeared not the pawn of his wife's ambition but the master of his own destiny.[6]

James Rees suggested a third possibility to Edwin Forrest, who adopted it in performance. Macbeth says "Tomorrow" and

at that moment he meets the eye of his wife—like an electric shock, the infernal spark acts upon his already overcharged brain—he starts, gazes as if upon the fabled basilisk, and mutters in fear and dread, as if in the presence of a supernatural being, "As he purposes." Here it is they fully understand each other.[7]

All three are perfectly legitimate readings at this point. But, although there are signs in the text that the idea of murdering Duncan presents itself first to Macbeth, Lady Macbeth later so completely overawes her husband that the first impression is supplanted by a much stronger one. The more she presses him the more reluctant he becomes: and when he finally goes to kill Duncan her hypnotic influence, the vision of the dagger and his "heat-oppressed brain" make him move like a ghost (II. 1. 56)—a mere ghost of himself, far from exercising complete freedom of will.

Just before the murder of Duncan and immediately afterwards Macbeth impresses us as a victim rather than a villain. The deed is done in horror and, as Bradley has finely said, "as if it were an appalling duty."[8] This is not to claim that Macbeth is simply a victim, only that he seems to be so when it matters most, at the cross-roads of the play, when he feels most intensely, speaks his most moving lines and is most fully himself. And we are given the same sense that he is a victim, it should be noted, by his general way of thinking and imagining. Unlike Hamlet, who tries to master his thought in his soliloquies, who even interrupts its headlong rush from the outside, as it were ("Why, what an ass am I!" "About, my brains!"[9]), Macbeth gets carried away by his thought, thought turns into vision, and he himself impresses us as a helpless, horrified

---

[6] D. Bartholomeusz, *Macbeth and the Players* (Cambridge, 1969), pp. 199, 144.

[7] Quoted by A. C. Sprague, *Shakespeare and the Actors (1660–1905)* (Cambridge, Mass.: Harvard University Press, 1945), pp. 233–34.

[8] Bradley, *Shakespearean Tragedy*, p. 358.

[9] *Hamlet*, II. ii. 577, 584.

onlooker. Just as the sorcerer's apprentice cannot stop the show of kings ("What, will the line stretch out to th' crack of doom?"— IV. i. 117) so he cannot halt his imagination once it begins to conjure forth tomorrow and tomorrow and tomorrow, or hounds and greyhounds, mongrels, spaniels, curs, shoughs, water-rugs and demi-wolves. The broken syntax of "If it were done when 'tis done" (I. vii. 1–12) also suggests Macbeth's helplessness, a mind bombarded by thoughts that it cannot hold back and yet, in this instance, dare not finish. And his hallucinations have a similar effect. Not only the ghost of Banquo, the dagger, the voices in the murder scene, the hands that pluck at his eyes, the stones that prate of his "where-about": throughout the play mysterious objects and noises float towards him out of the unknown, across the normal boundaries of space and time, always threateningly, so that his characteristic mode of perception also presents him to the audience as a victim, a sufferer who demands the audience's sympathetic response.

. . . We must ask how Shakespeare adjusts the response as he goes along, both for and against his hero, and how completely he changes it in the fourth act.

Most of the play's defensive maneuvers have been noticed before. Macbeth benefits from an unusual perspective: he speaks all the best verse, he alone engages the audience repeatedly in soliloquy, and in his inward-looking honesty, if not in his speech addressed to others, he represents the play's most sympathetic human value. He appeals to us as his own accuser, so that we can participate simultaneously with his moral and his criminal nature (when the poetry and perspective demand it, in the first two acts). In addition he benefits from minor dramatic stratagems that are less obvious—for instance, the silence of Banquo's ghost (III. iv). Instead of calling for revenge, in the traditional manner, the ghost never competes with Macbeth verbally, which allows Macbeth's point of view to dominate the scene—and to prevail with the audience.

On the other hand, Shakespeare departed from his source, Holinshed's *Chronicles*, in order to "heighten Macbeth's guilt and deliberately take away, it would seem, characteristics which might attract an audience's sympathy":[10] Holinshed's Duncan is a man of many faults, his Macbeth has grievances against Duncan that Shakespeare dropped, and, after seizing the throne, his Macbeth ruled virtuously for ten years. Though the theatre audience could not know of these changes we may say that, far from consistently enforcing sympathy for his hero, Shakespeare took the opposite course as well.

In *Macbeth* the line of response zigzags on, at least in the first three acts, very much as in the other tragedies, except that different technical tricks are used. Consider, for example, the Christian imagery and its effect. Macbeth differs from almost all other Shakespearian villains in expressing deeply religious convictions, not once but many times, endorsed by the full force of some of Shakespeare's best poetry. He believes in "mine eternal jewel," he feels "the deep damnation of his taking-off," and, at the extremest push, his whole being aches for Christian comfort:

> But wherefore could not I pronounce "Amen"?
> I had most need of blessing, and "Amen"
> Stuck in my throat.
> (III. i. 67; I. vii. 20; II. ii. 31–33)

Paradoxically, these very passages define Macbeth's guilt and at the same time enforce the audience's sympathetic response. Intense Christian feeling fills the imaginative foreground and, while it lasts, crowds out all awareness of Macbeth's guilt. But of course it cannot last, and the line of response soon resumes its zigzag course, until it reaches Act IV.

That the play sags in Act IV is generally admitted. Malcolm's long interview with Macduff (IV. iii) is usually blamed, yet Macbeth's scene with the Weird Sisters may be just as great a weakness. Magnificently theatrical with its cauldron, its chanting hags, its screaming and silent apparitions, the scene presents a tragic hero dwarfed by gadgetry who, chameleon-like, seems to take on the local colour, becoming something of an automaton himself. And Macbeth also affects us as a mere shadow of himself for another

[10] At this point I quote and paraphrase William Rosen, *Shakespeare and the Craft of Tragedy* (Cambridge, Mass.: Harvard University Press, 1960), pp. 53–57.

reason. He can still soliloquise, yet his feelings now seem to lie at the verbal surface: he talks about them, but we are no longer deeply moved. He has lost his magic. As R. B. Heilman has said, "We expect the tragic protagonist to be an expanding character, one who grows in awareness and spiritual largeness; yet Macbeth is to all intents a contracting character, who seems to discard large areas of consciousness as he goes."[11] Nowhere else in the play is Macbeth made to shrink as suddenly as in IV. i. Distracted by the gadgetry we may not immediately notice it: the scene nevertheless damages our "sympathetic" relationship with the hero, and the play's suspense henceforth hangs on a much weaker thread—our detached interest in the second set of prophecies.

In IV. i Macbeth not only contracts as a person, he also shrinks in the play's perspective. Face to face with the Weird Sisters in I. iii he could hold his own. Now, as the Weird Sisters' "masters" (IV. i. 63) rise out of darkness, their "unknown power" scales him down: he thinks himself a free agent, he believes that he can conjure and compel them to answer him, but his words are mere bluster, the unknown powers only show what they want to show, and in the end they cruelly expose his helplessness:

> Another yet? A seventh? *I'll see no more!*
> And yet the eighth appears, who bears a glass
> Which shows me many more; and some I see
> That twofold balls and treble sceptres carry.
> *Horrible sight!*
>
> (IV. i. 118 ff.)

His first meeting with the Weird Sisters made Macbeth seem important to the audience; the second, in IV. i , has the opposite effect, making him unimportant, a point obliquely enforced by his 'frustrated rage.

The play's perspective continues to work against him in the next two scenes (IV. ii, iii), where his enemies talk about him and he cannot defend himself. Nevertheless we should notice that Shakespeare protects Macbeth, as far as he can: though the two scenes help to turn the audience against the tragic hero, how gently and circuitously Shakespeare goes about his business! Lady Macduff's

---

[11] Robert B. Heilman, "The Criminal as Tragic Hero," *Shakespeare Survey* 19 (1966): 13.

prattle with her young son reduces the seriousness of what might have been said, Macbeth's name is never mentioned, and, if I am correct in thinking that no deaths are shown, the audience has to wait till IV. iii. 204 before it knows the worst. Malcolm's extravagant self-accusations in the next scene also help to shield Macbeth from the audience's hostility, blunting its edge by first directing it upon a false target. In addition Malcolm himself shoots beside the mark in at least one particular:

> I grant him bloody,
> Luxurious, avaricious, false, deceitful,
> Sudden, malicious, smacking of every sin
> That has a name; but there's no bottom, none,
> In my voluptuousness. Your wives, your daughters,
> Your matrons, and your maids, could not fill up
> The cistern of my lust . . .
>
> (IV. iii. 57 ff.)

We have seen no sign of a *luxurious* (or lascivious) Macbeth, the idea contradicts our impression of his character, and when Malcolm obliquely insists upon the point, by talking of his own voluptuousness, we react uneasily to his testimony. What, after all, can he know of Macbeth except from hearsay? Malcolm and Macduff only see "black Macbeth" from the outside, whereas the audience knows him from his soliloquies and hesitates to accept the external image. Shakespeare, moreover, prevents the audience from giving its full confidence to Malcolm and Macduff by endowing them, initially, with a self-conscious eloquence that comes close to attitudinising:

> Let us seek out some desolate shade, and there
> Weep our sad bosoms empty.
>   . . . new sorrows
> Strike heaven on the face, that it resounds
> As if it felt with Scotland and yell'd out
> Like syllable of dolour.
>
> (IV. iii. 1–8)

At this point they have a reason for speaking so strangely. Yet their speech remains vaguely unconvincing: though they understand the world and its ways a little better than Lady Macduff and her son, Malcolm and Macduff still prattle like innocents when compared with Macbeth, who has looked into the abyss. They speak of things beyond their ken, until Ross brings the news about Macduff's family: and then, significantly, Macduff's rage turns swiftly from Macbeth to himself, which partly deflects the audience as well.

> Sinful Macduff,
> They were all struck for thee—nought that I am;
> Not for their own demerits, but for mine,
> Fell slaughter on their souls. Heaven rest them now!
>   (IV. iii. 224 ff.)

In these three transition scenes (IV. i–iii) the audience response to Macbeth changes decisively. Shakespeare nevertheless ensures that antipathy will not go too far: the third one urges the case against "devilish Macbeth" most explicitly, without permitting Malcolm and Macduff to win the audience's whole-hearted assent. And this much-maligned scene marks another important transition: the longest and slowest scene in the play, it introduces a new tempo, arresting the play's onward-rushing momentum just before Lady Macbeth's sleep-walking, where time stands still.

Although the fifth act continues the process of spiritual "contraction" we also see some signs of the earlier Macbeth, which help to complicate our response to his death. The honesty of his two stock-taking meditations reminds us of his great soliloquies, his habit of stating the case against himself:

> My way of life
> Is fall'n into the sear, the yellow leaf;
> And that which should accompany old age,
> As honour, love, obedience, troops of friends,
> I must not look to have; but, in their stead,
> Curses not loud but deep, mouth-honour, breath,
> Which the poor heart would fain deny, and dare not.
>   (V. iii. 22 ff.)

These lines ask not so much for our *pity* as for our *respect*. And the same is true of his speech when he hears of the queen's death: whatever the precise meaning of "She should have died hereafter," we cannot accuse him of *bovarysme*, of endeavouring to escape reality. Unlike the other tragic heroes, who had reacted so powerfully to the deaths of Portia, Ophelia, Desdemona and Cordelia, Macbeth feels very little, makes no pretense that it is otherwise, and, thinking of his own death as well, faces the facts. "Out, out, brief candle!" His honesty extorts our respect—unless the actor insists on pity instead, as did J. P. Kemble, a possible but I think undesirable alternative:

> When the news was brought, "The queen, my lord, is dead," he seemed struck to the heart; gradually collecting himself he sighed out, "She should have died hereafter." Then, as if with the inspiration of despair he hurried out distinctly and pathetically the lines "To-morrow, and to-morrow, and to-morrow" . . . rising to a climax of desperation that brought down the enthusiastic cheers of the closely packed theatre.[12]

As Macbeth proceeds from one murder to the next his capacity to feel contracts, and his feeling for Lady Macbeth withers away as well. How deeply he loved his "dearest partner of greatness" (I. v. 10) before the murder of Duncan we cannot really tell, but after it she ceases to matter to him. He plans the murder of Banquo alone, and in the banquet scene she reveals that they are slipping apart. Informed that Macduff "denies his person," she replies, "Did you send to him, *sir?*"—to the husband she had once taunted as "the poor cat i' th' adage." A history of the marriage in a monosyllable! The other tragic heroes continue to radiate life-affirming emotions in the fourth and fifth acts, giving or begging for forgiveness, freely expressing love or admiration—emotions that the audience responds to and reflects back upon them. Not so Macbeth: when his wife dies he loses his last human link with the past, the only person left who might have lifted him to emotional heights, and he expresses little more than defeat and weariness. "She should have died hereafter . . ."

In the fifth act Shakespeare denies Macbeth some of the emotions that appear to be indispensable in the other tragedies. No love, no fellow-feeling. Not even tears from the depths of some divine despair: only dry-eyed regrets and sudden bouts of desperation. Macbeth contracts within himself, and his relationships with others shrink and lose their humanity as well. We see him in the company of servants, messengers, a doctor, Seyton—unwilling hangers-on, rats that would leave the sinking ship (even Seyton's slowness in answering Macbeth's call—V. iii. 19 ff.—adds to this impression). And yet, although the play's imagery points to Macbeth's shrinking—

[12] W. Macready (quoted by Bartholomeusz, *Macbeth and the Players*, pp. 135–36), who admired Kemble's rendering.

> Now does he feel his title
> Hang loose about him, like a giant's robe
> Upon a dwarfish thief.
>
> (V. ii. 20–22)

we must not make too much of this process. For what is the logical conclusion?

> Though the death of Macbeth brings the play to a close, that death, we are made to feel, is no loss. "The time is free" (V. viii. 55) cries Macduff, displaying the "usurper's cursed head." And Malcolm speaks of "this dead butcher and his fiend-like queen" (V. viii. 69). The fall of the protagonist brings no tragic release, no feeling of woe or wonder, for Shakespeare mutes such feelings by transferring interest from Macbeth's personal plight to society's salvation . . .[13]

If there is any significance in the Folio's title, *The Tragedie of Macbeth*, the protagonist's death should certainly bring tragic release. Shakespeare, I believe, steers towards such a response by stressing the external image of the hero, Macbeth as seen by others, and in particular by repeating one word, *tyrant*, which is used by both Siwards, Macduff and Malcolm: "Thou liest, abhorred tyrant!" "Tyrant, show thy face!" "The tyrant's people on both sides do fight." True as it may be, the external view fails to give the whole truth; and the more Macbeth's enemies insist upon it, the more we are inclined to resist it. Hearing him described as *tyrant, usurper, butcher* and so on, an audience that has thrilled to a competent actor's rendering of the terrible soliloquies cannot but feel that a man's outer life is a tale told by an idiot, full of sound and fury, signifying very little, and that the inner life is all in all.

The responsibility for drawing such a conclusion is left with the audience. Shakespeare, however, took his precautions—not only by using words like *tyrant* that are meant to leave us dissatisfied, but also by preparing in two other ways for our final response to his hero's death. "*Enter Macduffe; with Macbeths head*" we read in the Folio. No other hero or villain in Shakespeare's mature work suffers an end so gruesome, though Iago and others are at least as guilty. Why should we be subjected to this horror?

The shocking climax with Macbeth's head follows another death, the whole point of which is to focus attention upon *response*. Siward

---

[13] Rosen, *Shakespeare and the Craft of Tragedy*, p. 102.

hears that his son died in battle. Unlike Macduff, who was struck speechless by similar news, Siward reacts with what can only be called heartiness:

> *Siward.*   Had he his hurts before?
> *Ross.* Ay, on the front.
> *Siward.*   Why, then, God's soldier be he!
>   Had I as many sons as I have hairs
>   I would not wish them to a fairer death.
>   And so—his knell is knoll'd.

Shakespeare meant us to wonder at such a phlegmatic grief, and makes Malcolm speak for us:

>   He's worth more sorrow,
> And that I'll spend for him.

But Siward persists:

>   He's worth no more.
> They say he parted well and paid his score;
> And so, God be with him!

Here, manifestly, Shakespeare raises the question of appropriate response—and then at once *"Enter Macduffe; with Macbeths head."* How carefully it was all planned!

Why had the severed head to be brought back? Precisely because it too focuses our response: we no sooner see it than we decide, if only unconsciously, that *this* is not Macbeth. The head, from which life has fled, represents the tyrant, the outer man; it serves as a ghastly reminder that there was an inner man. No one, of the survivors, can speak for the Macbeth of the soliloquies: we, the audience, have to do so for ourselves, and the play's tragic effect depends upon our accepting this challenge.

Between the Divine
and the Absurd: *King Lear*

by Susan Snyder

It is a striking fact that, although Shakespeare's main source for *Lear* was a tragicomedy, he himself added or expanded most of the comic elements I have been discussing: double plot, green world, upended hierarchies, commentary by the Fool, disguise. All together they carry strong suggestions of a final comic ordering—or they would if the outcome of Shakespeare's play were not so well known. As familiarity with *Hamlet* diminishes the uncertainty we ought to be sharing with the hero in the early acts of the play, so familiarity with *Lear* mutes the full effect of these implications of comic pattern. If we did not know what was coming, we would surely recognize and respond to the play's evident thrust beyond madness and misery to growth, reintegration, and new harmony.[1] We might recognize too that this comic movement, carried on as it is in terms of serious moral issues instead of the more purely social concerns of romantic comedy, points to an analogue with the Christian divine comedy of redemption. It is analogue only, because for reasons that I shall explore later Shakespeare placed the action of *Lear* in an emphatically non-Christian milieu. But in the sequence of pride, fall, recognition of guilt, forgiveness, and reconciliation, Christian audiences might well see something akin

[1] Marvin Rosenberg reports that spectators at a Berkeley production of *Lear* who were unfamiliar with the play found a happy ending "continually possible—even promised." *The Masks of King Lear* (Berkeley and Los Angeles, 1972), p. 10.

to their faith's basic pattern of evitability: sin and its consequences dissolving in new opportunity, the birth of the new man.

Sure enough, the last scene of Act IV brings a moving reconciliation between Lear and Cordelia. The Prodigal Son undercurrent joins with more overt allusions to Cordelia as savior—holy water, going about her father's business, redeeming nature from the general curse.[2] Lear's perception moves from death and hell to new life. And mercy supersedes justice:

> *Lear.* If you have poison for me I will drink it.
> I know you do not love me; for your sisters
> Have, as I do remember, done me wrong:
> You have some cause, they have not.
> *Cordelia.*   No cause, no cause.
>   (IV. vii. 72–75)

The scene is so charged and so satisfying that the unknowing audience could easily forget that Edmund, Goneril, and Regan are still at large, and feel that here was the end of the story. It is only after Lear and Cordelia exit that Shakespeare looks beyond the reunion to remind us of the coming battle:

> *Kent.* 'Tis time to look about; the powers of the king-
>   dom approach apace.
> *Gent.* The arbitrement is like to be bloody.
>   (93–95)

With this swing from security to fear begins the peculiar rhythm that dominates the last act of *Lear* and makes it different from the final acts of all Shakespeare's other tragedies. It is a very crowded act. As one event or announcement succeeds another, we are cast up and down by turns, hope alternating with fear. The battle is done almost before we know it has started; Edgar lets us down suddenly with the news that Lear and Cordelia have been defeated and taken prisoner. But hopes rise again immediately afterwards when Lear appears, not in despair but serenely happy. His lyrical "let's away to prison" speech reduces to insignificance the battle and its outcome ("who's in, who's out") and thus *refines* our expecta-

---

[2] IV. iii. 30; IV. iv. 23–24; IV. vi. 208; cf. Bethell, *Shakespeare and the Popular Dramatic Tradition*, pp. 59–61. Nicholas Brooke finds in Cordelia's mixture of "sunshine and rain at once" (IV. iii. 18) an anticipation of a redemptive conclusion—"the aftermath of storm . . . watery but astonishingly hopeful." *Shakespeare: "King Lear"* (London, 1963), p. 36.

tions, redirects them toward a more appropriate resolution. Surely it is right for the painfully educated new Lear to turn his back on the vanities of power, rather than to regain his throne by martial victory. Lear imagines his earthly paradise so beautifully that we forget it will be inside a prison. . . .

Does this strain of grotesquerie [reversals, startling events, the Fool's language, Gloucester's leap] prepare us for the final absurdity of Cordelia's death? Not directly, certainly. The essence of grotesque, after all, is that it intrudes unexpectedly. And, as we have seen, the rhythm of Act V keeps renewing hope until Lear enters carrying the dead Cordelia. On the other hand, the earlier shocks and dislocations have a similar spirit. They will probably connect with each other somehow, so that later ones reverberate beyond their particular moments. Subjective responses must vary from one spectator to the next (or, in the same spectator, from one occasion to the next), yet surely there is a common element of unease, unease not at the center of consciousness, but around the edges, waiting to close in at the shattering non sequitur of Cordelia's death.

If I am right, then Shakespeare has, in a way, prepared us for the end even while necessarily leaving us unprepared and open to shock. The question remains, to what purpose? Are we supposed to feel that the last shocking joke is the point, that the intimations of positive moral evolution in the divine comedy pattern were there only to show up the folly of perceiving order in an orderless universe? Or should we see Cordelia's death and Lear's last agony as underlining the pain of the human condition but leaving the redemptive pattern more or less intact? Probably critical opinion still leans more toward the second alternative, although Barbara Everett, Nicholas Brooke, William Elton, and John D. Rosenberg, among others, have argued for more pessimistic readings.[3] At one extreme, R. W. Chambers celebrates *Lear* as Shakespeare's *Pur-*

---

[3] Everett, "The New *King Lear*," *Critical Quarterly* 2 (1960): 325–39; Brooke, "The Ending of *King Lear*," in *Shakespeare 1564–1964*, ed. Edward A. Bloom (Providence, R.I., 1964), pp. 71–87; Elton, *"King Lear" and the Gods*, passim; Rosenberg, "King Lear and His Comforters," *Essays in Criticism* 16 (1966): 135–46. Everett, Elton, and Rosenberg all canvass the optimistic criticism before arguing against it.

gatorio; at the other, Jan Kott proclaims it Shakespeare's *Endgame*.[4] The play's stage history shows something of the same split. While eighteenth- and nineteenth-century productions generally cut or prettified the grotesque elements, some twentieth-century ones have opted emphatically for absurdity—notably that of Peter Brook in 1962.

The pessimists have sequence on their side, certainly. In terms of events, blind chance, or malevolent fate, has pretty much the last word. After the play action has come to its grim close, one can look back over the whole to see what happens to purpose and plan on several levels. On the surface, several characters initiate plots of some sort, to get power or love, to save or destroy. None of them, good or bad, ultimately succeeds. On a deeper level are the obscurely motivated wanderings of Lear and Gloucester. These *acquire* a purpose not intended by the wanderers and only partly engineered by Edgar, a positive pattern seemingly ascribable to an orderly, though awesome, providence that guides faulty men through suffering to wisdom. Taken together, these levels suggest a universe like that of *Hamlet,* in which human schemes go awry while some power beyond the human directs events toward a larger order. In *Lear,* however, there is still another level, one only suggested in *Hamlet,* to which belong those grotesque incongruities that mock all human dignity and meaning. The grotesquerie might have been contained, if not resolved, in a framing order, as the graveyard scene is in *Hamlet.* But Act IV, with Lear and Gloucester secure in their redemption, is not the end of the story. When Cordelia and Lear die as they do, the play seems finally to say, "This universe, after all, has no concern for men's moral growth, in fact has no mind; those momentary janglings that you shuddered at before shrugging them off as peripheral—they are the point." Pelican yields to pillicock.

The play does say this, but it says more. Even Brook, who more or less realized the *Endgame-Lear* on stage, found he had to cut or

[4] Chambers, *King Lear,* p. 47–52; Kott, *Shakespeare Our Contemporary,* 2nd ed. (London, 1967), pp. 100–33. Wilson Knight has it both ways, in separate essays in *The Wheel of Fire,* presenting an optimistic purgatorial interpretation in "The *Lear* Universe" and exploring the implications of absurdity in "*King Lear* and the Comedy of the Grotesque." Knight does not integrate the two views.

undermine certain parts of the text that worked against the Becket-
tian bleakness. The practical compassion shown by Cornwall's servants to the blinded Gloucester was omitted, as was Edmund's
repentant "some good I mean to do, / Despite of mine own nature"
(V. iii. 243–44); and Edgar's (or Albany's) couplets that conclude
the play were spoken against a rumble of thunder presaging
another storm. Brook's decisions help to define the affirmative
elements in *Lear*. The servants can do little enough for Gloucester,
yet their disinterested impulse to help offers more hope for the
human spirit than Brook's vision would allow. Since we know
nothing beforehand of these nameless men and see nothing of
them afterward, their act may perhaps imply something about
humanity in general. In any case, its significance is in its quality
rather than its efficacy. Those who find values affirmed amid the
despair of *Lear* tend to locate them in the characters as opposed to
the course of events, in the constant loyal goodness of some and the
spiritual growth of others. Without ignoring the Gonerils and
Oswalds who exist alongside the Cordelias and Kents, without
denying that the good go down as well as the corrupt, this view
finds meaning "not in what becomes of us, but in what we
become."[5]

Brook's impulse to sabotage the final speech points us to another
aspect of affirmation in *Lear*:

> The weight of this sad time we must obey;
> Speak what we feel, not what we ought to say.
> The oldest hath borne most; we that are young
> Shall never see so much nor live so long.
>   (V. iii. 323–26)

While the words are muted and sad enough, their message is not
despair. If the first line is meant as a response to Kent's speech just
before, in which he rejects a share in rule and in life itself, then "we
must obey" counters "my master calls me; I must not say no." That
is, we must accede to life, not death. At any rate, the word *obey*
suggests order, as does the balanced form of the last three lines.
And the order sought is significantly different from the hypo-

---

[5] Maynard Mack, *"King Lear" in Our Time* (Berkeley and Los Angeles: University of
California Press, 1965), p. 117. Heilman's equivalent value is "the quality of [the good
characters'] living"; Robert B. Heilman, *This Great Stage* (Baton Rouge: Louisiana State
University Press, 1948), p. 289.

critical forms with which the evil began in Act I. "What we ought to say," with its reminder of the love test, yields to "what we *feel*" (My italics). This speech is probably Edgar's; Albany has already showed the same spirit in his attempts to provide for the future of the state. First he aspires to a moral settling of accounts: the king will be restored, friends will be rewarded, enemies will be punished (298–304). He breaks off to witness yet another horror, Lear's last agony. Although events once again have mocked human orderings, Albany, instead of subsiding into despair, tries again to pick up the pieces: "Friends of my soul, you twain / Rule in this realm and the gor'd state sustain" (319–20). Starting as a passive neutral, Albany has, during the course of the action, defined himself by choosing human fellowship as the only alternative to men's preying upon one another like monsters of the deep. Now left, by Lear's defeat and Cornwall's death, sole ruler of Britain, he gives up the throne—first to the rightful king, and then after Lear has died to Kent and Edgar, presumably out of a sense of his own unworthiness. Again this last scene recalls the first, again with a significant difference: Albany's unselfish offer of power is the opposite of Lear's self-serving abdication. Although in order that this structural point be made Albany must decline active participation in rule, his words here—"friends of my soul . . . the gor'd state sustain"—express continued concern for the private and public bonds that tie men together. Enid Welsford has observed that in the early part of *Lear* the bad characters are firmly allied while the good are divided among themselves; toward the end the reverse is true.[6] Albany's words to Edgar and Kent throughout the scene have underlined that community of the good, even surrounded by terrifying disorder. As for the bad characters, Goneril has preyed on Regan and on herself, and Edmund has departed further from the solidarity of evil at the last, to make common cause with the good. Edmund's impulse to save Cordelia and Lear is ineffective, as future events may frustrate Albany's hopes for the gored state, but the impulse itself marks Edmund's reentry (or entry) into the human community.

The final movement of *Lear*, then, is not all pillicock. Some elements counter the pervasive absurdity. Yet this negative, rather

[6] Cited by Irving Ribner, *Patterns in Shakespearian Tragedy* (New York, 1960), p. 135 n.

grudging formulation will not do for the many readers and spectators who find the play exalting. Are Bradley and all the others who see transcendent victory at the end simply refusing to face the bleak facts? Certainly the facile optimism of some finds sweetness in the uses of adversity with too little attention to the actual experience of the two old men—grinding agony, exhaustion, death. Others import back into the story the Christian otherworldly comfort that Shakespeare so rigorously excluded from it, so that they can imagine Lear and Cordelia united again beyond the grave. There is exaltation in *Lear*, I believe, but it is *tragic* exaltation. Far from depending on the next world, its premise is that this world—imperfect, limiting, indifferently cruel, perhaps senseless—is all there is. Lear's universe is preeminently the scene of tragic heroism as I described it in the Introduction, and Lear himself is the unaccommodated but also unaccommodating hero. "Pour on; I will endure" (III. iv. 18). He does more than that. Mocked and trivialized by his Fool and by his own silliness, battered by storms within and without, Lear keeps on asking. His pursuit of justice does not stop with the half-truth that he is more sinned against than sinning, or with the abortive trial of Goneril and Regan, or even with his anarchic intuition that all are guilty and hence none can justly punish: "Handy-dandy, which is the justice, which is the thief?" This question, with all the reservations it implies about human justice, is allowed to stand; and no divine justice comes to answer the later, more terrible question, "Why should a dog, a horse, a rat have life, / And thou no breath at all?"[7] Yet in a world where "none does offend," Lear has nevertheless insisted on his moral responsibility, offering himself to Cordelia for punishment because he has wronged her: "You have some cause." Not finding morality outside, he has created it inside. Like other tragic heroes, Lear in adversity realizes more and more of his self. The final words of the play pay tribute to that fullness of enduring and learning: "the oldest," Lear, has suffered and lived more fully than any who come after him will. Like Hamlet in particular—not the Hamlet who saw heaven ordinant and divinity shaping our ends but the Hamlet of the graveyard scene—Lear seems in his energetic, questing response to absurdity to be *creating* a self, defining it against nothingness.

---

[7] III. ii. 59–60; III. vi ; IV. vi. 154–55; V. iii. 306–7.

Creation is a divine act. It may perhaps seem strange to talk of human beings performing divine acts in a play whose characters appeal so often to the gods. Religion is omnipresent in *Lear.* Its content, however, is problematic. Scholars have tried to piece together a consistent theology from the many religious invocations and explanations, but with little success. The comments contradict each other; and the action confirms Gloucester's "as flies to wanton boys are we to th' gods" at least as much as it confirms Edgar's "the gods are just." In fact, if we mean by "gods" anything more than "the way things turn out," they do not seem to exist in the play at all. Omnipresent yet nonexistent, the gods invoked in *Lear* carry a dual meaning, indicating simultaneously that men need a divinity greater than their own selves and that those selves are after all the only source of that divinity. Any divine comedy they achieve is self-generated, without support from a larger order.

Notice, for example, that prayers to these gods are almost never answered. Lear exhibits from time to time the patience he has prayed for, Cordelia's appeal that her father be restored to his senses meets with some short-range success, and Edgar does eventually prosper as the remorseful Gloucester twice prays he will.[8] One could say, more doubtfully, that Edmund's goddess Nature stands up for bastards, at least for a while. In general, though, prayers go unanswered so regularly that asking for a divinely initiated action just about guarantees it will not happen. The gods do not strike Goneril blind and lame, do not keep Lear from madness or even from humiliating tears, do not find out and punish their enemies in the storm, do not crack Nature's molds and destroy the world, do not reward Gloucester's kindness to Lear or keep him from further despair after his attempted suicide, do not cause the right side to win the battle, and most of all do not save Cordelia from death.[9] Either the heavens are empty or their divinities are perverse, alien to any moral system we can understand. At times the result is so ironically at odds with the prayer that one suspects a malicious intelligence behind it. The reward for Gloucester's kindness is his savage blinding by Cornwall; the stormy blasts and eye-piercing flames that Lear calls down on Goneril fall in fact on himself and Gloucester.

[8] II. iv. 270; IV. vii. 14–17; III. vii. 91; IV. vi. 40.

[9] II. iv. 161–64; I. v. 43–44; II. iv. 276–77; III. ii. 49–51; III. ii. 6–8; III. vi. 5; IV. vi. 220–21 (cf. V. ii. 8–10); V. ii. 2; V. iii. 256.

On the other hand, it gradually becomes apparent that images of the gods in *Lear* have a close subjective relation to the characters who offer them. Kind and protective themselves, Kent and Cordelia see the gods as kind and protective. Edgar and Albany, who value justice, see them as just. For Lear in his anger at his elder daughters, they are wrathful and punishing, but after he is reborn into humility, they smile on self-sacrifice. For Gloucester after he has sheltered Lear from the storm, the gods are kind; when he despairs they are wantonly cruel; after he is brought from despair to acceptance they are "ever-gentle."[10]

Edmund's goddess Nature is clearly a projection of his own lawless, amoral energy. His address to her in the second scene of Act I serves dramatically to introduce him to the audience, but after this speech, which in any case is more self-definition than plea, Edmund forgets he has a tutelary deity. He refers to things divine only twice, to bolster his pose of righteousness when he is doing down first his brother and then his father:

> . . . I told him [Edgar] the revenging gods
> 'Gainst parricides did all their thunders bend.
>
> > (II. i. 45–46)

> O heavens! that this treason were not, or not I the
> detector!
>
> > (III. v. 11–12)

Aside from these pious frauds practiced on Gloucester and (rather unnecessarily, one would think) on Cornwall, Edmund is as silent on religious matters as the other bad characters are. Regan has one conventional exclamation (II. iv. 166), while Goneril and Oswald say nothing of the gods. It would appear that besides differentiating images of the divine according to temperament and moral condition of the imager, the play distinguishes more generally between the good characters who invoke their gods in earnest and the bad ones who call on them hypocritically or not at all. This might indicate that the gods are real after all, but I think there is a better explanation.

[10] I. i. 182; IV. vii. 14; V. iii. 170; IV. ii. 78–80; I. iv. 275–89; II. iv. 160–66; V. iii. 20–21; III. vii. 34; IV. i. 37–38; IV. vi. 219. I share the premise that the characters religious conceptions reflect their own natures with various critics, e.g., J. C. Maxwell, "The Technique of Invocation in *King Lear,*" *Modern Language Review* 45 (1950): 142–47; Knights, *Some Shakespearean Themes,* pp. 132–33; Elton, *"King Lear" and the Gods,* passim. My conclusions differ from theirs, however.

The strongest evidence that men make divinities rather than the other way round is that again and again conclusions about what the gods are like and what they should do follow and grow out of *human* initiatives. A good example is Lear's meditation on poverty during the storm. He says, "I'll pray," but then he talks not to gods but to men, the poor naked wretches and those in power who should be taking thought for them:

> Poor naked wretches, wheresoe'er you are,
> That bide the pelting of this pitiless storm,
> How shall your houseless heads and unfed sides,
> Your loop'd and window'd raggedness, defend you
> From seasons such as these? O, I have ta'en
> Too little care of this! Take physic, pomp;
> Expose thyself to feel what wretches feel,
> That thou mayst shake the superflux to them,
> And show the heavens more just.
>
> (III. iv. 28–36)

The gods come in only at the end, and they come as result rather than cause. When human rulers like Lear learn to distribute wealth justly, then the heavens will be revealed as just.

Words and action follow this pattern at several significant points. When Albany hears that Cornwall has been killed for blinding Gloucester, he says,

> This shows you are above,
> You justicers, that these our nether crimes
> So speedily can venge!
>
> (IV. ii. 78–80)

Does it show any such thing? A *man* has punished Cornwall, not the "visible spirits" sent down from heaven that Albany conceives as the proper agents of retribution (IV. ii. 46–47). What "proves" the existence of heaven is a purely human action. The scene of Cornwall's punishment itself ends in a similar way:

> 2 *Servant.* Let's follow the old Earl and get the Bedlam
>   To lead him where he would . . .
> 3 *Servant.* Go thou. I'll fetch some flax and whites of eggs
>   To apply to his bleeding face. Now heaven help
>   him!
>
> (III. vii. 102–6)

First comes the desire to help; then it is projected onto the gods.

In the Dover cliff scene, we actually watch Edgar invent new gods for his father. Picking him up after his "leap," Edgar proclaims Gloucester's life a miracle and instructs him about the makers of that miracle: "Think that the clearest gods, who make them honours / Of men's impossibilities, have preserved thee" (IV. vi. 73–74). Both the impossibility and the miraculous preservation are, of course, Edgar's own work. He is converting his father away from the casual murderer-gods Gloucester has earlier called up from his despair. Interestingly, Gloucester himself has shown an impulse toward a more positive belief soon after the "flies to wanton boys" pronouncement, in a speech that more or less parallels Lear's meditation on social justice. Like Lear, he is stirred by his own misery to feel for others:

> Here, take this purse, thou whom the heavens' plagues
> Have humbled to all strokes. That I am wretched
> Makes thee the happier. Heavens, deal so still!
> Let the superfluous and lust-dieted man
> That slaves your ordinance, that will not see
> Because he does not feel, feel your power quickly;
> So distribution should undo excess,
> And each man have enough.
>
> (IV. i. 65–72)

What has happened to him seemed senseless only a moment ago, yet now he perceives a purpose in it: heaven strikes at the comfortably hard-hearted ones to make them, in Edgar's later phrase, "pregnant to good pity." Why does Gloucester see this just now and not before? Because he has felt the good pity and initiated, by himself, the distribution that undoes excess—"take this purse." He finds meaning in heaven's act only through his own act.

Religion in *King Lear*, then, does not contradict heroic self-creation but reinforces it. Men make gods in their own images. Shakespeare is not Marlowe, however, and the play does not celebrate the all-sufficient ego. Edgar's insistence that his father attribute his rescue from death to the "clearest gods" reminds us that, even though the gods have no objective reality, it is a sign of moral health to invoke them. The implication is that men must create gods out of themselves but not make self their god. They need to refer their lives to larger ideals of order and community, even if the order receives no support from an indifferent universe, and community cannot save them from undeserved suffering.

In a sense, *King Lear* is a play about religion in the making. Shakespeare created for it a thoroughly pagan milieu quite unlike that of his source play, which is steeped in Christian allusion and assumption. The play world of *Lear* is emphatically, if not totally, primitive. Elton thinks that Shakespeare de-Christianized the story in order to make his own play demonstrate the breakdown of belief in providence. He sees the "poor naked wretches" speech as an indictment of cosmic injustice, with Lear's recognition of his own injustice as an incidental irony.[11] I would argue rather that this recognition is central: it is Lear's acknowledgment that if justice is to exist, he as man and ruler must make it happen. Cosmic injustice is still there, but all is not therefore cheerless, dark, and deadly. Shakespeare's decision to examine man's ethical and metaphysical position in the universe without the *donnés* of Christian revelation is in line with the general tendency of his maturing art. Charlton points out, for example, that in *Richard III* it is assumed that the wages of sin is death, while *Macbeth*, in the next decade, reveals the internal necessity of that principle, by demonstrating its roots in "the bare rudiments of human nature."[12] One sees the same impulse to discard orthodox frameworks and start with human beings alone in the development of Shakespeare's political drama. The divine scheme of sin and retribution that is prominent in the *Henry VI–Richard III* tetralogy is much less noticeable in the *Richard II–Henry V* group, where problems of government are explored mainly in human terms. Shakespeare went farther in the same direction when he abandoned English history, with its patriotic imperatives, for the emotional neutrality of Rome. In *Julius Caesar*, *Antony and Cleopatra*, and especially *Coriolanus*, he used that freedom to address fundamental questions about the individual's relation to the state without any prior assumption in favor of the state. He could hardly ask whether English prosperity and continuity were worth all they demanded (though perhaps he comes close to asking it through Hal's rejection of Falstaff). He could and did question the value of Rome. *Hamlet,* after some flirtation with absurdity, finally asserts an external guiding providence; five years later, in *Lear*, Shakespeare removes providential sureties and leaves

---

[11] *"King Lear" and the Gods*, pp. 225–26.
[12] H. B. Charlton, *Shakespearian Tragedy* (Cambridge, 1944), p. 141.

his characters alone to destroy themselves or to create a positive ethic out of their own need. The play's values of love, forgiveness, and fellow-feeling gained through suffering are indeed those preached by Christianity. The point is that, rather than being handed down from on high, they take root in and grow up from the ground of human desperation. Furthermore, in an apparently random universe with no afterlife in which ultimate justice is meted out, following that ethic must be its own reward. Victories won through it are personal, limited, and nonenduring.

I suggest as the shaping emotion of tragedy a tension between recognition of death's rightness and protest against its wrongness. This is to say that tragedy's ground is the disputed border—or no-man's-land—between a just and orderly pattern for life on the one hand and an amoral patternlessness on the other. Shakespeare in *King Lear* is not rewriting the *Purgatorio* or anticipating *Endgame*; he is setting one vision against the other, and in their uneasy coexistence lies the play's peculiar tragic force. Dante and Beckett at their respective poles offer not tragedy but two kinds of comedy. What is important to realize here is that each kind in its way diminishes man somewhat. He is either a figure in a preestablished scheme, following the way laid out for him by a higher intelligence, or he is an aimless atom in a universe of aimless atoms. Where the two comic visions are held in balance, with neither dominating, individual choice and perseverance have special significance. The universe of tragedy, and preeminently of *Lear*, intimates pattern but fails to complete it; some pieces of the jigsaw are forever missing, and some of those on hand will never fit. Man is heroic in these circumstances when, like Lear, he has the capacity to create a larger self even out of the destructive element—to make his own meaning.

Dramatic Judgement in *King Lear*

by Harriett Hawkins

In *King Lear*, Shakespeare's great tragedy about truth and falsehood, no equivocations on the part of the characters are admitted or permitted. Like chess pieces, the characters in *King Lear* are initially divided into black ones and white ones, and they are divided according to whether they stand on the side of truth or on the side of falsehood:

> *Lear.* So young and so untender?
> *Cordelia.* So young, my lord, and true.
>
> (I. i. 105–6)

> *Kent.*   To plainness honour's bound
> When majesty falls to folly. Reserve thy state;
> And in thy best consideration check
> This hideous rashness. Answer my life my judgment:
> Thy youngest daughter does not love thee least;
> Nor are those empty-hearted whose low sounds
> Reverb no hollowness.
>
> (I. i. 146–52)

> *Fool.* They'll have me whipp'd for speaking true: thou'lt
> have me whipp'd for lying.
>
> (I. iv. 180–81)

The play's several spokesmen for truth are insulted, banished, stocked, tortured, and forced to go into disguise by other characters, but they nevertheless remain absolutely honest spokesmen for the truth and for the right. The liars, on the other hand, remain rich, secure, gorgeous, and powerful for a time, though the hollow

falsity of all their pretensions to any form of humanity finally is
dramatically exposed for ever:

> *Edgar.* Maugre thy strength, youth, place, and eminence,
>   Despite thy victor sword and fire-new fortune,
>   Thy valour and thy heart—thou art a traitor;
>   False to thy gods, thy brother, and thy father;
>   Conspirant 'gainst this high illustrious prince;
>   And, from th'extremest upward of thy head
>   To the descent and dust below thy foot,
>   A most toad-spotted traitor.
>
> (V. iii. 131–38)

In what is a very significant contrast to Macbeth, certain of the
vicious characters in *King Lear*—Cornwall, Regan, and Goneril—
suffer hardly at all before they die, and they never once condemn
themselves. To the very end they remain comfortably smug in their
evil. Furthermore, they experience no general recognition of the
good, and they do not inevitably even face retributive justice from
the good characters. Nevertheless, the vicious characters in *King
Lear* are summoned to judgement, and their judgement may be the
most damning of all judgements. For the deaths of Cornwall,
Goneril, and Regan touch no one, on or off the stage, with any pity
or awe or, indeed, with any emotion whatsoever. If Albany can
dismiss the death of Edmund (who is by far the most interesting,
intelligent, and sensitive villain in the play) as "but a trifle here," the
deaths of Cornwall, Goneril, and Regan are even more dismissible.
So far as everybody in the theatre is concerned, their deaths are
ultimately and completely insignificant. Indeed, throughout this
play, Shakespeare gives these characters the emotional appeal of
faceless, soulless automatons. They never come to life dramatically
or emotionally. Even in their love affairs they are as malicious,
cowardly, and cruel as they are when, in a group, they humiliate or
torture old men:

> *Edmund:*   Yet Edmund was belov'd.
>   The one the other poison'd for my sake,
>   And after slew herself.
> *Albany.* Even so.
>
> (V. iii. 239–41)

"Even so." So what? There is not even any emotional interest on
our parts, here, in relegating Shakespeare's goats to the eternal

brimstone. They are like indistinguishable, stinging, buzzing insects (Edmund himself apparently cannot find any significant difference between Goneril and Regan), and one feels just about the same amount of emotion at their deaths as one might feel while watching the death throes of a swarm of hornets.

By contrast, the stage action *"Enter* Lear, *with* Cordelia *dead in his arms"* arouses as much human emotion as it is possible for art to elicit. However many times this play has been read, the impact of King Lear grieving over Cordelia summons forth overwhelming pity, tears, horror, the desire to help, a shriek that this cannot be, for life must not be so cruel. It arouses righteous indignation, outrage, pain, love for the old King, a complete recognition of what he must feel and a full understanding of the depth of his loss. Compared to the dramatic impact of the death of Cordelia, the deaths of a hundred Edmunds and a thousand Regans could only be considered trifles. And in spite of the fact that the death of Cordelia appears to have no significance whatsoever in terms of any gods, or any "Absolute," the emotional responses which this death generates in the theatre and which are such completely human ones—grief, pity, love, terror—are of awesome human significance in and of themselves.

The tremendous flow of feeling which goes out to King Lear from the other characters and from the audience does not, of course, help Lear himself. Unlike Macbeth, the Lear of the last act has all that "should accompany old age." He has the "honour, love, obedience, troops of friends" that Macbeth so grievously missed. But they are of no comfort to Lear bending over Cordelia. "A plague upon you, murderers, traitors all!" he says to the characters and to the audience who have endured with him to the end. Still, the sheer humanity of Lear's fury directed against everyone who has survived his daughter only increases our pity, our understanding, our love for him. So far as we are concerned, the humane pity, the passion and the insight and the love which King Lear summons from everyone in the theatre, is *le vrai Jugement dernier.* And *King Lear* itself represents the very highest kind of art, defined by Proust as "that which is the most real, the most austere school of life."

Certain very austere facts of ordinary life dominate this tragedy. They are the harshest truths of human experience, and they are divorced from any of the comforts of theology or fiction. Certain good characters in the play (like Kent and Cordelia) receive no earthly reward for their loyalty, and no reward in the after-life is promised to them. If these characters are honest and true, this is because their own moral integrity requires them to be honest and to be true, and in maintaining their own moral integrity they have all the reward that they are going to get. It is also true that death is completely random, completely arbitrary. The message to the prison could have saved Cordelia. Similarly, Cornwall might have recovered from his wound. In this tragedy, we are never encouraged to consider death as a punishment for crime. Death is simply the inevitable end of life which can come, at any time, to the good and to the evil alike. Characters can therefore choose death as an escape from life whenever they wish. Gloucester constantly contemplates suicide, and Goneril commits suicide. This is one of the choices left to the individual characters. Another such choice is the choice of values.

On the one hand, the characters in *King Lear* may choose to adopt for themselves the values that permit human beings to live together in honour, peace, social harmony, and love:

> Good my lord,
> You have begot me, bred me, lov'd me; I
> Return those duties back as are right fit,
> Obey you, love you, and most honour you.
> Why have my sisters husbands, if they say
> They love you all? Haply, when I shall wed,
> That lord whose hand must take my plight shall carry
> Half my love with him, half my care and duty.
> Sure I shall never marry like my sisters,
> To love my father all.
>
> (I. i. 94–103)

Alternatively, the characters in this play may choose to reject all these values, and this rejection, by its very nature, clearly permits people to prey on each other like "monsters of the deep":

> *Edmund.* A credulous father! and a brother noble,
> Whose nature is so far from doing harms
> That he suspects none; on whose foolish honesty
> My practices ride easy! I see the business.
> Let me, if not by birth, have lands by wit:
> All with me's meet that I can fashion fit.
>
> (I. ii. 170–75)

> *Cornwall.* True or false, [this letter] hath made thee Earl of
> Gloucester.
>
> (III. v. 16–17)

> *Goneril.*   . . . the laws are mine, not thine.
> Who can arraign me for't?
>
> (V. iii. 157–58)

Very frequently in this play the underlying motives for choosing either of these alternatives are given no dramatic importance whatsoever. It is as if Shakespeare were trying to show us that choices for right and wrong, that the deeds of good and evil based on these choices, are more important than any reasons for such choices and deeds. Remembering his experiences in German concentration camps, the psychoanalyst Bruno Bettelheim observed that "when the chips were down it was utterly unimportant why a person acted the way he did; the only thing that counted was how he acted."[1] Similarly, in the crisis situations of *King Lear*, we judge the characters completely on the basis of the decisions that they make and act upon, and the reasons for their decisions or actions are of no great concern to us.

Certainly no gods in this tragedy will intervene to prevent the rejection of all humane[2] values, nor will they intervene to punish those who reject these values. The only evil, the only justice, the only mercy, and the only miracles that occur in this play result from the actions of men. We see that the monsters who prey on others may finally turn on each other and kill each other off, just as Goneril kills Regan. We see that honourable men like Edgar may finally rise to fight against evil. But these fates, these facts, obviously reflect the very common human consequences of very common human evil. They do not (necessarily) reflect some Divine Judgement in favour of the good. Similarly, the bonds which hold society together—the values of kinship, honesty, friendship, loyalty, kindness, and love—are very basic social values. No supernatural sanction is given to them. To choose to abide by them is, in *King Lear*, to choose full humanity, but this choice (given the fact

[1] Bruno Bettelheim, *The Informed Heart* (London, 1970), p. 25.

[2] Sir Peter Medawar's dictionary definition of "humane" seems as good a definition as any: " 'humaneness,' according to the dictionary, means 'characterized by such behaviour or disposition towards others as befits a man,' " *The Future of Man* (London, 1960), p. 56.

that other human beings are perfectly free to behave in monstrous ways) will not preclude cruel suffering. It may in fact increase it. Certainly, within their dramatic lifetimes the good characters in *King Lear* suffer more, not less, than the evil ones. Indeed, taking a stand for moral and social order, in this play, is consistently shown to be harder and more dangerous than deliberately rejecting any social or moral obligations that might interfere with self-interest. To tell the truth, to do one's moral or social duty to others, is to face banishment, torture, or death:

> *Lear.*   Kent, on thy life, no more!
> *Kent.* My life I never held but as a pawn
> To wage against thine enemies; nor fear to lose it,
> Thy safety being motive.
>
> (I. i. 153–56)
>
> *Gloucester.* If I die for it, as no less is threatened me, the King my old master must be relieved.
>
> (III. iii. 18–19)
>
> *Cordelia.* No blown ambition doth our arms incite,
> But love, dear love, and our ag'd father's right.
>
> (IV. iv. 27–28)

Kent, Gloucester, Cordelia, the Fool, and others decide to take their stands at great cost to their personal safety and comfort. And if, as this play suggests that it may be, death is the death-obliterate and not necessarily the entrance to another form of life, then the characters who choose the good are treated far more cruelly by Shakespeare himself than the characters who choose evil, since they suffer so much before they die. On the other hand, the good characters do all come to life before they die. They help each other, they can trust each other, they all finally give or finally receive unconditional love, and they go down as human beings who have taken a stand on the side of humane values. In a moving account of the prisoners whose integrity triumphed over all the horrors of Dachau and Buchenwald, Bruno Bettelheim gives us a keen insight into the brave stands taken by the good characters in *King Lear*:

> . . . to survive as a man not a walking corpse, as a debased and degraded but still human being, one had first and foremost to remain informed and aware of what made up one's personal point of no return, the point beyond which one would never, under any circumstances, give in to the oppressor, even if it meant risking and

losing one's life. It meant being aware that if one survived at the price of overreaching this point one would be holding on to a life that had lost all its meaning. It would mean surviving—not with a lowered self-respect, but without any.[3]

By taking their stands on the side of moral and social order, Kent, Cordelia, Gloucester, Edgar, and the Fool claim for themselves and (so far as the audience is concerned) they ultimately inherit the kingdom of humanity which the banally portrayed villains, the play's "walking corpses," never even enter. At their most debased and degraded, the good characters remain human beings, not beasts, while their rich, secure persecutors are metaphorically identified with the lowest forms of life on the play's evolutionary scale.

Interestingly, if obviously, in the beginning of the play, Edmund seems far more interesting than Edgar. Thereafter, however, while Edmund never (until his one attempt at a good deed in the end) deviates from his originally defined bastardy, Edgar goes (and grows) through a series of drastic mutations. He goes all the way down to Poor Turlygood, poor Tom ("Edgar I nothing am") and then—always serving his father—he moves up to his triumphant victory as the (literally and figuratively) "true" son and heir of the Earl of Gloucester who is able to recognize evil and overcome it. Gloucester himself, in the beginning, is callow and crass. His first real moral commitment costs him his eyes. But Gloucester does learn to "see," because he learns to "feel" (IV. i. 69–70), while he was able to do neither in the opening scenes of the play. Gloucester finally dies a death which combines the two ultimate human passions, the extremes of joy and sorrow. When he experienced them, his heart "burst smilingly." And that is not the worst way for a man to die.

Lear, of course, goes through the greatest mutation of all. He begins as a petty old tyrant who flings away love and integrity and truth as if he were unloading counterfeit money. But Lear ends his life as "the King himself." Precisely how Lear feels when he dies will always remain a great dramatic mystery, but there is never any question where he dies. To that question, everybody in the theatre can only answer in the words of Kent, "In your own kingdom, Sir." By the end of the play Lear deserves all the love and the respect he

[3] *The Informed Heart,* pp. 145–46.

wanted so much at the beginning. He has learned to know himself utterly ("Forget and forgive, I am old and foolish"), and where he once insisted upon being protected and pitied, Lear learns to pity and to protect others at some of the very darkest moments in his •life. He pities his Fool in the storm (III. ii. 66–73) and he comforts Cordelia on their way to prison. There is no doubt that this mighty old man "might have saved" his daughter if only Shakespeare had let him get there in time. Shakespeare himself sends King Lear out into the tempest and then forces Lear to experience all the worst things that a man can experience, and King Lear endures to the end. For this reason, Lear is the greatest of Shakespeare's dramatic affirmations of the human capacity to grow, to learn, to feel, and to remain an unconditionally royal lord of earth in spite of all the physical suffering human beings may share with the humblest animals, and in spite of experiencing a degree of emotional suffering which no animal can know.

And this is why, despite all the justifiable intellectual arguments that *King Lear* makes a grotesque mockery of human aspirations set against an indifferent and absurd Absolute, the play still, to the common reader, represents an affirmation of the human capacity to surmount all inhuman indifference, all absurdity. We ourselves, as human beings watching Shakespeare's great tragedy, cannot be indifferent to the King Lear of the final acts, nor does Lear ever seem to us (even in his most grotesque moments) merely an illustration of life's absurdity. We cannot even remain indifferent to his followers. Shakespeare will not permit us to do so. Certainly he makes everyone in the audience feel the highest admiration for Kent, who never once requests any admiration from anyone, but who categorically, by word and by deed, defines himself as a man:

Lear. What art thou?
Kent. A man, sir.
Lear. What dost thou profess? What wouldst thou with us?
Kent. I do profess to be no less than I seem, to serve him truly that will
    put me in trust, to love him that is honest, to converse with him that
    is wise and says little, to fear judgment, to fight when I cannot
    choose . . .

(I. iv. 9–17)

Kent never expects any reward for being "a man." His unselfishly loyal service to the King is never fully recognized by Lear. But it is recognized by the audience. From their point of view, Kent dares do "all that doth become a man." He never compromises with his integrity—with his truth to himself or his truth to others. He takes a firm stand against evil. He loves, he serves. He is one of the characters who literally and figuratively inherits the kingdom in the end, and "Who will inherit the kingdom?" is perhaps the most crucial question raised, and answered, throughout this play.

Obviously, by any standards of calculated self-interest, Kent is a complete fool. The Fool himself makes this clear. But the Fool also makes it clear that those who subordinate everything to self-interest are knaves who, in the long run, will prove to be even greater fools:

> That sir which serves and seeks for gain,
>   And follows but for form,
> Will pack when it begins to rain,
>   And leave thee in the storm.
> But I will tarry; the fool will stay
>   And let the wise man fly.
> The knave turns fool that runs away;
>   The fool no knave, perdy.
>
>   (II. iv. 76–83)

In the last analysis, by his treatment and judgement of the characters in *King Lear*, Shakespeare makes the conventional worldly wisdom of the vicious characters appear ultimately foolish. And their selfishness appears supremely foolish in terms of the most basic standards by which common humanity evaluates the quality of human life. Kent's life has human value and significance. The life of Regan does not.

For if men like Lear, Kent, Edgar, and the Fool are faced not only by human evil, but by an indifferent universe as well, then they can, they must, help each other to surmount this indifference. Indeed, in this play, they are obliged to do so in order to give meaning to their own lives and to the lives of others. Clearly the only meaning they can give to life is a human meaning. The storm does not care whether or not it is afflicting King Lear. Kent does care. Because the characters cannot expect intervention from any Absolute, it is up to them to create their own heavens or hells, their own kingdoms, on earth. The universe, the world, the stage of all human actions, permits all forms of life to occupy it. It impartially

allows the existence of the highest and the lowest forms of life—
toads, monsters of the deep, and men. The sun, the storms, the
universe which these forms of life inhabit, appear to be completely
neutral towards them all. So there is no point in either blaming the
universe for not abiding by specifically human values, or blaming it
for human failures to abide by them:

> This is the excellent foppery of the world, that, when we are sick in
> fortune, often the surfeits of our own behaviour, we make guilty of our
> disasters the sun, the moon, and stars; as if we were villains on necessity;
> fools by heavenly compulsion; knaves, thieves, and treachers, by spher-
> ical predominance; drunkards, liars, and adulterers, by an enforc'd
> obedience of planetary influence; and all that we are evil in, by a divine
> thrusting on . . .
>
> (I. ii. 110–20)

Writing about the future of man, Sir Peter Medawar concludes that
men have been passing responsibility for their own actions to some
metaphysical force or other for too long:

> Think only of what we have suffered from a belief in the exis-
> tence and overriding authority of a fighting instinct; from the doc-
> trines of racial superiority and the metaphysics of blood and soil;
> from the belief that warfare between men or classes of men or
> nations represents a fulfilment of historical laws. These are all
> excuses of one kind or another, and pretty thin excuses. The
> inference we can draw from an analytical study of the differences
> between ourselves and other animals is surely this: that the bells
> which toll for mankind are—most of them, anyway—like the bells on
> Alpine cattle; they are attached to our own necks, and it must be *our*
> fault if they do not make a cheerful and harmonious sound.[4]

We can draw precisely the same inference from Shakespeare's analytical study of the differences between men (who can choose to be
good or evil) and animals (to whom the human definitions of good
and evil do not apply) throughout *King Lear*. In no other play by
Shakespeare is the "scene" of so little influence on the characters.
The great stage of the world, in this play, is only a stage, a setting
for human actions. A court can be the scene where deeds of great
virtue or great viciousness are acted out by men. So can a heath. A
castle can be a refuge or a torture chamber, entirely depending on
how people behave within it. So can a hovel. How people act, how
they treat each other, is all that matters.

---

[4] *The Future of Man*, p. 103.

How people act, how they treat each other, is all that matters, also, in the last judgement issued in the New Testament: "I was hungry and you fed me." Time after time, in so many great works of the human intellect, traditionally "divine" truths and judgements turn out to be the basic human truths and judgements. These works, these truths, do have a kind of divinity, because they have a universality (so far as human experience is concerned) that transcends time, space, and all the convulsive changes in theological dogma and intellectual fashion. For instance, whoever speaks the epilogue to *King Lear* appears to use the universally inclusive "we" (as well as the royal "we") when he says it is imperative that, at whatever cost, people speak the truth:

> The weight of this sad time we must obey;
> Speak what we feel, not what we ought to say.

And certainly the very greatest artists, philosophers, and scientists have always told the truth as they felt and saw it, no matter what their historical situations may have told them that they "ought to say." And with astonishing frequency they independently arrive at exactly the same conclusions. Over and over again they give us the same truths. Maybe this is another reason why certain truths have taken on a numen—they frequently come from the most intelligent and the most sensitive human beings that have spoken to other human beings over the centuries. But the main reason they survive so triumphantly is surely because they *are* truths. Many of the inferences arrived at in *King Lear*, for instance, are arrived at by quite a different route in the following quotation from Proust's *The Captive*:

> All that we can say is that everything is arranged in this life as though we entered it carrying the burden of obligations contracted in a former life; there is no reason inherent in the conditions of life on this earth that can make us consider ourselves obliged to do good, to be fastidious, to be polite even, nor make the talented artist consider himself obliged to begin over again a score of times a piece of work the admiration aroused by which will matter little to his body devoured by worms, like the patch of yellow wall painted with so much knowledge and skill by an artist who must for ever remain unknown and is barely identified under the name Vermeer. All these obligations which have not their sanction in our present life seem to belong to a different world, founded upon kindness, scrupulosity, self-sacrifice, a world entirely different from this, which we

leave in order to be born into this world, before perhaps returning to the other to live once again beneath the sway of those unknown laws which we have obeyed because we bore their precepts in our hearts, knowing not whose hand had traced them there—those laws to which every profound work of the intellect brings us nearer and which are invisible only—and still!—to fools.[5]

The fact that Shakespeare dramatically exhibits his truths about human values by showing human beings in a world without any divine order, while Proust feels that the identical human values may ultimately reflect some divine order, does not matter. The truths hurled out at us by both artists are the same. And if Shakespeare and Proust permit us, in very differing ways, to know, to see, to feel, their truths, then their works have done all that human art—the living likeness of truth that transcends the artist's time and space—ever can do for us. Whether or not we consider ourselves obliged to act upon these truths remains our own affair.

[5] Marcel Proust, *The Captive*, trans. C. K. Scott Moncrieff (New York, 1932), pp. 509–10.

Quarto and Folio *King Lear*
and the Interpretation of Albany
and Edgar

by Michael J. Warren

The two texts of *King Lear* present obvious editorial and critical problems. The Quarto of 1608 prints about 283 lines that are
not printed in the 1623 Folio; the Folio prints about 100 that are
not printed in the Quarto.[1] A variation of nearly 400 lines in a text
of around 3,300 lines is significant;[2] in addition, there are also a
very large number of variant substantive readings. However, far
from alarming editors and critics to the delicate problems involved
in printing and discussing a single play called *King Lear*, this wealth

"Quarto and Folio *King Lear* and the Interpretation of Albany and Edgar," by
Michael J. Warren. From *Shakespeare: Pattern of Excelling Nature*, ed. David Bevington
and J. L. Halio (Newark: University of Delaware Press, and London: Associated
University Presses, 1978), pp. 95–97, 99–105. Copyright © 1978 by Associated University Presses. Reprinted by permission of Associated University Presses Inc.

Author's Note: This paper is an enlarged version of that delivered at the International Shakespeare Association Congress in Washington, D.C., in April 1976. As a
consequence of delivering the paper I have become aware that three scholars are
currently writing dissertations arguing for the distinctness of the Quarto and Folio
texts of *King Lear*: Steven Urkowitz of University of Chicago, Georgia Peters Burton of
Bryn Mawr College, and Peter W. M. Blayney of Cambridge University; each of us has
arrived at the same major conclusion independently of the others. I would like to
thank my colleague Professor John M. Ellis for his helpful advice and criticism with
respect to the argument of the first part of this paper.

[1] I am using the figures cited by Alfred Harbage on p. 1104 of his appendix to his
text of *King Lear* published in *The Pelican Shakespeare* (Baltimore, 1969), pp. 1104–6.

[2] *The Pelican Shakespeare* states that *King Lear* is 3,195 lines long; *The Norton Facsimile: The First Folio of Shakespeare*, ed. Charlton Hinman (New York, 1968), gives *King
Lear* 3,301 lines.

of material has been treated as an ample blessing from which a "best text" of Shakespeare's *King Lear* may be evolved. Indeed, the standard methods of bibliography and editing—the application of critical principles "to the textual raw material of the authoritative preserved documents in order to approach as nearly as may be to the ideal of the authorial fair copy by whatever necessary process of recovery, independent emendation, or conflation of authorities"[3]—such methods and the accepted assumptions of the origins of each text have led to the editorial habit of establishing and publishing a *King Lear* text that is produced by a process of conflation, by the exercise of a moderate and quasi-scientific eclecticism, and by a studied disregard for the perils of intentionalism.[4] In a recent article Kenneth Muir writes:

> Until the work of bibliographers and textual critics in the present century, editors chose readings from either text, according to taste. It is now generally agreed that, whatever the basis of the Quarto text, the Folio text of *King Lear* is nearer to what Shakespeare wrote; but, even so, editors are still bound to accept a number of readings from the inferior text and, since there were cuts in the prompt-book from which the Folio text was derived, a number of long passages.[5]

This statement reveals certain clear attitudes of editors to their task. It is assumed that there is one primal lost text, an "ideal *King Lear*" that Shakespeare wrote, and that we have two corrupted

---

[3] Fredson Bowers, *Textual and Literary Criticism* (Cambridge, 1966), p. 120.

[4] Harbage, "Note on the Text": "In 1608 a version of *King Lear* appeared in a quarto volume sold by Nathaniel Butter at his shop at the Pied Bull. Its text was reproduced in 1619 in a quarto falsely dated 1608. Various theories have been offered to explain the nature of the Pied Bull text, the most recent being that it represents Shakespeare's rough draft carelessly copied, and corrupted by the faulty memories of actors who were party to the copying. In 1623 a greatly improved though 'cut' version of the play appeared in the first folio, evidently printed from the quarto after it had been carefully collated with the official playhouse manuscript. The present edition follows the folio text, and although it adds in square brackets the passages appearing only in the quarto, and accepts fifty-three quarto readings, it follows the chosen text more closely than do most recent editions. However, deference to the quarto is paid in an appendix, where its alternative readings, both those accepted and those rejected, are listed. Few editorial emendations have been retained, but see . . ." (p. 1064). See also G. Blakemore Evans, "Note on the Text" of *King Lear*, in *The Riverside Shakespeare* (Boston, 1974), pp. 1295–96, and Kenneth Muir, "Introduction" to *King Lear* (Arden Shakespeare) (Cambridge, Mass., 1959), pp. xix–xx.

[5] Kenneth Muir, "King Lear," in *Shakespeare: Select Bibliographical Guides*, ed. Stanley Wells (Oxford, 1973), p. 171.

copies of it. It is hypothesized that F is a less corrupt version of the ideal text than Q, though both preserve features of the ideal original; and that while there is more corruption in Q, some uncorrupted elements remain that can mitigate the admittedly lesser corruption of F. The concept of the "ideal *King Lear*" is problematic here, first, because its existence cannot be known, and second, because in the absence of such knowledge it is nevertheless further assumed that all alterations of any nature from that imaginary text are by hands other than Shakespeare's. Such an assumption is based on no evidence, and is counter to our experience of authors and their habits—for example, the modification of texts after first publication by Jonson, Pope, Yeats, James, and Pinter. Of course, it is conceivable that this standard hypothesis may indeed be true, but the confidence with which it is assumed is unwarranted, and the lack of a constant awareness that it is an assumption leads to poorly founded judgments. For instance, a statement such as "editors are still bound to accept a number of readings from the inferior text" is merely an editor's justification of the right to be eclectic; although editors may well be advised at times to adopt readings where comparison of texts indicates simple misprints or nonsensical readings, circumspection and wariness are always necessary, for nonsense may merely be sense we do not yet understand, and further we cannot know that alterations between Q and F are not authorial in origin. Most editors admit that the examination of the two texts leads to the conclusion that editing has taken place, and yet they are generally reluctant to take that editing seriously.

Having asserted the necessity of a decent skepticism in relation to the concept of the "ideal" text, I wish to argue that in a situation where statements about textual status are never more than hypotheses based upon the current models of thought about textual recension, it is not demonstrably erroneous to work with the possibility (a) that there may be no single "ideal play" of *King Lear* (all of "what Shakespeare wrote"), that there may never have been one, and that what we create by conflating both texts is merely an invention of editors and scholars; (b) that for all its problems Q is an authoritative version of the play of *King Lear*; and (c) that F may indeed be a revised version of the play, that its additions and omissions may constitute Shakespeare's considered modification of the earlier text, and that we certainly cannot know that they are not.

Of course, I am once more introducing, after over fifty years of relative quiescence, the specter of "continuous copy": not, I would hope, in the confident, fantastic, and disintegrationist mode of Robertson and Dover Wilson, but in a skeptical and conservative way. In his famous lecture *The Disintegration of Shakespeare*, E. K. Chambers dismissed the excesses of his contemporaries as much by the force of ironic rhetoric and an attractive appeal to common sense as by any real proof; but he nowhere succeeded in denying the possibility of authorial reworking. He instanced the few cases of recorded extensive revision as indicative that revision of any kind was rare; and he asserted as follows: "That any substantial revision, as distinct perhaps from a mere abridgement, would entail a fresh application for the Master's allowance must, I think, be taken for granted. The rule was that his hand must be 'at the latter end of the booke they doe play'; and in London, at least, any company seriously departing from the allowed book would run a considerable risk."[6] Which is an interesting hypothesis; but what in this connection would constitute "substantial revision" or "serious departure"? Chambers to the contrary, that same common sense which leads me to praise him in his rejection of disintegrationist excesses leads me nevertheless to believe that a play like *King Lear* may have undergone revision beyond "mere abridgement"—what Chambers, following Henslowe, might classify as "altering"—without the necessity of resubmission to the Master of the Revels.

In putting forward this argument I have ignored many of the complexities of relation that have been the stuff of textual debate for many years. I have done so because they are merely the current working hypotheses of the editing world, and because they are not immediately relevant to my contention. I would maintain that Q and F *King Lear* are sufficiently dissimilar that they should not be conflated, but should be treated as two versions of a single play, both having authority. . . .

. . . I wish to argue that Q and F reveal significant differences in the roles of Albany and Edgar, differences sufficiently great that one is obliged to interpret their characters differently in each, and, especially in relation to the alterations in the last scene, to appreci-

---

[6] E. K. Chambers, *The Disintegration of Shakespeare* ([London], 1924), p. 17.

ate a notable contrast in the tone and meaning of the close of each text. These differences go beyond those which may be expected when two texts descend in corrupted form from a common original; they indicate that a substantial and consistent recasting of certain aspects of the play has taken place. In brief, the part of Albany is more developed in Q than in F, and in Q he closes the play a mature and victorious duke assuming responsibility for the kingdom; in F he is a weaker character, avoiding responsibility. The part of Edgar is shorter in F than in Q; however, whereas in Q he ends the play a young man overwhelmed by his experience, in F he is a young man who has learned a great deal, and who is emerging as the new leader of the ravaged society.

In both texts Albany speaks little in the first act. Neither Albany nor Cornwall speaks in the first scene in Q; their joint exclamation "Deare Sir forbeare" (I. i. 162) appears in F only.[7] In the fourth scene, which Goneril dominates in both texts, Q lacks two of the eight brief speeches that F assigns to Albany, and a phrase that completes a third. Missing are "Pray Sir be patient" (I. iv. 270) and "Well, you may feare too farre" (I. iv. 338), and the phrase "Of what hath moued you" (I. iv. 283), which in F succeeds "My lord, I am guiltlesse, as I am ignorant." Albany, who is bewildered and ineffectual in either text, is more patently so in Q, where he is given no opportunity to urge patience in response to Lear's question—"is it your will that wee prepare any horses" (F: "Is it your will, speake Sir? Prepare my Horses") (I. iv. 267)—and no opportunity to warn Goneril of the unwisdom of her acts. Goneril's part also is smaller in Q than in F—she lacks I. iv. 322–43—but she dominates the scene nevertheless.

However, when Albany enters in the fourth act after a period in which he does not ride to Gloucester's house with Goneril and is mentioned only in the context of the always incipient conflict

---

[7] For convenience I shall cite line numberings based on Muir's Arden edition throughout this essay; apparent inconsistencies occasionally result from the Arden relineation. All quotations from Q are from *King Lear, 1608 (Pied Bull Quarto)*: Shakespeare Quarto Facsimiles No. 1, ed. W. W. Greg (Oxford, 1939); all quotations from F are from *The Norton Facsimile: The First Folio of Shakespeare*, ed. Charlton B. Hinman (New York, 1968). The text will normally make clear whether Q or F is being quoted; on occasions when the text is not specified and the lines under discussion appear in both Q and F with only insignificant differences in spelling and punctuation, I quote from F alone.

between himself and Cornwall, his reappearance is different in
quality in each text. In both texts the scene begins with Oswald
reporting Albany's disaffection (IV. ii. 3–11) while Goneril scorns
"the Cowish terror of his spirit" (IV. ii. 12). In F Albany's speech on
entering is very brief:

> Oh *Gonerill*,
> You are not worth the dust which the rude winde
> Blowes in your face.
>
> (IV. ii. 29–31)

However, Q continues:

> I feare your disposition
> That nature which contemnes ith origin
> Cannot be bordered certaine in it selfe,
> She that her selfe will sliuer and disbranch
> From her materiall sap, perforce must wither,
> And come to deadly vse.
>
> (IV. ii. 31–36)

And Goneril's prompt dismissal "No more, the text is foolish" leads
to a longer speech of powerful moral reproach, likening the sisters
to tigers, and reaching its climax in the pious pronouncement that

> If that the heauens doe not their visible spirits
> Send quickly downe to tame this vild offences, it will come
> Humanity must perforce pray on it self like monsters of the
> deepe.
>
> (IV. ii. 46–50)

The speeches that follow in Q are much reduced in F, and both
Albany and Goneril lose lines. The cuts in Goneril's part are largely
references to Albany as a "morall foole," statements critical of his
mild response to the invasion of France; her stature is not notably
diminished by the loss. The reduction of Albany's part, by contrast,
severely reduces his theatrical impact. In F he is left with barely six
lines between his entrance and that of the messenger, and there is
no sense of the new strong position that lines such as the following,
even allowing for Goneril's belittling rejection, establish in Q:

> *Albany.* Thou changed, and selfe-couerd thing for shame
> Be-monster not thy feature, wer't my fitnes
> To let these hands obay my bloud,
> They are apt enough to dislecate and teare
> Thy flesh and bones, how ere thou art a fiend,

> A womans shape doth shield thee.
> *Goneril.* Marry your manhood mew . . .
>
> (IV. ii. 62–68)

In Q the succeeding lines of moral outrage at the news of the blinding of Gloucester present Albany as a man of righteous wrath,
outraged by injustice; the same sequence in F presents Albany as
equally outraged, but because of the brevity of his previous rebukes
he appears more futile in context, less obviously a man capable of
action. The cutting diminishes his stature.

Although Albany does assert himself in the fifth act in both texts,
he is much stronger in Q by virtue of the presence of three passages that are not his in F. At his entrance he asserts control over
the situation in both texts with his first speech; Q reads:

> Our very louing sister well be-met
> For this I heare the King is come to his daughter
> With others, whome the rigour of our state
> Forst to crie out, . . .
>
> (V. i. 20–23)[8]

The speech continues in Q but not in F:

> where I could not be honest
> I neuer yet was valiant, for this busines
> It touches vs. as *France* inuades our land
> Not bolds the King, with others whome I feare,
> Most iust and heauy causes make oppose.
>
> (V. i. 23–27)

The inclusion of this passage in Q gives immediate prominence to
the complexity and scrupulousness of Albany's understanding of
the political and moral issues. More important, however, are the
two alterations in the closing moments of the play: at V. iii. 251 Q
assigns to Albany the order "Hast thee for thy life," which F gives to
Edgar; and Q assigns the final four lines to Albany, which again F
gives to Edgar. I shall discuss these changes more fully as I deal
with Edgar, but it is sufficient to point out at this stage that Albany
is in command throughout the last scene in Q while in F he is
considerably effaced at the close.

In both Q and F Edgar presents far more complex problems
than Albany, not least because he is intrinsically a more complex

---

[8] At V. i. 21 F reads, "Sir, this I heard," for "For this I heare."

and difficult character even before textual variations are considered. Edgar's part, which in conflated texts is second only to that of Lear in length,[9] is reduced in size in F, but unlike Albany, Edgar receives some new material which, however it is interpreted, tends to focus attention more precisely upon him.

The differences in Edgar's role between Q and F in the first act are not of major significance: at I. ii. 98–100 Q includes and F omits an exchange between Edmund and Gloucester about Edgar that reveals more about Gloucester's character than Edgar's; F omits Edmund's imitative discourse upon the current crisis and Edgar's ironic reply "How long haue you been a sectary Astronomicall?" (I. ii. 151–57); and F includes a passage not in Q in which Edmund proposes concealing Edgar in his lodging, and recommends going armed, to the surprise of his brother (I. ii. 172–79). More important variations appear in the third act. At III. iv. 37–38 in F (after a stage direction *"Enter Edgar, and Foole,"* which contradicts Kent's speech a few lines later, "What art thou that dost grumble there i'th' straw? Come forth"), Edgar utters a line that Q lacks: "Fathom, and halfe, Fathom and halfe; poore *Tom*"; this offstage cry makes a chilling theatrical introduction to Edgar-as-Tom, and it is moreover the event that, coupled with his entrance, appears to propel Lear finally into madness. Later in the third act F omits material that Q includes. F lacks the trial of Goneril that Lear conducts with the support of Edgar and the Fool (III. vi. 17–56). While F provides the Fool with a new last line in the play, "And Ile go to bed at noone" (III. vi. 88), it omits Kent's tender speech over Lear in Q which begins "Oppressed nature sleepes" (III.vi.100–104). However, very important alterations in this middle section of the play follow immediately; they are F's omission of the soliloquy with which Edgar closes III. vi in Q and F's minor amplification of Edgar's first speech in the fourth act, two speeches that provide the transitions to and from the climactic scene of the blinding of Gloucester. These alterations need to be discussed in the larger context of the character and function of Edgar in the play.

In recent years serious challenges have been made to the traditional conception of Edgar as the good, devoted, abused but patient, loving son. Some of this examination has led to the for-

---

[9] See *Pelican Shakespeare*, p. 31.

mulation of extreme positions in which Edgar has appeared as
almost as culpable and vicious as Edmund, dedication to an ideal of
selfless virtuous support being interpreted as an unconscious psychic violence, a dangerous self-righteousness that must exercise
itself on others. It is unnecessary, however, to censure Edgar so
strongly to accommodate some of the distance that one frequently
feels from him; one may allow him his virtue while still seeing its
weakness. Speaking much in aside and soliloquy, Edgar is distanced theatrically from many of the events of the play. However,
despite his involvement with Lear in the mad scenes, he also
appears at times to be distanced emotionally from the events
around him; his moral commentary reflects his response to the
events, his assessment of his philosophical position in their light.
The problem is that his response is frequently inadequate. As the
play proceeds Edgar is obliged to confront the shallowness of his
rationalizations, and yet much of the time he nevertheless appears
impervious to the new knowledge that is being forced upon him.
He possesses a naively pious and optimistic faith in the goodness of
the world and the justice of the gods, and in his own youthful,
romantic vision of his role in this world of conflict. In his mind his
father's despair will be conquered by his endless encouragement;
the triumphant climax will be the restoration to Gloucester of the
knowledge of his son's existence and readiness to go off to recover
his dukedom for him. The mode of Edgar's thought is Christian
romantic-heroic, in which virtue usually triumphs splendidly. That
it bears little relation to the realities of the universe in which the
play takes place is evident; but it does save Gloucester from abject
misery, and provides incidentally a happy, well-deceived death for
him. We can appreciate Edgar's love and concern for his father,
while doubting the maturity of many of his judgments.

It is in the context of this conception of Edgar, which is appropriate to either text, that I wish to demonstrate the major alterations
in the role. When the soliloquy beginning "When we our betters see
bearing our woes" is spoken at the close of III. vi in Q (III. vi.
105–18), we are aware of Edgar's ability to comment upon the
king's suffering, the power of fellowship, and his capacity to
endure; in F, which lacks these meditations, Edgar has played a
very small part in a rather brief scene, and the play rushes to the
blinding of Gloucester. But F compensates for these cuts by

expanding the speech with which Edgar opens the fourth act in both texts by adding an extra sentence. The speech reads:

> Yet better thus, and knowne to be contemn'd,
> Then still contemn'd and flatter'd, to be worst:
> The lowest, and most deiected thing of Fortune,
> Stands still in esperance, liues not in feare:
> The lamentable change is from the best,
> The worst returnes to laughter.
>
> (IV. i. 1–6)[10]

But F continues:

> Welcome then,
> Thou vnsubstantiall ayre that I embrace:
> The Wretch that thou hast blowne vnto the worst,
> Owes nothing to thy blasts.
>
> (IV. i. 6–9)

And then Gloucester enters. In both texts Edgar expresses the philosophic confidence of the man who has reached the bottom, but in F Edgar speaks still more facilely courageous lines of resolution against fortune just prior to having the inadequacy of his vision exposed by the terrible entrance of his father. What the revision in F achieves is this. The play is shortened and speeded by the loss from III. vi and the opening of IV. i of about fifty-four lines (three minutes of playing time at least). The absence of Edgar's moral meditation from the end of III. vi brings the speech at IV. i. 1 into sharp focus, isolating it more obviously between the blinding and the entrance of Gloucester; in F the two servants do not remain onstage after Cornwall's exit. The additional lines at this point emphasize the hollowness of Edgar's assertions; while the quantity of sententiousness is reduced, its nature is made more emphatically evident. Edgar gains in prominence, ironically enough, by the loss of a speech, and the audience becomes more sharply aware of his character.

The last act reveals major alterations that surpass those briefly described in the discussion of Albany. In both texts Edgar describes the death of his father with rhetorical fullness and elaborate emotional dramatization (V. iii. 181–99). In Q, however, he is given an additional speech of seventeen lines (V. iii. 204–21) only briefly

---

[10] At IV. i. 4 Q reads "experience" for "esperance."

interrupted by Albany, in which he reports his meeting with Kent. The removal of this speech not only speeds the last act by the elimination of material of no immediate importance to the plot, but also reduces the length of the delay between Edmund's "This speech of yours hath mou'd me, / And shall perchance do good" (V. iii. 199–200) and the sending of an officer to Lear. It also diminishes the sense of Edgar as the immature, indulgent man displaying his heroic tale of woe, for in F Albany's command "If there be more, more wofull, hold it in" (V. iii. 202) is obeyed; in Q by contrast Edgar nevertheless continues:

> This would haue seemd a periode to such
> As loue not sorow, but another to amplifie too much,
> Would make much more, and top extreamitie . . .
>
> (V. iii. 204–7)

and the speech reveals Edgar's regard for his own dramatic role in the recent history:

> Whil'st I was big in clamor, came there in a man,
> Who hauing seene me in my worst estate,
> Shund my abhord society, but then finding
> Who twas that so indur'd . . .
>
> (V. iii. 208–11)

F, then, maintains the fundamental nature of Edgar as philosophical agent through the play, but in the last act reduces somewhat his callowness, his easy indulgence of his sensibility in viewing the events through which he is living. In so doing F develops Edgar into a man worthy to stand with the dukes at the close of the play, capable of assuming power.

The elevation of Edgar at the close and relative reduction of Albany that distinguish F from Q can be documented from three other places. At V. iii. 229[11] in Q Edgar says to Albany "Here comes Kent sir," but "Here comes Kent" in F. The transfer of the command "Hast thee for thy life" (V. iii. 251) from Albany in Q to Edgar in F gives Edgar a more active role in the urgent events; indeed, Q may indicate that it is Edgar who is to run. All Edgar's lines after "Hast thee for thy life" are shared by Q and F apart from the last four, which Q assigns to Albany. Though they are partial

[11] This is the Arden placing that follows F; Q places this line in the middle of Albany's next speech at V. iii. 232.

lines at most, they are susceptible of quite different interpretations according to whether Edgar speaks the last lines or not. If one considers Edgar's behavior in Q in the light of his lachrymose speech about Kent and his apparently subordinate role to Albany, he appears to be silenced by Lear's death: initially in Q he cries out "He faints my Lord, my Lord" (V. iii. 311), then appeals to Lear, "Look vp my Lord" (312), only to say after Kent has assured him of the death, "O he is gone indeed" (315), and to fall silent for the rest of the play. By contrast, F omits the "O" in this last statement, and then gives Edgar the last lines. In Q, then, Edgar concludes the play stunned to silence by the reality of Lear's death, a very young man who does not even answer Albany's appeal, "Friends of my soule, you twaine, / Rule in this Realme" (V. iii. 319–20), so that Albany reluctantly but resolutely accepts the obligation to rule: "The waight of this sad time we must obey" (323). This characterization of Edgar is a far cry from the Edgar of F who comes forward as a future ruler when he enables Albany to achieve his objective of not ruling; F's Edgar is a young man of limited perceptions concerning the truth of the world's harsh realities, but one who has borne some of the burdens and appears capable of handling (better than anybody else) the responsibilities that face the survivors.[12]

In summary, Q and F embody two different artistic visions. In Q, Edgar remains an immature young man and ends the play devastated by his experience, while Albany stands as the modest, diffident, but strong and morally upright man. In F Edgar grows into a potential ruler, a well-intentioned, resolute man in a harsh world, while Albany, a weaker man, abdicates his responsibilities. In neither text is the prospect for the country a matter of great optimism, but the vision seems bleaker and darker in F, where the young Edgar, inexperienced in rule, faces the future with little support.

In discussing these two texts I have focused on what seem to me to be the two major issues of the revision; I have not attended to the absence of IV. iii from F, nor to the relatively minor but nev-

---

[12] If this distinction between the presentations of Edgar in the two texts is made, the subtitle of Q makes more than merely conventional sense in its place: "*With the unfortunate life of* Edgar, *sonne* and heire to the Earle of Gloster, and his sullen and assumed humor of TOM of Bedlam."

ertheless significant differences in the speeches of Lear, the Fool, and Kent. However, I submit that this examination of the texts and the implications of their differences for interpretation and for performance make it clear that they must be treated as separate versions of *King Lear*, and that eclecticism cannot be a valid principle in deciding readings. Conflated texts such as are commonly printed are invalid, and should not be used either for production or for interpretation. Though they may give their readers all of "what Shakespeare wrote," they do not give them Shakespeare's play of *King Lear*, but a play created by the craft and imagination of learned scholars, a work that has no justification for its existence. The principle that more is better, that all is good, has no foundation. What we as scholars, editors, interpreters, and servants of the theatrical craft have to accept and learn to live by is the knowledge that we have two plays of *King Lear* sufficiently different to require that all further work on the play be based on either Q or F, but not the conflation of both.

Poetry and the Structure of Belief in *Antony and Cleopatra*

by Janet Adelman

From the first words of the play ("Nay, but"), our reactions have been at issue. We are given judgments that we must simultaneously accept and reject; we are shown the partiality of truth. But finally we are not permitted to stand aside and comment with impunity any more than Enobarbus is: we must choose either to accept or to reject the lovers' versions of themselves and of their death; and our choice will determine the meaning of the play for us. But the choice becomes increasingly impossible to make on the evidence of our reason or our senses. How can we believe in Enobarbus's description of Cleopatra as Venus when we see the boy actor before us? The Antony whom Cleopatra describes in her dream is not the Antony whom we have seen sitting on stage in dejection after Actium or bungling his suicide. Although the lovers die asserting their postmortem reunion, all we see is the dead queen and her women, surrounded by Caesar and his soldiers. The stage action necessarily presents us with one version of the facts, the poetry with another. This is the dilemma inherent in much dramatic poetry; and the more hyperbolical the poetry, the more acute the dilemma. Critics are occasionally tempted to read *Antony and Cleopatra* as a very long poem; but it is essential that we be aware of it as drama at all times. For how can one stage hyperbole? Reading the play, we might imagine Antony a colossus; but what shall we do with the very human-sized Antony who has been before us for several hours? In a sonnet, for instance, an assertion contrary to fact will be true within the poem; standards must be imported from outside the work by which to find the assertions improbable. As Shakespeare points out, not every girl be-sonneted has breasts whiter than snow, despite the assertions of her son-neteer. But a play carries its own refutation within itself: even with the most advanced stage technology, the action and the human actors will undercut these assertions even as they are made. Pre-cisely this tension is at the heart of *Antony and Cleopatra*: we can neither believe nor wholly disbelieve in the claims made by the poetry.

The poetry of the last two acts is generally acknowledged as the sleight-of-hand by which Shakespeare transforms our sympathies toward the lovers, in despite of the evidence of our reason and our senses. Although even Caesar speaks in blank verse, the language of most richness and power is in the service of the lovers: it is the language in which Enobarbus creates Cleopatra as Venus and the lovers assert the value of their love and their death. In this play, the nay-sayers may have reason and justice on their side; but as Plato suspected when he banished poetry from his republic, reason and justice are no match for poetry. The appeal to mere reason will not always affect fallen man; according to Renaissance theorists, it was precisely the power of poetry to *move*, occasionally against the dic-tates of all reason, that made it at once most dangerous and most fruitful. And modern critics are as wary of the power of poetry as their predecessors: the poetry in *Antony and Cleopatra* is almost always praised, but the praise frequently coincides with the suspi-cion that it has somehow taken unfair advantage of us by befud-dling our clear moral judgment. It is that doubtless delightful but nonetheless dubious means by which the lovers are rescued from our condemnation at the last moment, rather as Lancelot rescues Guinevere from her trial by fire. We are pleased but suspect that strictest justice has not been done. If it is true that Shakespeare uses the poetry to dazzle our moral sense and undo the structure of criticism in the play, then we may find *Antony and Cleopatra* satisfy-ing as a rhetorical showcase, but we cannot admire the play as a whole. It is refreshing to find this charge made explicit by G. B. Shaw, who clearly enjoys expressing his contempt for a poet who finds it necessary to rescue his lovers from our moral judgment by means of a rhetorical trick:

Shakespear's Antony and Cleopatra must needs be as intolerable to the true Puritan as it is vaguely distressing to the ordinary healthy citizen, because after giving a faithful picture of the soldier broken down by debauchery, & the typical wanton in whose arms such men perish, Shakespear finally strains all his huge command of rhetoric & stage pathos to give a theatrical sublimity to the wretched end of the business, & to persuade foolish spectators that the world was well lost by the twain. Such falsehood is not to be borne except by the real Cleopatras & Antonys (they are to be found in every public house) who would no doubt be glad enough to be transfigured by some poet as immortal lovers. Woe to the poet who stoops to such folly! . . . When your Shakespears and Thackerays huddle up the matter at the end by killing somebody & covering your eyes with the undertaker's handkerchief, duly onioned with some pathetic phrase . . . I have no respect for them at all: such maudlin tricks may impose on tea-house drunkards, not on me.[1]

The final poetry, detached from character and situation, does indeed give us the glorified vision of love that Shaw mistrusted, a vision not wholly consistent with the merely human Antony and Cleopatra, though Antony is far more than a debauchee and Cleopatra anything but typical, no matter how wanton. But the poetry is not a rhetorical Lancelot. Its assertions and the problems they present to our skepticism have been inherent throughout: and if the poetry strains our credulity toward the end, the strain itself is a necessary part of our experience. Are the visions asserted by the poetry mere fancies, or are they "nature's piece 'gainst fancy"? Precisely this tension between belief and disbelief has been essential from the start. When the lovers first come on stage, very much in the context of an unfriendly Roman judgment, they announce the validity of their love in a hyperbolical poetry which contrasts sharply with Philo's equally hyperbolical condemnation. Here, at the very beginning, two attitudes are set in juxtaposition by the use of two equally impossible images which appeal to two very different modes of belief. Philo uses hyperbole as *metaphor:* "his captain's heart / . . . is become the bellows and the fan / To cool a gipsy's lust" (I. i. 6–10). This is the deliberate exaggeration which moral indignation excites; it does not in any sense call for our literal belief. The hyperbolical metaphor is morally apt, and that is all. The Roman metaphor is carefully delineated as metaphor: it never pretends to

---

[1] Bernard Shaw, *Three Plays for Puritans* (London, 1930), pp. xxx–xxxi.

a validity beyond the metaphoric. But what of the lovers? "Then
must thou needs find out new heaven, new earth" (I. i. 17); "Let
Rome in Tiber melt" (I. i. 33). Strictly speaking, these hyperboles
are not metaphor at all. Antony's words assert his access to a hyperbolical world where such things actually happen, a world beyond
the reach of metaphor. They claim, like Cleopatra's dream, to be in
the realm of nature, not of fancy. His words do not give us the
protection of regarding them merely as apt metaphors: they make
their claim as literal action. We may choose to disbelieve their
claim; but in doing so, we are rejecting a version of reality, not the
validity of a metaphor. And precisely this kind of assertion will
become more insistent—and more improbable—as the play progresses.

The poetry of the final acts should not take us unaware: if at the
last moment it surfaces, like the dolphin who shows his back above
the element he lives in, the whole of the play and a good deal of
Shakespeare's career should have prepared us for its appearance.
The validity of the imaginative vision as it is asserted in the poetry
is a part of Shakespeare's subject in *Antony and Cleopatra*. But the
play is not therefore "about" the vision of the poet: we are presented with lovers creating the image of their love, not with poets
poetizing. For the association of love with imagination or fancy is
one of Shakespeare's most persistent themes. Love in Shakespeare
almost always creates its own imaginative versions of reality; and it
is almost always forced to test its version against the realities
acknowledged by the rest of the world. Theseus in *Midsummer
Night's Dream* tells us that the lover, like the lunatic and the poet, is
of imagination all compact (V. i. 7–8): in that play, "fancy" is generally used as synonymous with "love." We remember Juliet, valiantly
making day into night in spite of the lark that sings so out of tune.
Imagination is essential to love; but if it is totally unmoored to
reality, it becomes love's greatest threat. Othello's love will turn to
hate as Iago poisons his imagination. . . .

Troilus and Cressida is Shakespeare's most horrifying vision of
untested imagination in love. In that sense, it is a necessary coun-
terpoise both to the earlier comedies and to *Antony and Cleopatra*.
For *Antony and Cleopatra* is *Troilus and Cressida* revisited: if *Troilus
and Cressida* portrays desire as a slave to limit, *Antony and Cleopatra*

asserts the power of desire to transcend limits; if Troilus's subjection to mere imagination nearly destroys him, Cleopatra's imagination of her Antony virtually redeems them both. Later, in the romances, the desires of the lovers will usually become their realities: the art itself is nature, and imagination purely redemptive. *Troilus* and the romances are in this sense at opposite ends of the scale: in *Troilus and Cressida,* our credulity is at the mercy of our skepticism, as Troilus himself will discover; in the romances, our skepticism is banished by an act of total poetic faith. But *Antony and Cleopatra* is poised in a paradoxical middle region in which skepticism and credulity must be balanced. In this sense, the perspectives of both *Troilus and Cressida* and the romances are included within *Antony and Cleopatra*; and it is precisely because of this inclusiveness that imagination can emerge triumphant.

The process of testing the imagination is essential to the assertion of its validity: for only through an exacting balance of skepticism and assent can it prove true. And more than any other play, *Antony and Cleopatra* insists on both our skepticism and our assent. For it is simultaneously the most tough-minded and the most triumphant of the tragedies, and it is necessarily both at once. Throughout, Shakespeare disarms criticism by allowing the skeptics their full say: the whole play is in effect a test of the lovers' visions of themselves. Cleopatra herself presents the most grotesquely skeptical view of her own play:

> . . . The quick comedians
> Extemporally will stage us, and present
> Our Alexandrian revels: Antony
> Shall be brought drunken forth, and I shall see
> Some squeaking Cleopatra boy my greatness
> I' the posture of a whore.
>
> (V. ii. 215–20)

Once she has spoken, this Roman version of her greatness becomes untenable; we know that Shakespeare's *Antony and Cleopatra* is not an item in Caesar's triumph. It is only in the context of "Nay, but" that we can answer "yes": if the imaginative affirmations were not so persistently questioned, they could not emerge triumphant. The extreme of skepticism itself argues for affirmation: and here the affirmations are no less extreme than the skepticism. Throughout the play, we are not permitted to see Cleopatra merely as a fallen woman: we are asked to see her in the posture of a whore. And when the time has come for affirmation, we are asked to believe not in the probable but in the palpably impossible: not that the lovers are worthy though misguided, but that they are semidivine creatures whose love has somehow managed to escape the bonds of time and space, and even of death. Whore or goddess, strumpet's fool or colossus: the play allows us no midpoint. After all the doubt which has been central to our experience, we are asked to participate in a secular act of faith. This is the final contrariety that the play demands of us: that the extreme of skepticism itself must be balanced by an extreme of assent.

When Cleopatra somewhat coyly asks poor Dolabella whether or not there could be such a man as the Antony she dreamed of, Dolabella denies the possibility of her dream. Her answer is immediate: "You lie up to the hearing of the gods" (V. ii. 95). The entire play has led us to the point where we, as well as Cleopatra, can find Dolabella's denial of the dream at least as suspect as the dream itself. In what sense do we come to believe in the lovers' assertions, and how are we led to this belief?

One of the paths of assent open to us is that which would see the lovers' paradoxical and hyperbolical assertions as accurate metaphors for psychological facts, as descriptions of the world as it appears to the lovers. Antony says, "Fall not a tear, I say, one of them rates / All that is won and lost" (III. xi. 69–70). If one of Cleopatra's tears is worth the world to Antony, then one tear *is* worth the world—insofar as we agree to see the world from his perspective. What we think of the bargain is, for the moment, irrelevant. In these matters there need be no "objective correlative": if Hamlet's situation drives him to despair, then it is for him a desperate situation. But does "His legs bestrid the ocean" mean only, "As far as Cleopatra was concerned, Antony's legs bestrid the ocean"? Do we accept the lovers' assertions only as evaluative truths, only as we would perforce accept the truth of the statement, "It looks red to me" (even though the object looks very blue to us)? Is Cleopatra's dream only one more judgment in the long series of partial and erroneous judgments in the play? I think not. To believe in these assertions only as psychological metaphors is Philo's Roman way and does not seem adequate to our experience. "Cleopatra dies at one with Antony in her love for him" simply does not do justice to our sense of affirmation when she says, "Husband, I come"; we cannot translate the impossible statement of fact into any possible statement of emotion without losing its force. As Cleopatra's dream of Antony is in the realm of nature, not of fancy, so these assertions leave the realm of fancy and begin to claim our belief as fact.

To the extent that we are engaged with the protagonist, his judgment will be our judgment; and to that extent it will be dramatic fact. Throughout most of *Antony and Cleopatra*, we are not permitted to become wholly engaged with the protagonists. In fact, most of the structural devices of the play prevent our engagement. . . . But toward the end of the play the dramatic technique changes radically. We tend more often to accept the lovers' evaluation of themselves, to take them at their word, because we are more often permitted to identify ourselves with them. The entire structure of framing commentary and of shifts of scene had forced us to remain relatively detached from them; after Act IV, Scene xii, it tends to disappear. No one intervenes between us and the lovers; there are no radical and disjunctive shifts in perspective. The final scene of the play is almost twice as long as the next longest scene (364 lines as opposed to 201 in Act III, Scene xiii): and it is Cleopatra's scene virtually from beginning to end. For once, she is allowed to undercut Caesar by her commentary: "He words me, girls, he words me" (V. ii.190). The Clown interrupts Cleopatra, but she turns his presence to her own account: his banter serves as an impetus to her immortal longings. Though he qualifies the solemnity of her death, he does not provide the radical shift in perspective that we have come to expect in this play. We can here take her as seriously as she takes herself, participate with her in the tragic perspective. The critical structure drops away from Antony in Act IV, Scene xiv, in much the same manner. And as we are permitted to become involved with the lovers, their evaluations tend to take on the status of emotional fact even in despite of the literal fact.

If the dramatic structure now permits us to become engaged with the lovers, it also works to give us the feeling of assent in spite of all logic. For most of the play, we have been subjected to the wear and tear of numerous short scenes, to the restless shifts of perspective. Now, as the lovers leave the world of business, we are permitted to rest. The scenes become longer and more leisurely;

the entire pace of the play slows. In some ways, the rhythm of the play suggests the rhythm of the sexual act itself, especially in the quiescent melting of its end. And as the lovers come together, even the quality of the language changes. The word "come," used so frequently by the lovers as they prepare to die, suggests that death is a reunion, not a separation—a suggestion not at all mitigated by the secondary sexual meaning of the word.[2] But the sound of the word may be as significant as its meaning. We move from the complexity, rapidity, and lightness of "Our separation so abides and flies, / That thou, residing here, goes yet with me; / And I, hence fleeting, here remain with thee" (I. iii. 102–4) to the simple slowness of "I come, my queen" (IV. xiv. 50). The restless tension in the language seems to be replaced by a new ease. If we participate in the lovers' sense of release from life, it is at least partly because we are ourselves released from the strain which action and language had imposed on us earlier.

At the same time, we are released from the doubts and scruples which have hedged us in throughout the play. Ultimately our sense of assent probably comes from the fact that the psychological roots of the play are our psychological roots too. Insofar as *Antony and Cleopatra* concerns overflow, the dissolution of boundaries, bisexuality, and the association of both death and sexual love with loss of self and ecstatic union, it touches many of us where we live. One of the most difficult problems in love of any kind is to strike a balance between the desire to give oneself wholly to another and the desire to keep oneself wholly intact. We have had both sides of this conflict exacerbated in us as we watch the play: and most of the time, the spokesmen for the terrors of dissolution and loss of self have had the upper hand. Antony's fear that he is losing his visible shape may come dangerously close to home: for it is to some extent the fear of everyone in love. When this fear at last becomes desire, when mere loss of self is transformed into "I come, my queen," we are bound to feel the release as well as Antony. As the lovers die asserting that death is union, they temporarily resolve the tension for us; and in that sense, their resolution is bound to be ours.

This sense of resolution prepares us, I think, for the leap of faith necessary at the end of the play; and if we are given the feeling of assent, the play supports our feeling with a logic of its own.

[2] The number of times the lovers use the word within the space of a few lines is astonishing. See IV. xiv. 50–101; IV. xv. 29–90; V. ii. 47; V. ii. 286–322.

Antony's assertion that he and Cleopatra will meet in Elysium has sometimes been regarded as evidence of his delusion-unto-death; but if it is a delusion, it must in some sense be our delusion too. The play has throughout insisted on the possibility of the impossible: Caesar is in fact at Toryne, however impossible; the Clown echoes the particular impossibility of a death which is not final in his tale of the immortal woman who reports how she died of the biting of the worm. Throughout, we have been told that death may be sleep. At Enobarbus's death, the Roman guardsmen assume that he is asleep; even when he does not awaken, they think that "he may recover yet" (IV. ix. 33). Even the crocodile "transmigrates" instead of dying. Cleopatra faints when Antony dies, and Iras assumes that "she's dead too" (IV. xv. 69). Her recovery gives us a precedent and a dramatic image for immortality.

Antony's impossibility is in some sense confirmed by Cleopatra's independent expression of the same impossibility: "I am again for Cydnus, / To meet Mark Antony" (V. ii. 227–28). These may be shared delusions, but they nonetheless create in us the sense that the lovers have grown together in death. The lovers are apart or acting at cross-purposes during most of the play: despite the verbal assertions of love and union, the sense we get is of their disunity. But after Antony dies, the feeling of union is gradually created, not only through Cleopatra's resolve to join him in death (as everyone has noted, she is not entirely resolute) but also through the dramatic structure. She begins to echo his phrases as though the lovers were in fact becoming one. But the lovers are not the only ones who assert their impossible reunion. Toward the end of the play, the possibility of the impossible is repeatedly confirmed by a striking technique: the assertions are reiterated by the most unexpected allies. In the end, the lovers do not need to rely on each other for support in their assertions: for their hyperbolical assertions are echoed by characters not ordinarily prone to the hyperbolical vision. Cleopatra finds in Antony's death the signs of the great Apocalypse: "darkling stand the varying shore o' the world"; "The soldier's pole is fall'n." But even the guardsmen greet Antony's suicide as an apocalyptic event:

> *Second Guard.*   The star is fall'n.
> *First Guard.* And time is at his period.
>   (IV. xiv. 106–7)

Both independently see Antony as a fallen star; we need not depend on the testimony of his mistress alone. Their reaction authenticates her hyperbolical vision. The lovers' assertions that death is a sleep in which they will be reunited are authenticated by the same means. Antony senses in Cleopatra's death the coming of night: "Unarm, Eros, the long day's task is done, / And we must sleep" (IV. xiv. 35–36). While she lived, she was "thou day o' the world" (IV. viii. 13); at her death, only darkness is left. Iras urges her mistress to sleep in strikingly similar language: "Finish, good lady, the bright day is done, / And we are for the dark" (V. ii. 192–93). For Cleopatra, the asp is the baby "that sucks the nurse asleep" (V. ii. 309). Antony's sleep will permit him to meet Cleopatra where souls do couch on flowers; Cleopatra calls for "such another sleep" (V. ii. 77) to repossess her dream of Antony. At the last moment in the play, even Octavius hints that perhaps death is a sleep which will permit them to be reunited: "she looks like sleep, / As she would catch another Antony / In her strong toil of grace" (V. ii. 344–46). The repeated assertion from unexpected perspectives forces us to consider that, despite all probability, the impossible may be true.

After Actium, Thidias bestows some excellent Roman advice on Cleopatra:

> Wisdom and fortune combating together,
> If that the former dare but what it can,
> No chance may shake it.
>
> (III. xiii. 79–81)

Roman wisdom consists in confining oneself to the possible; but Egyptian wisdom always dares more than what it can. Antony may be a strumpet's fool (I. i. 13), but Octavius is after all only fortune's knave (V. ii. 3). Cleopatra tells us as she lifts Antony into the monument that wishers were ever fools. Perhaps so: but there are many kinds of folly.[3] Enobarbus in his Roman wisdom knows that "The loyalty well held to fools does make / Our faith mere folly" (III. xiii.

---

[3] When Charmian advises Cleopatra to cross Antony in nothing, she teaches "like a fool" (I. iii. 10); though age gives Cleopatra freedom from childishness, it cannot give her freedom from folly (I. iii. 57). Antony leaves her, deaf to her "unpitied folly" (I. iii. 98).

42–43); yet his refusal to abide by his folly finally kills him. For despite the judgment of our reason, man is most noble when he is most foolish: when Enobarbus has obeyed his reason, he feels himself "alone the villain of the earth" (IV. vi. 30). Antony in his foolish passion kills himself at the news of Cleopatra's death; but his folly insures his nobility. Wishers and fools may see more deeply than men of reason: the Soothsayer who sees a little into nature's infinite book of secrecy (I. ii. 9) is a fool:

> *Charmian.* . . . prithee, how many boys and wenches must I have?
> *Soothsayer.* If every of your wishes had a womb,
>   And fertile every wish, a million.
> *Charmian.* Out, fool! I forgive thee for a witch.
>   (I. ii. 35–39)

Cleopatra, like the Soothsayer, is both witch and wisher: and not all her wishes are fertile. But in the end, her folly is the folly of vision; and the whole play moves us toward the acknowledgment of its truth.

Throughout, the play has insisted on the unreliability of all report and the uncertainty of truth itself . . . Is Mardian's false report false after all? It becomes true after the fact when Cleopatra does kill herself for Antony. And what of the Clown's witness for the immortal worm, "a very honest woman, but something given to lie, as a woman should not do, but in the way of honesty" (V. ii. 251–53)? Not all judgments are equally verifiable: Cleopatra's dream of Antony is not susceptible of proof in the way that Pompey's prediction of his whereabouts is. The play teaches us that there are different modes of belief for different kinds of statement. It forces us to acknowledge a fundamental paradox of the human imagination: that occasionally truth can be told only in lies. Cleopatra's dream is her lie in the way of honesty; it is the central paradox of the play that we must both deny it and find it true. Like the other assertions of the impossible, it remains in the unverifiable domain of the true lie. And however impervious to logic this domain is, it occasionally comes closer to our experience than the tidy categories of logic can. There are lies and dreams that are more true than truth itself; the hyperbolical version of their story which the lovers present at the end of the play is one of these lies. The poetry in which the lovers create their version of the story may be only true lies; but the paradoxical true lie may be the only sort of truth available to us in this world. . . .

In *Antony and Cleopatra,* when the poetry conflicts with the literal situation, it nonetheless can make some claim to our belief. Cleopatra's dream has a certain validity, although it is a dream; in the romances, the dream is usually revealed as the reality. For the metaphors of the earlier plays become the literal actions of the romances. Lear says to Kent in the storm,

> . . . where the greater malady is fix'd
> The lesser is scarce felt. Thou'ldst shun a bear;
> But if thy flight lay toward the roaring sea,
> Thou'ldst meet the bear i' th' mouth.
> (*King Lear* III. iv. 8–11)

Lear expresses the most extreme situation imaginable here by the metaphor; but in *The Winter's Tale,* precisely this metaphor will become the literal action. Antigonus will be caught between the bear and the raging sea and will face the bear in the mouth. In *Hamlet,* we are told about the flights of angels that will sing the prince to his rest; in *The Tempest,* we see Ariel singing Ferdinand to his rest. Pericles hears the music of the spheres and sleeps: in his dream, Diana appears and reveals the real pattern behind his apparently random wanderings. His dream is not a poetic assertion or a metaphor but a vision which is literally true: for Diana herself appears on stage before us. We are given momentary access to a truth usually concealed; the miraculous takes place before our eyes. The impossible is no longer a matter of poetic assertion: it actually takes place on stage. When Hermione steps down from her pedestal in *The Winter's Tale,* the impossible has been achieved. In these plays, the symbolic pattern asserted in the poetry takes precedence over any considerations of realism: each play dares far more than what it can. No one would think of questioning Hermione about her perverse sadomasochistic desire to torment Leontes by remaining hidden until Perdita is found or about her living arrangements during that period; nor in fact do we take the rationalization that she has remained hidden very seriously. We know that she has come back to life. We do not, that is to say, seek to explain the impossible away. Instead, we gladly accept the impossibility for the sake of the symbolic pattern: she must remain hidden until her daughter has grown up and returned; only thus can the validity of the natural process of regeneration be asserted.

In both romance and tragedy, then, the poetry and the action are in accord: in tragedy, the poetry is usually at the service of the action; in romance, the action is usually at the service of the poetry. *Antony and Cleopatra* stands between the two: poetry and action conflict; and each makes its own assertions and has its own validity. We do not literally believe in such poetic assertions as the postmortem reunion, and we certainly do not see them achieved on stage; but at moments the symbolic pattern of reunion begins to take precedence over any literal-minded questions about how precisely the lovers plan to be together. At these moments, the modes of tragedy and romance are competing; and we must be willing to acknowledge the claims of both. At the end of *Antony and Cleopatra*, death bolts up change for Cleopatra, and she becomes almost statuelike in her attainment of stasis: "I am marble-constant: now the fleeting moon / No planet is of mine" (V. ii. 239–40). Octavia is subject to Cleopatra's scorn for being more "a statue, than a breather" (III. iii. 21) in life; but Cleopatra will attain her eternity by becoming statuesque in death. This transformation is emblematic of the power accorded art in this play: the poetic assertion itself will confer a kind of eternity. In *The Winter's Tale*, art or poetic assertion becomes a literal fact of nature: the statue moves from her pedestal and comes to life. And in *Antony and Cleopatra* the art does not remain lifeless: the poetic assertion moves into the realm of nature. Cleopatra overpictures the mere picture of Venus; her Antony is nature's piece 'gainst fancy. The art here is not pure nature, as it is in *The Winter's Tale*: it is after all the *imagination* of an Antony which is nature's piece. The assertion remains poised in the middle region, where we can neither believe it nor disbelieve it: and finally this balance is essential to the whole.

If the lovers create themselves as immortals and demand that we participate in their creation, they are nonetheless subject to the ironic vision which has informed the play throughout. In the course of the play, we may find ourselves moved from a position of detachment to a position of engagement: but in the totality of the experience, one perspective does not cancel the other out. If our belief is essential, so is our doubt. But what do we make of a play that strives so hard to command our belief, but only in the context of our doubt? What, finally, is the "meaning" of *Antony and Cleopatra*? Perhaps that no one "meaning" can account for any event in the knot intrinsicate of life. Literary criticism frequently assumes that the knot can be untied: that every work will have a single explicable meaning. But this assumption may be counter to the process of Shakespeare's art, which usually functions to suggest that our experiences are larger than the intellectual formulations in which we attempt to embody them. Norman Rabkin eloquently warns against the "fallacy of misplaced concreteness":

> [Critics assume that] what can be brought by self-contained argument to a satisfying conclusion is what is worth discussing, and responses that don't work into the argument must be discounted. . . . But it is time to recall that all intellection is reductive, and that the closer an intellectual system comes to full internal consistency and universality of application . . . the more obvious become the exclusiveness of its preoccupations and the limitations of its value. . . . In fact, the ultimate irreducibility to a schema may be the hallmark of the work of art and the source of its power.[4]

No one interpretation of *Antony and Cleopatra* can hope to account for the complexity of its experience: certainly no interpretation which demands that it conform to a purely tragic model. To overlook the elements of comedy and romance in *Antony and Cleopatra* and demand that it conform entirely to our expectations of tragedy is in effect to request the crocodile to confine his activities to either land or water and stop perpetually wandering between the two: it is a crime against the nature of the beast. Comedy, tragedy, and romance are here distinct versions of life: limited and human attempts to understand the nature of an action which remains essentially baffling. Each will inevitably find significance in different and partial aspects of experience: none in the whole. But the play will not allow us partial vision: as *Antony and Cleopatra* moves among several perspectives, it suggests the futility and the validity of each; only in its generic impurity can it embrace the whole.

The fluidity of interpretation characteristic of the Renaissance allows all the variety of the play to be held in suspension at once,

4 "Meaning and Shakespeare," in *Acta of the World Shakespeare Congress*, ed. Clifford Leech (1972).

with no straining after singleness and certainty of meaning. In general, the Renaissance was more at home with diversity than we are: the sensibility which nourished the fruitful confusions of Renaissance syncretism has been destroyed by the triumph of the scientific intellect. Underlying syncretism is the conviction that there is one essential truth which may be embodied in apparently contradictory ways—a conviction wholly alien to our assumption that opposites are irreconcilable. We want the play to conform tidily to our system: Rome or Egypt, Reason or Passion, Public or Private. But in fact the play achieves a fluidity of possibility far more akin to our actual experience than any of our systems can be. As Maynard Mack says of the play,

> To such questions, *Antony and Cleopatra*, like life itself, gives no clear-cut answers. . . . Those who would have it otherwise, who are "hot for certainties in this our life," as Meredith phrased it, should turn to other authors than Shakespeare, and should have been born into some other world than this.[5]

If an act of criticism can be imagined as a struggle between the critic and the author, then it must be conceded that the author has won, hands down. For this play achieves its most stunning effects with an ease which leaves criticism gasping behind: "By Isis, I will give thee bloody teeth" (I. v. 70); "Pity me, Charmian, / But do not speak to me" (II. v. 118–19); "No more a soldier" (IV. xiv. 42); "Husband, I come" (V. ii. 286). Finally, there is only one conclusion:

> Kneel down, kneel down, and wonder.
>
> (II. ii. 19) .

5 "Introduction" to *Antony and Cleopatra* (Baltimore: Pelican, 1959), p. 23.

Shakespeare's Last Tragic Heroes

by G. K. Hunter

The word which most clearly leads the modern eye straight from *Lear* to the Last Plays is the word "reconciliation." *Lear* is seen as the greatest of the tragedies because it not only strips and reduces and assaults human dignity, but also because it shows with the greatest force and detail the process of restoration by which humanity can recover from this degradation. Lear is exiled from his throne, his friends, his dependents, his family, even from his own reason and his own identity:

> Does any here know me? This is not Lear:
> Does Lear walk thus? speak thus? Where are his eyes? . . .
> Who is it that can tell me who I am?
>
> (I. iv. 255)

But what is lost on one side of madness and exile is seen to become unimportant when set against what is discoverable on the further shore:

> We two alone will sing like birds i' th' cage . . .
> And take upon's the mystery of things
> As if we were God's spies.

When Lear leaves the warmth, the society, the "civilisation" of Gloucester's castle he might seem to be leaving behind him all of the little that is left to make life bearable. But the retreat into the isolated darkness of his own mind is also a descent into the seed-bed of a new life; for the individual mind is seen here as the place from which a man's most important qualities and relationships draw the whole of their potential. Lear continues to assert his

"Shakespeare's Last Tragic Heroes," by G. K. Hunter. In J. R. Brown and B. Harris, *The Later Shakespeare*, Stratford-upon-Avon Studies No. 8 (London: Edward Arnold Publishers Ltd., and New York: Holmes and Meier, 1966.) Reprinted by permission.

innermost perceptions (that justice is a word with meaning, that
there is an order in nature, broken by ingratitude and immorality),
and continues to do so even when it is only through madness that
he can pursue the tenor of his own significance, when it is only in
this context that he can set at naught the palpable success of
opposite views. But by preserving these "mad" assumptions the
hero is, in fact, preserving the substance of a moral life, of which
dignity and social acceptance are only the shadows.

Lear stands on the edge of his exile and states his vision of what
he sees to be involved:

> . . . But for true need—
> You heavens, give me that patience, patience I need.
> You see me here, you gods, a poor old man,
> As full of grief as age; wretched in both.
> If it be you that stirs these daughters' hearts
> Against their father, fool me not so much
> To bear it tamely; touch me with noble anger,
> And let not women's weapons, water-drops,
> Stain my man's cheeks!
>   (II. iv. 269)

The hero here sees himself as an inextricable part of a universal
order. What has happened to him is no less involved in the divine
dispensation than are his own feelings. The speech is one of a
convulsive series of efforts to *understand* what has happened, in
terms that relate to his assumptions, an effort that drives him
through madness to the strange hushed acceptance that has been
thought to reappear only in the Last Plays.

The same emphasis on his own complicity appears in the first
scene on the heath:

> Let the great gods
> That keep this dreadful pudder o'er our heads,
> Find out their enemies now. Tremble, thou wretch,
> That hast within thee undivulgèd crimes
> Unwhipp'd of justice. Hide thee, thou bloody hand;
> Thou perjur'd, and thou simular man of virtue
> That art incestuous; caitiff, to pieces shake,
> That under covert and convenient seeming
> Hast practis'd on man's life. Close pent-up guilts,
> Rive your concealing continents, and cry
> These dreadful summoners grace. I am a man
> More sinn'd against than sinning.
>   (III. ii. 49)

The last two lines of this great plea for justice allow that Lear is himself a man of sin; what they cry for is not revenge so much, but a fairer distribution of punishment, so that Lear's condition on the heath may find its echo in the punishment of the hypocrites, and so be recognized as an inevitable part of the condition of man. Lear in exile absorbs humanity, and assimilates it to his own condition, rather than (as one might expect) rejecting it.

With this in mind one may look at another exile speech, from a play that has been called "the still-born twin of *Lear*"[1]—*Timon of Athens*:

> Piety and fear,
> Religion to the gods, peace, justice, truth,
> Domestic awe, night-rest, and neighbourhood,
> Instruction, manners, mysteries, and trades,
> Degrees, observances, customs and laws,
> Decline to your confounding contraries
> And let confusion live. Plagues incident to men,
> Your potent and infectious fevers heap
> On Athens, ripe for stroke. . . . Breath infect breath,
> That their society, as their friendship, may
> Be merely poison! Nothing I'll bear from thee
> But nakedness, thou detestable town!
> (IV. i. 15)

Timon outside Athens' walls fixes his gaze not on his own condition, seen as a part of a universal evil, but on the evil society of Athens, seen as radically distinct from the self who is leaving it. Lear's speeches show anger and self-pity of course, but his self-regard does not explain all the sentiments that appear in them; they are not merely documents of a desperate mind; there is also a genuine insight into an objective reality. Timon's sentiments, on the other hand, do not tell us anything very penetrating about Athens. Lear's effort to understand makes his vision more complex; Timon's hatred merely simplifies. His mind remains so monomaniacally fixed in hatred of society that it is obviously as dependent on Athens now as it was in the old days of acceptance. The mind in exile is not here a point of refuge and new growth; Timon remains the creature of his society, only maimed by his inability to accept it.

---

[1] J. Dover Wilson, *The Essential Shakespeare* (1932), p. 131.

This difference between the exile speeches of Lear and Timon is symptomatic of a difference between the two plays; *Timon* does not explore the condition of the outcast as symbolic of basic humanity, but only shows the outcast *set against* his society; the change is even characteristic of a difference between the tragedies which lead up to *Lear* and those which lead down on the other side of the watershed. The tragedies normally thought of as following *Lear*—*Timon, Macbeth, Coriolanus, Antony and Cleopatra*—are all in some sense plays of exile; there is an obvious physical exile in *Timon* and *Coriolanus*, and a more complex psychological exile from social normality in *Macbeth* and *Antony*. And all of them are plays of exile in the *Timon* rather than the *Lear* sense, for in none does the individual hero succeed in creating a new world of value inside himself, finding the point of growth which will absorb and transmute the world as it is. The temporizing and compromising society is rejected, but the rejection leaves the hero maimed and incomplete. There is no sense in which Lear (or Hamlet or Othello, for that matter) is diminished by his failure to accept integration into society; but there is a real sense in which this is true of the later heroes.

The whole behaviour of Timon shows the curious paradox of the man, superlatively endowed and favoured by Fortune, who thinks that it is his privilege to move through society like an earthly god:

> He moved among us, as a muttering king,
> Magnificent, would move among his hinds.[2]

He dispenses largesse with an open, undiscriminating hand; he refuses reward; he never counts the cost. It is certainly magnificent; but it is also inhuman. The word *inhumanity* is no doubt merely appropriate to a god, and can be seen as a proper part of his praise; but when used of Timon, a man, the word can only be pejorative:

> For bounty, that makes gods, does still mar men.
> (IV. ii. 41)

And this paradox applies equally in both halves of the play. For Timon the indiscriminate hater of men has the same hunger for the absolute as Timon the indiscriminate lover. If we recoil from the inhumanity of the former we must also recoil from the latter.

The censure that I see aimed at Timon's indiscriminateness seems to be paralleled by a similar censure aimed at the Senate. The Senate refuses to allow particular cases or to see any mitigating circumstances in the crime of Alcibiades's anonymous friend. With Angelo-like incapacity to discriminate law from justice, they rest on the assertion, "We are for law," and banish Alcibiades for questioning this. But at the end of the play, when they themselves are the victims, they take an opposite view:

> We were not all unkind, nor all deserve
> The common stroke of war. . . .
> . . . All have not offended;
> For those that were, it is not square to take,
> On those that are, revenge: crimes, like lands,
> Are not inherited . . . Like a shepherd
> Approach the fold and cull th' infected forth,
> But kill not all together.
>
> (V. iv. 21)

Alcibiades, and the play as a whole, accepts the plea; he makes his victory an occasion for compromise:

> I will use the olive with my sword,
> Make war breed peace, make peace stint war, make each
> Prescribe to other, as each other's leech.
>
> (V. iv. 82)

But in the very same speech we have his appreciation of the magnificence of Timon who never learned to compromise. The paradox of an absoluteness which simultaneously exalts and maims the hero remains unresolved at the end of the play.

The life of Alcibiades, who fled and conspired against his country, provides a natural bridge between Timon, who forecast his career (as Plutarch tells us), and Coriolanus, who formed his Roman "parallel." Certainly Shakespeare's *Coriolanus* provides the obvious instance of exile and hatred to be compared with that in *Timon*. And, again, the speech spoken at the point of exile serves to focus the attitude of the hero:

> You common cry of curs, whose breath I hate
> As reek o' th' rotten fens, whose loves I prize
> As the dead carcasses of unburied men

That do corrupt my air—I banish you.
        . . . Despising
For you the city, thus I turn my back;
There is a world elsewhere.

                                        (III. iii. 122)

The gesture is magnificent, but the same reservation still applies: it
is inhuman, or rather anti-human. The "world elsewhere" of Coriolanus does not turn out to be in the least like Lear's world of
introspective anguish and revaluation; it is only the same Roman
political world, at a certain geographical remove, and equally resistant to the monomaniac individual. And however proud that individual, he continues to need a populace, a city, that accepts his
dominance. *Coriolanus* makes quite clear what is only implicit in
Timon: the political nature of the scrutiny to which these later
heroes are subjected. The aspirations of Hamlet, Othello, and Lear
relate centrally to their families; their principal effort is to comprehend and adjust the strains and tensions arising in that context; the
wider sphere of politics is present only as a background.[3] But the
difficulties of the later heroes involve organized society in a much
more direct way: Macbeth, Coriolanus, Antony all feel the pressure
to pursue a political course which runs against their natural indi-
vidualities. Moreover the "family life" of Coriolanus, as of Macbeth
or Antony, is only a particular aspect of this general social pressure.
Volumnia, the type of the Roman matron, sees home as a parade-
ground for training in leadership; the pressure of her love is always
exercised for a political end. Indeed the play shows a paucity of
relationships which are entirely private in intention. One might
indeed allow Virgilia to be unswayed by public interests; but it is
notorious that Virgilia is the most ineffectual character in the play.
There is no evidence that her love is any more listened to than that
of Flavius the steward in *Timon*, who is dismissed as statistically
meaningless, too exceptional to count; in the political or social
contexts of these plays the humble and disinterested love of the

---

[3] Brutus might seem to be an exception to the division being attempted here: he is
an "early" hero, whose dramatic life is concerned with politics and hardly at all with
family. But Brutus cannot justly be assimilated into the later group of heroes: he is
indeed made the opposite to Caesar, as a man whose real life remains obstinately
"private" even when he is caught up in political action. His private integrity is not
threatened by his public failure.

private individual can exercise little power, for the careers of their heroes are too little attuned to such cadences.

A unique feature of these late plays is of relevance here. *Macbeth, Coriolanus, Antony and Cleopatra* has each as its deuteragonist a woman of mature years and of amply developed political instincts. Each of these exercises on the protagonist a dominating influence which is eventually destructive of his life. In the homes dominated by these women the domestic emotions, love, loyalty, mutual comfort, thus become the prey of political ambition; and the mind of the hero is left with no counters to stake against the devouring claims of the political world.

The loss of a domestic scene whose values of trust and repose are believed by the hero to be distinct from those of the jostling political world, providing him therefore with an alternative vision of life—this loss is probably to be associated with a decline in the sense of an immanent sustaining metaphysical order, also characteristic of the last tragedies. In this respect, as in some others, *Macbeth* is obviously a transitional play. In the earlier tragedies—*Hamlet, Othello, Lear*—the political world is peripheral; the real conflict occurs inside the protagonist, whose struggle it is to absorb the assumptions of the world he lives in and transmute them into something metaphysically meaningful; the effect of Brutus, Hamlet, Othello, and Lear is to moralize through their sufferings the self-interested assumptions of those who live around them and have power over them. But Coriolanus and Antony do not try to make this effect; they make gestures of opposition to the world they live in, gestures towards apparent alternatives, but their opposition is more apparent than real; neither Corioli nor Egypt really exists on a different plane from Rome, nor does Timon's cave offer a meaningfully alternative life to that of Athens. These exiles make claims that have a metaphysical resonance, but the real effects in the play are determined on the lower plane of *Realpolitik*. In *Macbeth*, on the other hand, the two worlds of politics and metaphysics exist side by side in a state of almost perfect balance, where personal ambition is seen as a breach of both orders simultaneously, and escape from politics to metaphysics turns out to be no escape at all. Macbeth has an agonized knowledge of what a true domestic relationship ought to provide:

> Honour, love, obedience, troops of friends,

but, of course, he tries to act as if he did not know, as if the stuff of ambition were the stuff of life.

In these terms it is probable that *Timon* also should count as a transitional play, though in a less obvious or satisfactory way; and one cannot avoid the suspicion that "transitional" here may be a mere synonym for "unfinished."[4] The possibility of political action in *Timon* is limited and complicated all the time by metaphysical assumptions about human nature. Timon sees man as either a blessed or an accursed creature, and this effectively prevents him from seeking to affect human life by leadership or any other political activity.

Lear's curses when he goes into exile ask the gods to intervene or at least to observe; Timon's only ask that the *human* observances of religion (seen as symptoms of order) should cease to exist. Coriolanus manages to curse his banishers without mentioning the gods at all. The gods are invoked constantly, of course, even in this markedly secular play. There is a notable example in Coriolanus's speech after his capitulation in Act V:

> Behold, the heavens do ope,
> The gods look down, and this unnatural scene
> They laugh at.
>
> (V. iii. 183)

But the gods who appear out of Coriolanus's heaven are quite different from those who, in *Lear*, "keep this dreadful pudder o'er our heads." Coriolanus's gods only reflect back the human scene; most often, indeed, they appear to be the mere conveniences of Roman political faction;[5] certainly a gulf of irony separates them from involvement in the tragedy of any one individual.

Their withdrawal from possible involvement further isolates the hero, leaves him alone with his own standards and the political urge to fulfil the sense of individual greatness in terms of distinction from and dominion over his fellows. Unfortunately for Coriolanus's fulfilment, the *distinction* and *dominion* are not entirely compatible. He desires to be a nonpareil, to behave

---

[4] See U. Ellis-Fermor, "*Timon of Athens*: An Unfinished Play," *RES* 18 (1942), reprinted in *Shakespeare the Dramatist* (1961).

[5] E.g., I. i. 191; I. viii. 6; I. ix. 8; II. iii. 142; III. i. 290; III. iii. 33; IV. vi. 36; V. iii. 104.

> As if a man were author of himself
> And knew no other kin.

He speaks of the people

> As if you were a god, to punish; not
> A man of their infirmity.

(III. i. 81)

Like Timon, he denies reciprocity. "He pays himself by being proud," his wounds "smart to hear themselves remembered." His condescensions are general, hardly at all concerned with individuals. An episode, which seems to mirror Shakespeare's desire to make this point obvious, is that in which we see Coriolanus pleading for the exemption of a Volsci who had once sheltered him—but he cannot remember his name. As the bastard Faulconbridge tells us:

> . . . new made honour doth forget men's names:
> 'Tis too respective and too sociable.

(*John*, I. i. 187)

Coriolanus's pretension to be a god takes him rather further into action than does Timon's, and this undoubtedly reflects his greater involvement in politics, his interest in leadership:

> He is their god; he leads them like a thing
> Made by some other deity than Nature,
> That shapes men better; . . .

(IV. vi. 91)

But his involvement is also his destruction. To fulfil his distinction above other men he has to seek dominion over them; but he is bound to fail in this because the distinction is too great; he is too inhuman. Indeed the more godlike he seeks to be, the more *inhuman* he becomes. The play has very usefully been seen in relation to Aristotle's celebrated dictum: "He that is incapable of living in a society is a god or a beast"; or (as the Elizabethan translation expanded it): "He that cannot abide to live in company, or through sufficiency hath need of nothing, is not esteemed a part or member of a City, but is either a beast or a God."[6] The ambiguity of Aristotle's remark is nicely adjusted to the ambiguity that I find in these last tragedies, the moral ambiguity of heroes who are both godlike

---

[6] See F. N. Lees, "Coriolanus, Aristotle and Bacon," *RES* NS 1 (1950), 114–25.

and *inhuman*. The inhumanity of Coriolanus is conveyed to us in terms both of a beast and of a machine. Sometimes the two are combined as in the following:

> He no more remembers his mother now than an eight-year-old horse. The tartness of his face sours ripe grapes; when he walks, he moves like an engine and the ground shrinks before his treading. He is able to pierce a corslet with his eye, talks like a knell, and his hum is a battery. He sits in his state as a thing made for Alexander. What he bids be done is finished with his bidding. He wants nothing of a god but eternity, and a heaven to throne in.
>
> (V. iv. 16)

Coriolanus, like Timon, and like Macbeth, searches for an *absolute* mode of behaviour, and like them he finds it; but the finding it is the destruction of humanity in him, as it was in them. And as far as it concerns personality, the process is as irreversible for Coriolanus as for Timon or Macbeth; he can, however, avoid that final stage, where the absoluteness of the individual demands to be guaranteed by the destruction of his society. He is unable to sustain the absoluteness of "Wife, mother, child, I know not"; but I do not think we should see the collapse before Volumnia as a great triumph of human love. The play's judgement on the beast-machine nature of "absolute" man stands unchanged. Only death can chillingly enough satisfy the hunger for absoluteness; and the final scene in Corioli, with its ironic repetition of the political and personal pattern already set in Rome, makes it clear that nothing in Coriolanus has altered or can alter. Greatness is seen as a doubtful and destructive blessing; love is powerless to change that. And this would seem to be as true of *Antony and Cleopatra* as of the other plays considered.

Antony and Cleopatra is, of all the tragedies after *Lear*, the one which has least obvious connection with the line of thought pursued here. But the connections exist, I think, and to pursue them is to remove some of the difficulties of this "most quintessential of Shakespeare's 'Problem Plays'" (as it has recently been called).[7] Is Antony an exile? I suggest that he is, though only in a different sense from Timon and Coriolanus. He is an exile from a world that we never see in the play, which existed splendidly in the past and will never be recovered again, a world in which

[7] E. Schanzer, *The Problem Plays of Shakespeare* (1963).

> his goodly eyes
> ... o'er the files and musters of the war
> Have glow'd like plated Mars
>
> (I. i. 2)

and where

> his captain's heart
> ... in the scuffles of great fights hath burst
> The buckles on his breast ...
>
> (I. i. 6)

The play is remarkable in the sense it gives of living in a second age; it is full of references to the heroes of the recent past; Julius Caesar and Pompey the Great still overshadow the world of the present, whose major characters were then being formed. In the past it had seemed possible to be both glamorous and efficient, heroic and political. But Antony's "heroic" gestures—challenging Caesar to single combat, seeking to fight again at Pharsalia—are seen to be quite inappropriate to the present in which he lives. The minor characters display this obviously enough: Ventidius, who knows how to avoid seeming to be a hero, is the real man of the time; Enobarbus tries to be, but fails miserably. Pompey indeed has the choice set before him more clearly than anyone else in the play, when Menas offers to cut the throats of the triumvirs; but Pompey feels he cannot stoop to success:

> Thou must know
> 'Tis not my profit that does lead mine honour:
> Mine honour, it.
>
> (II. vii. 74)

He "will not take when once 'tis offer'd," and thus (as Menas sees) he becomes (at that very moment) a man of the past.

It is in the contrast between Antony and Octavius, of course, that this split in the world of the play is developed most fully. Octavius suffers from none of the scruples which affect Pompey; his treatment of Lepidus may serve to characterize his whole mode of proceeding;

> ... having made use of [Lepidus] in the wars 'gainst Pompey, presently denied him rivality, would not let him partake in the glory of the action; and not resting here, accuses him of letters he had formerly wrote to Pompey; upon his own appeal, seizes him.
>
> (III. v. 7)

He is everywhere marked by the celerity and decisiveness of his moves. "Tis done already" and "most certain" are his typical locutions; when he fights, "this speed of Caesar's / Carries beyond belief." There is no sense in which Caesar, like the other major characters, is still living in the past. Time is not for him a destroyer, but a whirlwind he rides to command the future.

Antony, on the other hand, is, as I have said, an exile from a glorious past that cannot be recovered. As an "ebb'd man," time is not his to command. In Egypt he is becalmed in the dramatic equivalent of Spenser's Lake of Idleness, Cleopatra having the role of Phaedria:

> But that your royalty
> Holds idleness your subject, I should take you
> For idleness itself.
>
> (I. iii. 91)

In this fertile and stagnant atmosphere of Nilus's mud, of

> The dull billows thick as troubled mire,
> Whom neither wind out of their seat could force,
> Nor timely tides did drive out of their sluggish source,
>
> (*Faerie Queene*, II. vi. 20)

time has a function other than that of developing the future out of the present:

> Now for the love of Love and her soft hours,
> Let's not confound the time with conference harsh;
> There's not a minute of our lives should stretch
> Without some pleasure now. What sport tonight?
>
> (I. i. 44)

The deviousness of Cleopatra, the sense of time stopping when Antony leaves her, the impossibility of forecasting her actions, her capacity to say and unsay—all these are means to bend the time of action into a hoop of enjoyment, the time of thinking into the time of the heart:

> And now like am'rous birds of prey
> Rather at once our Time devour
> Than languish in his slow-chapt pow'r.
> (Marvell, "To his coy mistress," 38)

In this atmosphere it is easy enough for Antony to be "heroic" (in the old, Herculean, sense of "generous," "large-scale"); but if heroism is to be more than sentimental self-indulgence, then it must allow also that every action, taken or avoided, is the moulding of the future. And this the play never allows us to forget, with its repeated reference to "our slippery people" who constantly shift their allegiance to the newcomer, to the primal law by which

> This common body,
> Like to a vagabond flag upon the stream,
> Goes to and back, lackeying the varying tide.
>
> (I. iv. 44)

Antony himself knows that

> The present pleasure,
> By revolution low'ring, does become
> The opposite of itself.
>
> (I. ii. 128)

But even Antony's capacity to break out of this Idle Lake where "we bring forth weeds / When our quick minds lie still," and to return to the Roman world of action, cannot heal the schism in the world of the present. Critics often write as if it was open to Antony to choose a complete and satisfactory life as a Roman, married to Octavia and sharing rule with Caesar. But Caesar himself knows better:

> I must perforce
> Have shown to thee such a declining day
> Or look on thine; we could not stall together
> In the whole world. But yet let me lament
>   . . . that our stars,
> Unreconcilable, should divide
> Our equalness to this.
>
> (V. i. 37)

In the present of the play the partial life lived by Octavius, and the other partial life, lived to the full by Antony, are as incapable of fusion as time present and time past. Octavius and Antony are affected equally by this; but Octavius can hardly be called an exile from the completer world of the past, for he never belonged to it; his speeches move in the present and the future. But Antony is an exile and is aware that he is an exile, living on borrowed time in an

inevitably hostile world. The idea is particularly well conveyed by
the continuous play on the word *Antony* as representing not only
the name of the man we see before us, but also the *Idea* of the man
as he was once, and as he ought to be:

> Since my lord
> Is Antony again, I will be Cleopatra.
>
> (III. xiii. 186)

> He comes too short in that great property
> Which still should go with Antony.
>
> (I. i. 58)

> O my oblivion is a very Antony.
>
> (I. iii. 90)

> I dream'd there was an Emperor Antony—
> . . . Think you there was or might be such a man?
>
> (V. ii. 76)

> yet t'imagine
> An Antony were nature's piece 'gainst fancy,
> Condemning shadows quite.
>
> (V. ii. 98)

> she looks like sleep,
> As she would catch another Antony
> In her strong toil of grace.
>
> (V. ii. 343)

The magic of an image of *Antony* has the power to hold the heroic
past alive for the moment of the present; but the magic is a kind of
confidence-trick. Nothing in the present really supports the idea;
and as soon as the charm of immediate power weakens (at Actium)
the empire shatters like quicksilver. The most telling of these
Antony references comes in his death-speech:

> Here I am Antony;
> Yet cannot hold this visible shape my knave.
>
> (IV. xiv. 13)

The effort to be *Antony*, to identify the actions of the present with
this heroic figure, is fully revealed in the necessity to die for it, and
so, by this means, to deny and defeat the reductive currents of time
and policy. Antony's choice here is as much a choice of the absolute
as is that of Coriolanus or Timon; but the absolute is of the

opposite kind. They choose detachment, hardness, inhumanity; he prefers the grand illusion of an absolute magnetism, loyalty, love:

> The nobleness of life
> Is to do thus [*Embracing*], when such a mutual pair
> And such a twain can do it.
>
> (I. i. 36)

This is magnificent, but it is undercut by self-indulgent sentimentality as surely as are the "victories" of Act IV. The will to be godlike must have set against it the fact that "the god Hercules whom Antony lov'd" leaves him when his fortunes decline. As in *Coriolanus*, the gods only reflect back what human beings have made for themselves.

The later tragedies offer the alternative absolutes of exclusion and inclusion, of denying the world and of swallowing it; death seals equally the opposite magnificences of Timon and Antony; but in neither case does the play conceal the price that has been paid for closing the uneasy gap between the absolute and the real— abandonment of the good ordinariness of a life lived among compromises, or the loss of a sense of reverence for the unknown in destiny, a sense of submission to the immanence of higher powers.

Timon in Context

Robert B. Heilman

The problem of self-knowledge is one that may take us some-what closer to the issue of quality in *Timon of Athens* than do other matters that have been much discussed, such as its structural defects, technical slips, and allegorical stiffness. In exploring the problem of self-knowledge, we can make use of four contexts which throw light on the art of *Timon*.[1] The first context is historical: Renaissance thought on the subject of self-knowledge. The second is the great tragedies: if one avoids the obvious conclusion that the greater make the lesser look still smaller, there are still differences in conception of character that are illuminating. The third context is that of the chronologically nearby plays—*Antony and Cleopatra, Coriolanus,* and *Cymbeline*; they illustrate *Timon* problems best of all, and therefore I give them fuller treatment than the great tragedies. Finally, there is the unusual context of other plays in later times: they help clarify the *Timon* theme and even make Shakespeare's play look ancestral.

As for Renaissance thought, two studies give useful information. Paul A. Jorgensen's *Lear's Self-Discovery* (1967) and Rolf Soellner's *Shakespeare's Patterns of Self-Knowledge* (1972) have summarized fully the extensive Renaissance ideas on the discovery, knowledge, and awareness of the self—the injunction *nosce teipsum* or *gnothi*

"*Timon* in Context" combines, with extensive revisions. "From Mine Own Knowledge: A Theme in the Late Tragedies," *The Centennial Review* 8 (1964): 17–38; and "Robespierre and Santa Claus: Men of Virtue in Drama," *The Southern Review* NS 14 (1978): 209–25. I am grateful to the editors of these journals for permission to reuse the original materials.

[1] Another context, that of theatrical history, has been well dealt with by M. C. Bradbrook, "Blackfriars: The Pageant of *Timon of Athens,*" in *Shakespeare the Craftsman,* The Clark Lectures, 1968 (New York: Barnes and Noble, 1969), pp. 144–67.

seauton, and the experience *anagnorisis*, to use the term, as many do for convenience' sake, in a more limited sense than Aristotle did— and have explored various plays through the medium of these ideas. We need not go into those background materials here; the point is that Jorgensen and Soellner have provided a historical justification for criticism that deals with the self-knowledge of tragic protagonists and treats it as essential to their having a "proper magnitude." Jorgensen remarks perceptively, "If *King Lear* is an ultimate drama of self-discovery, this may help to explain why it is also perhaps the most totally compelling of all Shakespeare's plays" (p. 2). Indeed so. Other tragedies seem equally compelling to critics who are convinced of the protagonists' self-knowledge, less compelling to critics who believe it is incomplete. One persistent interpretation of Othello has been that his bias is more toward self-justification than full self-recognition; this has stirred up defenses of his moral self-awareness that seem now to be on the ascendant in the critical sky. Various critics (Kenneth Muir, for instance) have noted a kind of limitedness in the latter parts of *Macbeth*; one way of accounting for this is a marked constriction of the moral awareness that made the earlier Macbeth a figure of genuine representativeness and magnitude. Yet here again we find contradictory opinions. Some critics detect, in the brilliant metaphorical flights of Macbeth in his later downhill days, a true awareness of his moral course. To others his poetry seems to describe the results of his deeds rather than perceive their quality, to paint an existential wasteland rather than confront its only begetter. In all these judgments, however, the issue of self-knowledge is important.

I have moved over from the historical context of ideas to the context of the major tragedies, and I now want to proceed in two ways from the context of the major tragedies to the context of the late tragedies. The first transition is via the dramatist's attitude that makes many people respond similarly to dramas in both periods. Shakespeare characteristically tends to present everything that can be said for his protagonists. Hence, even when these figures are or become more constricted in consciousness, less completely aware of what they have been and done and are, they still tend to make us focus on what is admirable in them and be less attentive to other aspects of their being. Thus in Macbeth we see primarily the fighting spirit of the trapped man; in Antony, a figure of magnanimity (the view of Dorothea Krook and others) and a partner in a love that, in transcending all other values, transfigures him; in Coriolanus, the ultimate man of integrity; and in Timon, the truly generous, self-forgetful man. On the other hand, such readings are not unchallenged; qualifications or doubts creep in from other quarters. Some readers argue that Macbeth hardly acknowledges the evil that he has done, that Coriolanus remains immature and blind to political reality, and that Timon's misanthropic outbursts are tedious and self-serving. Probably Antony calls forth most diversity of response: true, almost no critics support the Roman view of life, but still there is some suspicion that the glorified Egyptian alternative does not quite escape a night-on-the-town triviality. A. L. French thinks that Antony's character is not up to the poetry that Antony speaks and that others use in speaking about him, and H. A. Mason similarly argues that Shakespeare magnifies Antony by "telling" rather than "showing," but Janet Adelman believes that the poetry triumphs over our disbelief. Norman Rabkin, usefully introducing the doctrine of "complementarity," rejects pro or con interpretations: we must live with contradictory impressions, calling on our "negative capability." To apply this doctrine in a slightly different way, we have to be aware both of the force and impressiveness of certain protagonists, and of their limits—in my view, a self-ignorance that holds them short of a possible magnitude.

The other transition from the major tragedies to the later ones lies in a contrast of motives. Lear, Othello, and Macbeth have in common a powerful egotistic passion, either foolish or evil, which drives them into disastrous actions—punitive, aggressive, or destructive—against others. They make us judge them as they compulsively strike savage blows, and so close off the possibility of becoming wiser without being sadder. Thus there is an immensely significant difference between them and the later heroes. For Antony, Coriolanus, and Timon believe—and partly or wholly persuade us to believe—that they possess, or represent, or practice a good that takes precedence over all other values. They are obsessed, as it were, with virtues that seem absolute, subject to no contingencies—in Antony, an erotic attraction apparently self-justifying and indeed salvationary; in Coriolanus, a military sense of honor that can ignore political reality or expect it to be acquiescent; and in Timon, a give-away impulse that can forget two problems, the limits of his distributable resources and the moral quality of beneficiaries.

Of these late heroes—the third context for a comment on *Timon*—Antony has most range: he can have glimpses of himself as failed general and statesman, as petty in honor and jealousy, as self-indulgent playboy. But he always hurries on; at no time does he say anything as plain and decisive as Enobarbus's "I have done ill," "I am alone the villain of the earth" (IV. vi. 18, 30). He cannot speak thus because, I suggest, he is at bottom the man of charm, that is, the man whose energy goes mainly into his impact on others. He charms all about him and, through them, us; then we unconsciously translate the quickly attractive into the durably laudable. The goal of this interpretation, however, is not to diminish Antony but to see that in him Shakespeare is exploring a certain kind of figure—the secular charismatic man. The implicit issue is: does the man of charm ever look within? Dare he? What substance might he find by which to estimate the thing done, the life lived? Or is charm itself a free-floating way of life, a slipping of all anchoring fixities that ordinarily define character and that might appear in one character as stabilities, in another as rigidities? Can he look within? The flow of his psychic energy is all outward; he is a kind of mesmerist. It is very difficult to imagine Antony looking inward and pondering the claims of this life or that life upon him, the authority of this imperative or that. An instinctive exciter of warm responsiveness can hardly inspect or challenge himself fundamentally, though he may briefly see that so visible a deed as the flight at Actium does not provide an image of greatmindedness. Further, the man of charm is himself charmed, by a woman who is all instinct and who embodies, better than any other Shakespeare heroine, an intuitive sense of how to achieve her ends.

In this remarkable union of charm and instinct there is, as it were, an autonomous realm, resistant to the reflective, to self-assessment; it simply is; it asserts itself by zest and magnetism; it is self-conscious only with respect to its own splendor and to unfriendly fortunes, not at all in the matter of how it may be placed by an assay of what lies beneath the dazzling surface. Shakespeare is here imagining a world where all vital powers conspire against self-knowledge. To say this may give some clue to a particular charm of the play, to the hypnotic effect of an *is* beyond reflection. When self-knowledge is present in a drama, it may pass like a disturbing current from characters to spectators. But when it is absent, its very absence gives spectators an extra measure of freedom to share in the gay abandonment, the brilliant unconcern of these special creatures who in a chosen, hedonistic island escape the cool and ordered central establishment of Caesar and Octavia; it frees us to join in all intoxications and in a rare union of disparate gratifications; to command the luxuries of the palace and yet dwell unfettered in bohemia, in a unique bohemia that grasps at cosmic unlimitedness and believes in its transcendent glory; and thus, gliding over the crude evidences of ordinary disaster, to mount to a final gilding in death and to discover, in despair of life, an erotic/ aesthetic triumph beyond mortality. Behind the facade of a lost world, sometimes a theme for sermons, flames a glittering life which, undisturbed by self-knowledge in the inhabitants, is warmly inviting to the romantic sensibility. The play all but enforces a romantic response. What is most bewitching, perhaps, is the brilliant "gypsy," Cleopatra. Amid her exotic splendors and rare mingling of playfulness and passion, there is subtly embedded the ultimate creation of the male erotic dream as fantasy of achievement. That dream is only secondarily of the enumerable charms, the intimated skills, the vital unpredictability, and the infinite variety; its essential image is the soul of the promiscuous woman faithful, in the end, to oneself alone.

There is a line of continuity from Antony to Coriolanus; both are military men, and Coriolanus has something of the personal power that we have seen in Antony. The patricians feel it, even the snubbed Roman plebeians feel it, and the Volscians are strongly moved by it; the tribunes of the people feel it, and Aufidius feels it (and in a noticeable structural parallel, the tribunes and Aufidius act to sterilize it). But whereas Antony is the man of charm, Coriolanus is the man of force; he is the warrior, intrepid, furious, able to take it, readier than most men to risk life in a cause. Antony, so to speak, has too little "character"; Coriolanus has too much. Whereas Antony is hedonistic, Coriolanus is ascetic—hardy in endurance (his most self-possessed moment is his departure into exile), a taut guardian against common self-indulgences, with a prophet's quickness to rage at and smite down what he sees as evil. Antony is equally at home in army tent, court, pub, or brothel, everywhere falling naturally into camaraderie; Coriolanus's taste is for battle alone, and he instinctively converts all life into a battle, with himself as the captain of rectitude triumphing over policy, pusillanimity, and perfidy—which are what he sees mainly in other men. He becomes a rigid Puritan Hotspur, a heroic tilter turned scourge and revenger. If Antony is the charmer, whose very stock in trade inhibits, despite his considerable stock of knowingness, persistence in self-knowledge, Coriolanus is the warrior whose unvarying military stance obstructs not only self-knowledge but the very awareness that there is anything to be known.

In battle Coriolanus is all but a parody of the hero, with his bloodiness, frenzied pursuit, noisy words of hate, and indifference to wounds. "My work hath not yet warm'd me" (I. v. 18), he says, in words that actually echo Prince Hal's burlesque of Hotspur ("he kills me some six or seven dozen Scots at a breakfast, washes his hands, and says to his wife, 'Fie upon this quiet life. I want work.' 'O my sweet Harry,' says she, 'how many hast thou kill'd today?' 'Give my roan horse a drench,' says he, and answers, 'Some fourteen . . . a trifle, a trifle'"—II. iv. 115 ff.). He is even more excessive when he rejects spoils and compliments (I. ix. 37–53); as he keeps harping on his distaste for praise (II. i. 185–86; II. ii. 76, 81), the selfless man becomes self-conscious; his ascetic rejection of adulation is strained, finally self-adulatory. So in his revulsion at political campaigning and in his tactless candor to the plebeians we can see integrity, yes, but interlaced with stubbornness and complacency, the pride that hates to flatter confounded with the pride of stiff-necked self-will. He supposes that he is exempt from the ritual humilities essential to political and indeed social existence; he has an illusion of immunity to custom. Character is made brittle by egotism.

When we are not in our pragmatistical mood, we spontaneously applaud the uncalculating, straightforward man of strength, identify with the pride that will not truckle, rage at imperfect actuality, condemn fickle mob and slick demagogue, find relief from the ways of the world by exploding into unreserved free speech.

Basically, Coriolanus acts in ways, and possesses qualities, that humanity values or admires or even envies. In his crisis we see the perennial confrontation of the good man and political reality. But this good man is a special case: he is intransigent in his self-asserted rectitude; his sense of an absolute moral "I" is fortified by his warrior's assurance that every antagonist is evil, his integrity is hardened into willfulness, his honor is turned macho. His "virtue" is literal and traditional—"manliness." What constitutes manliness? For Coriolanus it is manifested only in cut-and-thrust direct attack. For his mother Volumnia, however—the woman who, ironically, managed to stunt her son's growth at military-academy level— manliness can encompass various courses: if primarily it means bloody conflict, still it need not deny actuality, and it can permit forgiveness. Except for a fleeting moment or two, Coriolanus cannot accommodate such a trinity of alternatives. In him Shakespeare explores the way in which singlemindedness can mean a single-track mind. A grasp of complexity is one fruit of maturity; Coriolanus never ripens into such an awareness. Aufidius, of whom Coriolanus thinks only as a manageable instrument but who reflects a great deal on Coriolanus's nature, sums him up aptly in his final epithet "boy"—the right term for a man whose experiences have all been single-valued and whom they have left unable to grasp ambivalent reality. In Coriolanus, Shakespeare studies the man of honor whose self-conscious virtue prevents his knowing either others or himself. This man understands the responses of others so poorly because he cannot look within to learn something about human motive and attitude. His own uncriticized feeling makes up all his knowledge; it does not dawn on him that his own half-truth view of life has made it possible for enemies to attack him with half-truths. He does not suspect that he has misunderstood the nature of political life, betrayed himself to demagogues, betrayed Rome, and then betrayed his commitment to the Volscians; least of all does he glimpse the self projected in all these passionate steps.

So much for the several contexts that in different ways prepare us for the problems of *Timon*. Timon, as we have seen, shares with Antony and Coriolanus a conviction of possessing or practicing a good, one that is uncontingent and self-justifying and hence seals off an awareness of other values that may have some claim, of the nature of the humanity with whom he deals, and of other motives that may complicate his own actions. Timon and Antony are both outgoing; by a union of instinct and will they please others, Antony through a charm that everyone feels, Timon by an easy generousness that nearly everyone enjoys. Antony loves loving, for which he gives up all; Timon loves giving, and he gives all. But Timon has still more in common with Coriolanus, different as are their surface styles. Both are givers, one of blood, the other of money; each one considers himself a creditor; each is convinced that his fellow citizens dishonorably reject his claims, berates them furiously, goes bitterly into exile, and is willing to see a military revenge upon his own city. If *Timon* was the earlier play, it could be a sketch for *Coriolanus*, which treats both the hero and his adversaries more complexly. If *Timon* was the later play, it represented either a decline in Shakespeare's artistic skill or, quality aside, his attraction to the problem of what happens to the benefactor who, when he is disillusioned, has a longer time to feel the impact of dissillusion. In both plays, of course, Shakespeare reduces the range of his character by allowing him virtually no self-awareness. Hence the vitality of each play derives, not from the growth of moral perceptiveness in the hero, but from the hero's extraordinary energy in the quite human activity of thinking well of the self instead of thinking truly of the self.

To return for a moment to the context of the greater tragedies and its usefulness for the study of the later group. In both groups, of course, all the protagonists are "good" men, not ones we draw away from because of some central evil in make-up; they are tragic heroes in the Aristotelian sense. But there is one marked difference between the men in the earlier group and those in the later group. Lear, Macbeth, and Othello all carry out actions that are evil or lead to evil, and Hamlet desperately wants not to do an evil deed. On the other hand, Antony, Coriolanus, and Timon are all presented, initially or throughout, as possessors or practitioners of a good (a transforming love, patriotism and integrity, generosity). Lear, Macbeth, and Othello must all recognize, as best they may, that they have done evil. But Antony (with brief intermittent exceptions), Coriolanus, and Timon rest fairly secure in the conviction that they have found the right path and embody genuine virtues (as Hamlet struggles desperately to do) and that when things have gone wrong, loss or disaster is due to some inadequacy or failure of the world in which they live. Finally, and most significantly, the major tragedies are wholly unambiguous in presenting wrong actions, whereas the later tragedies are ambiguous in presenting actions that are deemed by tradition or by those who perform them to be good. Up to a point, of course, the plays affirm the values enacted or accepted. But the plays as wholes inhibit our total assent to what appears to be affirmed. We are not invited unquestioningly to accept romantic love, valorous independence, and material openhandedness as absolute or transcendent virtues, or even to be sure that they are possessed in pure form. Hence, of course, our inconsistent responses to the heroes as exemplars of virtue. In one reading, Timon is admirably generous, his friends are execrably greedy, ungrateful, and unreciprocating, and his inevitable turning upon them generates a brilliant rhetoric of excoriation. Other readers find Timon silly, his polemics tiresome, and his history all too allegorical; that is, his sudden conversion from philanthropic man to violent misanthropy is pat and mechanical.

The weakness of the play, however, lies in Timon's longwinded obtuseness rather than in his turnabout in mid-drama. Shakespeare is not wrong to convert philanthropy into misanthropy; what connects these attitudes psychologically is that both are univalent and therefore uncomplicated. One simplicity does easily change into another. Love, as we know, is quickly metamorphosed into hate; extremes meet. Timon's misanthropy is plausible but is overpresented, as if the dramatist had got addicted to it. In vituperation Timon goes on and on. Why? Because abuse is very necessary to him. Compare Lear: as long as he can flay Goneril and Regan, he can avoid acknowledging his own responsibility for decisions that have turned out disastrously. But in time Lear goes beyond abuse and on into recognition of himself as erring man. Shakespeare never lets Timon grow in this way. Timon's prolonged denunciations register not only disgust with evil but—I suggest—self-protection. As long as he can go on madly cataloguing human shortcomings, he can feel superior to other men. As long as he can think the world only a cesspool of ingratitude, he need ask himself no hard questions about ·his extraordinary benefactional sprees. As long as he can lash evil, he need take no look at his earlier philanthropic operation, at its quality, and at his own motives. To say this is not to ignore or deny the satirical cast of the play, especially the second half; it is rather to say that our attention is deflected from the satire by the problem of the satirical voice. Timon does not gain magnitude by becoming a madder Apeimantus, the professional misanthrope whose self-worshipping attacks on others are so histrionic that to their victims they seem hardly more than an annoying but endurable case of un-Athenian conduct (hence he does not come across as Fool to Timon's Lear). The Thersites-Bosola vein, with the mechanized hyperbole of vilification, ceases to hold; one's interest shifts from the mouthings to the mouth, and the mind and motives that govern it.

What could Timon, consciously or unconsciously, be protecting himself from? With only a little bit of self-awareness Timon might discover and acknowledge several truths about his give-away program. The first is that the exhaustion of resources has its penalties. Surely we are to sympathize with the efforts of the loyal steward Flavius to persuade "noble Timon" to take a sensible look at his shrinking capital. To give away everything has at least the disadvantage of making one unable to give help when other suppliants appear, as they are sure to do; but then, too, it renders one materially defenseless in a world that is less likely to assist than shun or take advantage of defenselessness. Total divestment of holdings is rational only if one intends to leave the world and become hermit or monk, a role that Timon in no way seeks.

Second, Timon might realize that his manic largesse is not so much a blessing to others as it is a way of leading them into temptation. Indiscriminate, mechanical handouts bring out the worst in people; it is not so much that they are irremediably corrupt in nature, or suffer from Calvinistic total depravity, as that the latent corruptibility of the human race is activated by opportunities thrust recklessly upon average human beings. (As Congreve's Lady Wishfort said, in a different context, "What's Integrity to an Opportunity?") Great laxness or great rigidity in the practice of a virtue renders one predictable; predictability leads to vulnerability, and vulnerability is tempting (both Coriolanus and Timon so manage their quite different virtues as to present an inviting vulnerability). Timon brings out the darker side of man by making robbery too easy. In modern idiom, he invites rape, which is never tolerable, but which in certain circumstances is close to inevitable.

Finally, Timon misconstrues prodigality with cash as generosity of spirit. This is to say, not that he is not generous, but that his giving does not quite manage to be an end in itself. Or for him the permissible pleasure of enjoying the pleasure of the recipients is not enough. Without knowing it, Timon banks on a quid pro quo; he acts the part of a charitable institution, but he has some acquisitive tendencies of his own. If he loves men, he is also in effect procuring their good will and gratitude. He is practicing what we might call timony—that is, a secular simony, a buying of good offices. Only an expectation that other men have made a compact with him—have obligated themselves to him—can explain the rancorous violence and indefatigability of his rants against Athenians and mankind.

It is such matters that Timon, were he capable of self-knowledge, might reflect upon. That he does not do so may mean that Shakespeare had worn out his earlier interest in self-awareness, or that for a time he was luxuriating in the simpler rhetoric of disillusionment—that disillusionment about the world that feeds on unpunctured illusion about oneself. Or perhaps he was temporarily fascinated by the energy that men put into self-justification, direct or indirect, and into apparently self-justifying lines of action—the abandonment to a virtue that seems absolute—even as these lines take them steadily toward destruction. We have to feel the energy; and the irony of outcomes that contradict expectations is effective. Still, it is difficult not to find in the protagonists' self-ignorance a limitation that accounts for the lesser status of some plays, most notably *Timon*. Few critics have tried to rescue it from a disesteem usually based more on structural or other technical defects than upon a major constriction of character, of adult humanity.

The final context for an estimate of *Timon* is that of several later plays, ironically enough all comedies, which deal independently with the Timon theme. They all tend to confirm the reading of *Timon* presented here. In Goldsmith's *The Good Natured Man* (1768) Honeywood believes that "universal benevolence is the first law of nature"; hence, just like Timon, he falls into a help-everyone habit that would leave him, like Timon, financially ruined did not a wise uncle administer a shock that makes him, unlike Timon, see what he has been up to: "How have I sunk by too great an assiduity to please! . . . [I] perceive my . . . vanity, in attempting to please all by fearing to offend any. . . ." Surely his words identify a Timon motive. The uncle debunks universal-benevolence people as "men who desire to cover their private ill-nature by a pretended regard for all . . ." (later a theme in Dickens). Though this is probably not applicable to Timon, still it would help explain the quickness of his complete about-face to total misanthropy. In Brecht's *The Good Woman of Setzuan* (ca. 1940) the issue is not the motive of the benefactor but the effect of benefactions upon beneficiaries: Shen Te, a female Timon and Honeywood, is called "good" by everyone; that is, she is susceptible to appeals for material help. Unlike Timon, she quickly sees what is happening: her gifts turn the recipients of them into rapacious spongers. To save herself from ruin by these leeches she must partly become a stern disciplinarian, that is, discriminate among petitioners, reject freeloaders, and make people earn what they get. (This tack leads to other complications not germane to the issue of timony.) Finally, the title character in Christopher Hampton's *The Philanthropist* (1970), Philip, is madly generous in another way: in his anxiety to "please"—the same word literally used of Honeywood and Shen Te, and applicable to Timon—he simply approves of, likes, agrees with, or praises everybody. What overtakes him is not financial, but spiritual, bankruptcy: others pity, ignore, scoff at, or desert him. (Cf. Camus's description of a character: "C., who plays at seducing people, who gives too much to everybody, but whose feelings never last, who needs to seduce, to win love and friendship, and who is incapable of both. A fine character to have in a novel, but lamentable as a friend.")[2] What is fascinating about Philip is his origin: Hampton created him by literally transforming Alceste, the title character of Molière's *Misanthrope*, into his opposite. Thus Hampton has perceived the subtle link between unlimited misanthropy and philanthropy, the convertibility of one into the other that Shakespeare had traced in the opposite direction.

Despite the validity of this central perception, *Timon* does not achieve what it might. The unrelentingness of Timon's practice, first in one mode and then in the other, makes his transformation,

² Albert Camus, *Notebooks 1935–1942*, tr. Philip Thody (New York: Knopf, 1963), p. 87.

though plausible, emblematic, and this quality rules out the qualifications, the complications, and above all the human self-understanding that seem probable and that later dramatists such as Goldsmith would find in the Timon type. The content of the later plays enables us to see that the materials are more effective in the comic treatment than in the style of unrelieved satirical melodrama. At the time he did *Timon,* however, Shakespeare was in his period of the single-valued protagonist, who either was inflexible from the start or gradually excluded alternatives. Now, suppose Shakespeare had come to *Timon* a little later when, in the period of the romances, he characteristically saw beneficent action or circumstance forestalling disaster until the erring agent could come into improved vision. One could imagine him altering sources and making Timon less univocal and more aware of his actions and himself. In *The Winter's Tale* Leontes, as stiffnecked as Coriolanus and Timon, is shocked into self-understanding, and in *Cymbeline* Posthumus and Iachimo are volubly self-condemnatory. Iachimo is Shakespeare's final variation on the theme of self-knowledge: he relishes thinking, or seeming to think, evil of himself. He makes a good thing of pointing the finger of blame at himself. He explores the posture, prolongs it, seizes stage with it (V. v. 153–209): self-knowledge is theatricalized as public self-accusation. Maybe this is easier when one has done a bad thing that has not prevented a good end than when one believes one has done only good things that have not prevented a bad end. But, as later dramatists show, even Timon types could see the light.

A final word on the trio of late tragedies. The heroes, if we take them at their simplest, exemplify three essential human virtues: devotion to a loved one, integrity in the world, and charity toward all. A great achievement of Shakespeare, in dealing with this group, is to avoid a simplistic attitude to the virtues. Instead he shows how the possessor of the virtue may hold to it questionably, and even suggests that the virtues themselves are contingent rather than absolute. But it is the spectators rather than the characters who gain this perception. For more perceptive men of virtue we have to go to earlier Shakespeare or later literature. As for the generous man: we have seen later Timons who could learn how charitableness becomes tainted. As for the man of integrity:

Molière's Alceste could partly grasp his errors; true, he did not clearly see that his integrity was badly infected by love of power, but he did know that there was some failure in himself. As for the lover, Antony—it is a hard case. But one thinks of the speaker in Richard Lovelace's lyric "To Lucasta, On Going to the Wars": "I could not love thee, dear, so much, / Loved I not honor more."

Chronology of Important Dates

	Shakespeare's Life	*Other Events*
1564	Shakespeare born at Stratford-upon-Avon (April 23).	
1576		James Burbage builds The Theater, England's first permanent playhouse, in outskirts of London.
1582	Shakespeare marries Anne Hathaway (November).	Hakluyt's *Voyages.*
1583	Daughter Susanna born (May).	
1585	Twins (Hamnet and Judith) baptized (February 2).	
1588		Defeat of Spanish Armada.
1590–92	*Henry VI, Parts 1, 2, and 3; Comedy of Errors.* Greene attacks Shakespeare as "upstart crow" in *Groatsworth of Wit* (first reference to Shakespeare as actor and playwright).	Spenser's *Faerie Queene,* I–III, and Sidney's *Arcadia* published (1590); Marlowe's *Tamburlaine* (1589–90) and *Dr. Faustus* (1592–93); Greene dies (1592).
1593–94	"Venus and Adonis" (1593) and "Rape of Lucrece" (1594) published; *Titus Andronicus, Taming of the Shrew, Richard III, Two Gentlemen of Verona;* Shakespeare joins Lord Chamberlain's Men as actor, playwright, and shareholder.	Theaters closed intermittently by outbreak of plague, notably February to year end, 1593.

1595–96	*A Midsummer Night's Dream, Richard II, Romeo and Juliet, King John, Merchant of Venice;* death of Hamnet (1596); Shakespeare family granted coat of arms (1596).	Sir Walter Raleigh's voyage to Guiana (1595); Spenser's *Faerie Queene*, IV–VI, published (1596).
1597–98	*1 and 2 Henry IV;* Shakespeare buys New Place (next-to-largest house in Stratford); Francis Meres praises Shakespeare as leading English playwright.	Bacon's *Essays* published (1597); Chapman publishes first installment of translation of Homer's *Iliad* (1598).
1599–1600	*Much Ado About Nothing, As You Like It, Henry V, Julius Caesar, Twelfth Night.*	Lord Chamberlain's Men construct the Globe Theater from the timbers of The Theater (1599); Spenser dies (1599).
1601–02	*Hamlet, Troilus and Cressida, All's Well That Ends Well;* death of Shakespeare's father (1601).	Unsuccessful rebellion by Earl of Essex, and his execution (1601); Ben Jonson active as playwright.
1603–04	*Measure for Measure, Othello.*	Death of Elizabeth and accession of James I (1603); Lord Chamberlain's Men become King's Men.
1605–06	*King Lear, Macbeth.*	
1607–08	*Antony and Cleopatra, Timon of Athens, Coriolanus;* marriage of Susanna (1607); death of Shakespeare's mother (1608).	King's Men acquire Blackfriars (private theater with exclusive clientele and evening performances) (1608–09).
1609–10	*Pericles, Cymbeline; Sonnets* published (1609).	
1611–12	*The Winter's Tale, The Tempest;* Shakespeare retires to Stratford.	Tourneur's *Atheist's Tragedy* (1611); Webster's *White Devil* (1612).
1613	*Henry VIII.*	Globe Theater burns while *Henry VIII* is played.
1616	Shakespeare dies (April 23).	Beaumont, Hakluyt, Cervantes die.
1623	Collected plays published in First Folio edition; Anne Hathaway dies.	Molière born (1622).

Notes on Contributors

JANET ADELMAN is Professor of English at the University of California, Berkeley. She has written *The Common Liar: An Essay on "Antony and Cleopatra"* (1973) and edited *Twentieth Century Interpretations of "King Lear"* (1978).

NICHOLAS BROOKE is Professor of English Literature at the University of East Anglia in Norwich. He is the author of *Shakespeare's Early Tragedies* (1968) and *Horrid Laughter in Jacobean Tragedy* (1979). In 1977 he delivered the Annual Shakespeare Lecture of the British Academy; his subject was "Shakespeare and Baroque Art."

REUBEN A. BROWER (1908–75) was Henry B. and Anne M. Cabot Professor of English at Harvard. He wrote *Hero and Saint: Shakespeare and the Graeco-Roman Tradition* (1971) and *Mirror on Mirror: Translation, Imitation, Parody* (1974), and coedited, with Helen Vendler and John Hollander, *I. A. Richards: Essays in His Honor* (1973).

JAMES L. CALDERWOOD is Professor of English at the University of California, Irvine, and has served as Associate Dean of Humanities. His books are *Shakespearean Metadrama* (1971), *To Be and Not To Be: Negation and Metadrama in "Hamlet"* (1983), and *Metadrama in Shakespeare's Henriad* (1979).

STANLEY CAVELL is Walter M. Cabot Professor of Aesthetics and the General Theory of Value at Harvard. His numerous publications include *Must We Mean What We Say?* (1969), *The Claims of Reason: Wittgenstein, Skepticism, Morality, and Tragedy* (1979), and *Pursuits of Happiness: The Hollywood Comedy of Remarriage* (1981).

ROSALIE L. COLIE (1925–72) taught at Barnard, Wesleyan, the University of Iowa, Victoria College (Toronto), and Brown. She wrote *Paradoxia Epidemica: The Renaissance Tradition of Paradox* (1966), *The Resources of Kind: Genre-Theory in the Renaissance* (1973), and *Shakespeare's Living Art* (1974, posthumous).

HARRIETT B. HAWKINS taught at Vassar from 1966 to 1978 and is now Senior Research Fellow at Linacre College, Oxford. She is the author of *Likenesses of Truth in Elizabethan and Restoration Drama* (1972) and *Poetic Freedom and Poetic Truth* (1976).

ROBERT B. HEILMAN is Professor Emeritus of English at the University of Washington. His earlier books were on Shakespeare, his later ones on dramatic genre. *Tragedy and Melodrama* (1968) and *The Ways of the World: Comedy and Society* (1978) both refer to a number of Shakespearean plays.

E. A. J. HONIGMANN is Joseph Cowen Professor of English at the University of Newcastle upon Tyne. He is the author of *Shakespeare: Seven Tragedies: The Dramatist's Manipulation of Response* (1976) and *Shakespeare's Impact on His Contemporaries* (1982).

G. K. HUNTER taught for some years at the University of Warwick and is now Professor of English at Yale University. He has written *Lyly and Peele* (1968) and *Dramatic Identities and Cultural Tradition: Studies in Shakespeare and His Contemporaries* (1978), and coedited with Philip Edwards and Inga-Stina Ewbank *Shakespeare's Styles: Essays in Honour of Kenneth Muir* (1980).

RICHARD L. LEVIN is Professor of English at the State University of New York at Stony Brook. His principal works are *The Multiple Plot in Renaissance Drama* (1971) and *New Readings vs. Old Plays: Recent Trends in the Reinterpretation of English Renaissance Drama* (1979).

KENNETH MUIR, King Alfred Professor of English Literature at the University of Liverpool from 1951 to 1974, is now Professor Emeritus. He edited *Shakespeare Survey* from 1965 to 1980, has served as Chairman of the International Shakespeare Association since 1974, and became Fellow of the Royal Society of Literature in 1978. His numerous works include *Shakespeare's Tragic Sequence* (1972) and *The Sources of Shakespeare's Plays* (1977).

NORMAN C. RABKIN, Professor of English at the University of California, Berkeley, was president of the Shakespeare Association of America in 1982. He has written *Shakespeare and the Common Understanding* (1967) and *Shakespeare and the Problem of Meaning* (1981), and edited *Approaches to Shakespeare* (1964).

MEREDITH ANNE SKURA is Associate Professor of English at Rice University. She has written *The Literary Use of the Psychoanalytic Process* (1981).

SUSAN B. SNYDER is Professor of English at Swarthmore College. She is the author of *The Comic Matrix of Shakespeare's Tragedies* (1979).

MICHAEL J. WARREN is Associate Professor of English at the University of California, Santa Cruz. He has written various articles on textual problems.

Selected Bibliography

Articles about Shakespeare's tragedies are too numerous even to sample here. Books are included selectively. The bibliography excludes works written before 1964, the date of Professor Harbage's earlier volume on the tragedies, and works written by the contributors to this volume, whose principal titles have already been provided. Titles of other works are found in the footnotes to the contributions.

I. *Works Dealing with Two or More of the Tragedies*

Barroll, J. Leeds. *Artificial Persons: The Formation of Character in the Tragedies of Shakespeare.* Columbia: University of South Carolina Press, ¹974.

Battenhouse, Roy W. *Shakespearean Tragedy: Its Art and Its Christian Premises.* Bloomington: Indiana University Press, 1969.

Bayley, John. *Shakespeare and Tragedy.* London and Boston: Routledge and Kegan Paul, 1981.

Berry, Ralph. *The Shakespearean Metaphor: Studies in Language and Form.* London: Macmillan, 1978.

Bevington, David, and Jay L. Halio, eds. *Shakespeare: Pattern of Excelling Nature.* Shakespeare Criticism in Honor of America's Bicentennial from the International Shakespeare Association Congress, Washington D.C., April 1976. Newark: University of Delaware Press, and London: Associated University Presses, 1978.

Bradbrook, M. C. *Shakespeare the Craftsman.* The Clark Lectures, 1968. New York: Barnes and Noble, 1969.
_____ *The Living Monument: Shakespeare and the Theatre of His Time.* New York and London: Cambridge University Press, 1976.

Brown, John Russell. *Free Shakespeare*. London: Heinemann Educational, 1974.

—— *Shakespeare's Dramatic Style*. London: Heinemann, 1970.

—— *Discovering Shakespeare*. New York: Columbia University Press, 1981.

Burckhardt, Sigurd. *Shakespearean Meanings*. Princeton: Princeton University Press, 1968.

Cantor, Paul A. *Shakespeare's Rome, Republic and Empire*. Ithaca: Cornell University Press, 1976.

Champion, Larry. *Shakespeare's Tragic Perspective*. Athens: University of Georgia Press, 1976.

Coursen, Herbert R. *Christian Ritual and the World of Shakespeare's Tragedies*. Lewisburg: Bucknell University Press, 1976.

Crane, Milton, ed. *Shakespeare's Art*. Chicago: University of Chicago Press, 1973.

Doran, Madeleine. *Shakespeare's Dramatic Language: Essays*. Madison: University of Wisconsin Press, 1976.

Edwards, Philip. *Shakespeare and the Confines of Art*. London: Methuen, 1968.

Fly, Richard. *Shakespeare's Mediated World*. Amherst: University of Massachusetts Press, 1976.

French, A. L. *Shakespeare and the Critics*. London and New York: Cambridge University Press, 1972.

French, Marilyn. *Shakespeare's Division of Experience*. New York: Summit Books, 1981.

Garber, Marjorie. *Coming of Age in Shakespeare*. London and New York: Methuen, 1981.

Goldman, Michael. *Shakespeare and the Energies of Drama*. Princeton: Princeton University Press, 1972.

Hawkes, Terence. *Shakespeare and the Reason: A Study of the Tragedies and the Problem Plays*. New York: Humanities Press, 1965.

—— *Shakespeare's Talking Animals: Language and Drama in Society*. London: Edward Arnold, 1973.

Hibbard, G. R. *The Making of Shakespeare's Dramatic Poetry*. Toronto: University of Toronto Press, 1981.

Holland, Norman. *Psychoanalysis and Shakespeare*. New York: McGraw-Hill, 1966.

Hunter, Robert G. *Shakespeare and the Mystery of God's Judgments*. Athens: University of Georgia Press, 1976.

Jones, Emrys. *Scenic Form in Shakespeare.* Oxford: Clarendon Press, 1971.
———— *The Origins of Shakespeare.* Oxford: Clarendon Press, 1977.

Kott, Jan. *Shakespeare Our Contemporary,* tr. Boleslaw Taborski. Garden City: Doubleday, 1964.

Leech, Clifford, and J. M. R. Margeson, eds. *Shakespeare 1971.* Proceedings of the World Shakespeare Congress, Vancouver, August 1971. Toronto: University of Toronto Press, 1972.

Mason, H. A. *Shakespeare's Tragedies of Love.* London: Chatto and Windus, 1970.

McElroy, Bernard. *Shakespeare's Mature Tragedies.* Princeton: Princeton University Press, 1973.

McFarland, Thomas. *Tragic Meanings in Shakespeare.* New York: Random House, 1966.

Nevo, Ruth. *Tragic Form in Shakespeare.* Princeton: Princeton University Press, 1972.

Proser, Matthew N. *The Heroic Image in Five Shakespearean Tragedies.* Princeton: Princeton University Press, 1965.

Simmons, J. L. *Shakespeare's Pagan World: The Roman Tragedies.* Charlottesville: University Press of Virginia, 1973.

Skulsky, Harold. *Spirits Finely Touched: The Testing of Value and Integrity in Four Shakespearean Plays.* Athens: University of Georgia Press, 1976.

Soellner, Rolf, *Shakespeare's Patterns of Self-Knowledge.* Columbus: Ohio State University Press, 1972.

Sypher, Wylie. *The Ethic of Time: Structures of Experience in Shakespeare.* New York: Seabury Press, 1976.

West, Robert H. *Shakespeare and the Outer Mystery.* Lexington: University Press of Kentucky, 1968.

Whitaker, Virgil K. *The Mirror Up to Nature: The Technique of Shakespeare's Tragedies.* San Marino: Huntington Library, 1965.

II. *Works Dealing with Single Plays*

HAMLET

Aldus, P. J. *Mousetrap: Structure and Meaning in Hamlet.* Toronto: University of Toronto Press, 1977.

Alexander, Nigel. *Poison, Play, and Duel: A Study in Hamlet.* London: Routledge and Kegan Paul, and Lincoln: University of Nebraska Press, 1979.

Charney, Maurice. *Style in Hamlet*. Princeton: Princeton University Press, 1969.

Davis, Arthur G. *Hamlet and the Eternal Problem of Man*. New York: St. John's University Press, 1964.

Farrell, Kirby. *Shakespeare's Creation: The Language of Magic and Play*. Amherst: University of Massachusetts Press, 1975.

Fisch, Harold. *Hamlet and the Word: The Covenant Pattern in Shakespeare*. New York: Ungar, 1971.

Gottschalk, Paul. *The Meaning of Hamlet: Modes of Literary Interpretation Since Bradley*. Albuquerque: University of New Mexico Press, 1972.

Gurr, Andrew. *Hamlet and the Distracted Globe*. Edinburgh: Published for Sussex University Press by Scottish Academic Press, 1978.

Muir, Kenneth, and Stanley Wells, eds. *Aspects of Hamlet*. Cambridge and New York: Cambridge University Press, 1979.

Prosser, Eleanor. *Hamlet and Revenge*. Palo Alto: Stanford University Press, 1967.

KING LEAR

Colie, Rosalie L., and F. T. Flahiff, eds. *Some Facets of King Lear: Essays in Prismatic Criticism*. Toronto: University of Toronto Press, 1974.

Davis, Arthur G. *The Royalty of Lear*. Jamaica, N.Y.: St. John's University Press, 1974.

Elton, William. *King Lear and the Gods*. San Marino: Huntington Library, 1966.

Goldberg, S. L. *An Essay on King Lear*. London and New York: Cambridge University Press, 1974.

Jorgensen, Paul. *Lear's Self-Discovery*. Berkeley and Los Angeles: University of California Press, 1967.

Mack, Maynard. *King Lear in Our Time*. Berkeley and Los Angeles: University of California Press, 1965.

Muir, Kenneth, and Stanley Wells, eds. *Aspects of King Lear*. Cambridge and New York: Cambridge University Press, 1982.

Reibetanz, John. *The Lear World: A Study of King Lear*. Toronto: University of Toronto Press, 1977.

Rosenberg, Marvin. *The Masks of King Lear*. Berkeley and Los Angeles: University of California Press, 1972.

OTHER TRAGEDIES

Adamson, Jane. *Othello as Tragedy: Some Problems of Judgment and Feeling.* Cambridge and New York: Cambridge University Press, 1980.

Bartholomeusz, Dennis. *Macbeth and the Players.* London: Cambridge University Press, 1969.

Butler, Francelia McWilliams. *The Strange Critical Fortunes of Shakespeare's Timon of Athens.* Ames: Iowa State University Press, 1966.

Evans, Robert O. *The Osier Cage: Rhetorical Devices in Romeo and Juliet.* Lexington: University of Kentucky Press, 1966.

Huffman, Clifford C. *Coriolanus in Context.* Lewisburg: Bucknell University Press, 1972.

Jorgensen, Paul. *Our Naked Frailties: Sensational Art and Meaning in Macbeth.* Berkeley and Los Angeles: University of California Press, 1971.

Krook, Dorothea. *Elements of Tragedy.* New York and London: Yale University Press, 1969. On *Antony and Cleopatra*, pp. 184–229.

Markels, Julian. *The Pillar of the World: Antony and Cleopatra in Shakespeare's Development.* Columbus: Ohio State University Press, 1968.

Muir, Kenneth, and Philip Edwards, eds. *Aspects of Macbeth.* Cambridge and New York: Cambridge University Press, 1977.

Muir, Kenneth, and Philip Edwards, eds. *Aspects of Othello.* Cambridge and New York: Cambridge University Press, 1977.

Riemer, A. P. *A Reading of Shakespeare's Antony and Cleopatra.* Sydney: Sydney University Press, 1968.

Rosenberg, Marvin. *The Masks of Macbeth.* Berkeley and Los Angles: University of California Press, 1978.

Soellner, Rolf. *Timon of Athens, Shakespeare's Pessimistic Tragedy.* Columbus: Ohio State University Press, 1979.